D0722457

DISCARDED
UNIVERSITY OF WINNIPEG
PORTAGE & BALMORAL
WINNIPEG, MAN.   R3B 2E9
CANADA

TRANSFORMATIONAL SYNTAX AND MODEL THEORETIC SEMANTICS

SYNTHESE LANGUAGE LIBRARY

TEXTS AND STUDIES IN
LINGUISTICS AND PHILOSOPHY

Managing Editors:

JAAKKO HINTIKKA, *Florida State University, Tallahassee*
STANLEY PETERS, *The University of Texas at Austin*

Editorial Board:

EMMON BACH, *University of Massachusetts at Amherst*
JOAN BRESNAN, *Massachusetts Institute of Technology*
JOHN LYONS, *University of Sussex*
JULIUS M. E. MORAVCSIK, *Stanford University*
PATRICK SUPPES, *Stanford University*
DANA SCOTT, *Oxford University*

VOLUME 9

P
291
·M25
1979

TRANSFORMATIONAL SYNTAX AND MODEL THEORETIC SEMANTICS

A Case Study in Modern Irish

by

JAMES McCLOSKEY

School of Celtic Studies, Dublin Institute for Advanced Studies, Dublin, Ireland

D. REIDEL PUBLISHING COMPANY

DORDRECHT:HOLLAND/BOSTON:U.S.A

LONDON:ENGLAND

Library of Congress Cataloging in Publication Data

CIP

McCloskey, James.
    Transformational syntax and model theoretic semantics.

    (Synthese language library; v. 9)
    "This piece of work began life as a doctoral thesis written at the University of Texas between 1976 and 1978."
    Bibliography: p.
    Includes index.
    1.   Grammar, Comparative and general–Syntax.   2.   Semantics.
3.   Montague   grammar.   4.   Irish   language–Grammar, Generative.
I.   Title.   II.   Series.   P291.M25   415   79–19269
ISBN 90–277–1025–2
ISBN 90–277–1026–0   pbk.

Published by D. Reidel Publishing Company,
P.O. Box 17, Dordrecht, Holland

Sold and distributed in the U.S.A., Canada, and Mexico
by D. Reidel Publishing Company, Inc.
Lincoln Building, 160 Old Derby Street, Hingham,
Mass. 02043, U.S.A.

All Rights Reserved
Copyright © 1979 by D. Reidel Publishing Company, Dordrecht, Holland
No part of the material protected by this copyright notice may be reproduced or
utilized in any form or by any means, electronic or mechanical
including photocopying, recording or by any informational storage and
retrieval system, without written permission from the copyright owner

Printed in the Netherlands

To the memory of my father

TABLE OF CONTENTS

FOREWORD

This piece of work began life as a doctoral thesis written at the University of Texas between 1976 and 1978. Now after a year in Dublin it is to become a book. Of the many people in the Department of Linguistics at Texas who shaped my interests and who helped me through the writing of the thesis, I must single out Lee Baker, Lauri Karttunen, Bill Ladusaw, Sue Schmerling and Stanley Peters for special gratitude. All of them have provided specific suggestions which have improved this work, but perhaps more importantly they provided a uniquely stimulating and harmonious environment in which to work, and a demanding set of professional standards to live up to.

To Ken Hale I owe a particular debt of gratitude – for two years of encouragement and suggestions, and particularly for a set of detailed comments on an earlier version of the book which led to many changes for the better.

I also thank my friends Per-Kristian Halvorsen and Elisabet Engdahl, both of whom took the trouble to provide me with detailed criticisms and comments.

In Dublin I am grateful to the School of Celtic Studies of the Institute for Advanced Studies for giving me the opportunity of teaching a seminar on many of the topics covered in the book and of exposing the material to people whose knowledge of the language is unequalled. Dónal Ó Baoill and Liam Breatnach have been particularly helpful.

I must also thank Kay Richardson of the D. Reidel Publishing Company for her help and for her patience in putting up with my dithering and repeatedly missed deadlines.

And, most of all, I must thank my wife Martha for putting up with me and my book.

Dublin, April 1979.

CHAPTER 1

INTRODUCTION

This book is an attempt to examine certain currently controversial issues in the theory of grammar in the light of data from a single language – namely, Modern Irish. Its primary aim is to develop a fragment of a grammar for the language – that is, a precisely-defined syntax and semantics for what I hope is an interestingly large body of data. The syntactic framework is that of transformational syntax; the semantic framework is that which has come to be known as Montague Grammar. I hope that the work may serve a number of different purposes.

Firstly, I have certain rather broad theoretical aims in mind. Most generally, I want to demonstrate the viability and attractiveness of a marriage between a transformational theory of syntax and a 'Montagovian' theory of semantic interpretation. This combination provides us with a theoretical framework of unique richness and precision for the exploration of problems at the interface of syntax and semantics.

More particularly, I want to defend a particular hypothesis about the nature of the relationship between syntactic and semantic structures, an hypothesis that lies at the heart of most work done within the framework of Montague Grammar. This is the claim that it is possible to define a semantic interpretation directly on the syntax of natural languages. The question of the proper relation between syntax and semantics is one that has been a focus of interest for workers within the paradigm of generative grammar for well over a decade now. Most work within that framework has assumed that it is not possible to define an adequate semantics directly on the syntax of natural language, but rather that one must assume the existence of an auxiliary language – 'semantic representation' or 'logical form' – which mediates the relationship between syntax and semantics. That is, one first maps syntactic representations of sentences of natural language onto representations in another (perhaps universal) formal language, and then one defines the semantic interpretation on this second language. The arguments for this position (to the extent that it has been argued for and not simply taken for granted) have mostly been presented in the absence of detailed semantic analyses or of detailed proposals about the nature of semantic theory. In all the recent discussions of 'logical form', for instance, (Chomsky, 1973, 1975, 1977, 1978; Sag, 1976a, 1976b; Williams, 1977; May, 1977) there has yet to appear a characterization of the syntax of logical form, or of its interpretation, or of the class of rules that map shallow structures onto representations in logical form. This lack of precision makes it extremely difficult to evaluate such proposals against empirical data. After all, the claim that 'logical form' is an essential mediator between syntax and semantics has substance only to the extent that interesting constraints can be placed on the set of rules that map syntactic representations onto logical form, and in the absence of concrete proposals about the form and functioning of such rules, it is impossible to know what such constraints might be.

Montague Grammar provides us with an interesting alternative to this position in a number of respects. Firstly, it provides us with the richest and most rigorously-defined theory at present available of what 'meaning' is and of how to associate meanings with the syntactic representations of phrases of natural language. The theory is rich enough that it allows for the discussion of interestingly large and complex bodies of data on natural language semantics. It also both allows us and requires us to work at a level of precision in semantic analysis which permits the formulation of analyses and hypotheses that are, in a serious way, testable against empirical data.

Secondly, most work that has been done within the framework of Montague Grammar is based on the hypothesis that it is possible to define semantic interpretations directly on the syntax of natural language. In other words, there is neither need nor justification for the postulation of a significant level of linguistic structure like 'semantic representation' or 'logical form'.

It is within this theoretical context that I would like the present work to be viewed. It is an attempt to defend the plausibility of the view that syntax can indeed be directly interpreted. Now clearly this claim is an interesting one only if it is clear that the syntactic base is not being distorted to suit our semantic purposes — that is, if it is clear that the syntax we are using captures the necessary syntactic generalizations. Put another way, the claim that syntax is directly interpretable amounts to the claim that syntactically motivated and semantically motivated analyses will be at least compatible with one another. I hope to show that with respect to the data to be considered here, syntactic and semantic considerations converge in an interesting way on a single analysis, that is, that the same syntax that accounts in a principled way for syntactic facts also provides a suitable basis for semantic interpretation. To this end, I will break with the usual practice of those who have worked in the tradition of Montague Grammar and begin by considering syntactic facts largely in isolation. In the first half of the book I present a detailed study of the syntax of relative clauses and questions. These two syntactic systems happen to be very closely related (more so than in most languages that I know of), and the attempt to give that relatedness formal expression raises certain interesting theoretical questions. Consideration of these matters will lead us into a discussion of several currently controversial issues in syntactic theory – concerning the existence of unbounded deletion rules and the role played by conditions such as the Subjacency Condition (Chomsky, 1973, 1977; Chomsky and Lasnik, 1977; Bresnan and Grimshaw, 1978) in the explanation of the phenomenon of island constraints (in the sense of Ross, 1967). Having defended a particular analysis on its own (syntactic) merits, we can go on in the second half of the book to show how this syntactic base can support, without modification, a rather elegant system of semantic interpretation.

These, then, are the theoretical concerns that underlie the discussion that follows. But theories tend, in the nature of things, and particularly in linguistics, to be rather ephemeral. Perhaps the most important end that might be served by this work is that of simply exploring a fairly large body of data from a language that has gone largely un-investigated within modern paradigms of research. Irish has the added attraction of belonging to an interesting typological minority – that of VSO languages – that has not received its fair share of attention from linguistic theorists. I hope that I have not let my predilection for theoretical argumentation predominate to the extent that those who do not share my theoretical concerns will find nothing to interest them in what follows.

Before getting on with it, I should probably issue certain caveats about the data to be discussed. I have called this book a study in Modern Irish, but there is in fact no such single language – Irish consists of three rather disparate dialect-groupings (Ulster, Connacht and Munster) and there exists no widely-spoken standard. The dialect chiefly represented in this work is Ulster Irish (as spoken in West Donegal). This is the dialect that I speak and know most about and the fieldwork that provided the basic data for the book was done, for the most part but not entirely, with native speakers of Ulster Irish. If one were to make the most careful statement possible, then one would say that the dialect described here is a rather conservative Ulster dialect, one largely free from English interference. That said however, I should point out that I am reasonably sure that the facts as described here hold for the other dialects as well, and that, as far as the sub-systems to be discussed are concerned, the dialects are substantially in agreement. At those points where dialect-differences that I know of exist I have noted that fact in the text or footnotes. None of these differences, I think, affect crucially any of the theoretical points I wish to make.

Much of the material I will be dealing with is discussed in traditional handbooks. Among the most useful of these is Cormac Ó Cadhlaigh's (1940) *Gnás na Gaeilge* (in Irish) and *Ceart na Gaeilge* (*A Treatise on Irish Syntax*) (in English) by the same author. There are also two useful works by Gerald O'Nolan, *Studies in Modern Irish* (1919) and his *The New Era Grammar of Modern Irish* (1934). There is one work that I know of that is devoted to a study of the syntax of Northern Irish – Séamas Ó Searcaigh's *Coimhréir Ghaedhilg an Tuaiscirt* (1939). A good modern synthesis (in Irish) is the *Graiméar Gaeilge na mBráithre Críostaí*, produced by the Christian Brothers in 1960.

CHAPTER 2

THE SYNTAX OF RELATIVE CLAUSES

2.1. BASIC DATA

Modern Irish has two productive Relative Clause strategies,[1] which, following traditional usage, I shall call the Direct and the Indirect Relative respectively. The two strategies exhibit certain differences of morphology, which will be discussed in due course, but the central difference between the two is that the Indirect Relative involves retention of a pronoun at the site of the relativized constituent inside the relative clause, while the Direct Relative involves removal of the relativized constitutent; that is, there is an intuitively felt 'gap' at the relativization site. As one might expect on the basis of the work of Keenan and Comrie (1977), the pronoun-retaining Indirect Relative is used when the relativized constituent is relatively inaccessible to its matched constituent outside the clause. One aspect of the accessibility relation has to do with the grammatical relation borne by the relativized NP within the relative clause.

Explicit rules in the traditional grammars are normally given only for the cases where the relative clause is simple – that is, contains no embedded clauses. We can begin by considering just these cases and leave more complicated situations till later. The usual account given is roughly as follows.

The Direct Relative (the type that uses a gap rather than a resumptive pronoun) is used when the relativization site is subject of its clause, as in (1):

(1)   **an fear a dhíol __ an domhan**
        the man   sold   the world

        ' . . . the man who sold the world'

I shall leave the particle *a* which introduces relative clauses in this and following examples unglossed for the moment, since its status is one of the things I want to discuss, and it is difficult to settle on a translation which would not prejudice the issue. Use of the Direct Relative is obligatory in a situation such as (1). Example (2) is ungrammatical because it marks the relativized subject with a resumptive pronoun and shows the morphology of the Indirect Relative.

5

(2)   *an fear a ndíolann sé an domhan
           *the man   sells   he the world

           ' . . . the man who sells the world'

There are certain situations however in which use of the pronoun-retaining
Indirect Relative is obligatory – if the relativized constituent is the object
of a preposition or a possessive modifier of a NP.[2]

(3)   an fear a dtabharann tú   an t-airgead do
           the man   give   you the money   to-him

           ' . . . the man to whom you give the money'

(4)   an fear a bhfuil a   mháthair san   otharlann
           the man   is   his mother in-the hospital

           ' . . . the man whose mother is in the hospital'

There are no grammatical examples corresponding to (3) or (4) with the
form of the Direct Relative.

If we restrict our attention to simple relative clauses, then there is just one
situation in which the choice between Direct and Indirect Relative types is
free. This is when the relativized constituent is the direct object of its clause.
Thus both (5), with a gap and the morphology of the Direct Relative, and
(6), with a resumptive pronoun and the morphology of the Indirect Relative,
are grammatical.

(5)   an scríbhneoir a molann na mic léinn é
           the writer   praise the students him

(6)   an scríbhneoir a mholann na mic léinn __
           the writer   praises the students

           'the writer whom the students praise'

In this situation, use of the Direct Relative, as in (6), is overwhelmingly more
frequent than use of the Indirect type, but that the Indirect type is also
possible is shown by the following selection of examples:[3]

(7)   fá   dhaoine a shiúil an saol agus a chaill a   gcreideamh
           about people   walked the world and   lost   their faith

           agus ar chuir an Misean Mór   ar ais ar staid na grásta iad
           and   put   the Mission Great back on state the grace   them

           ' . . . about people who wandered the world and lost their faith
           and whom the Great Mission brought back to a state of grace'.

(8)   **an fear a bhí marbh ... agus gur thóg Íosa ón**
         the man   was dead   and   raised Jesus from-the

         mbás é
         death him

         ' ... the man who was dead ... and whom Jesus raised from
         the dead'

(9)   **an rud seo a tharla   agus gur fhoillsigh an Tiarna dúinn é**
         this thing   happened and   revealed   the Lord   to-us it

         ' ... this thing that happened and that the Lord revealed to us'

(10)   **Ní   éigin áirithe a bhí aige   á iarraidh ar Dhia agus nár**
         thing some certain   was at-him asking-it on God and NEG

         thug Dia dó   é
         gave God to-him it

         ' ... something that he was asking God for and which God did
         not give him'

What is usually said on this matter is that the Indirect Relative type, as in
(7)–(10), is used only if use of the Direct Relative type would give rise to a
troublesome ambiguity. Examples like (11) are of course ambiguous, because
there is no way to tell whether the missing constituent is subject or direct
object in its clause.

(11)   **an file a mhol   na léirmheastóirí**
         the poet   praised the critics

         'the poet that praised the critics'

         'the poet whom the critics praised'

This ambiguity can be resolved by using the Indirect Relative. This is per-
mitted in the case of direct objects, but not in the case of subjects. For a
discussion of this matter, see McCloskey (1977c).

   This much is certainly true, but it seems to me that there are other factors
which influence the choice of one type over the other. For example, consideration of the examples quoted above, as well as the collection in Ó Cadhlaigh
(1940, pp 376–377) suggests that if the relative clause is the final one in a
conjoined series, then the Indirect Relative is more likely to turn up. For the
purposes of this study I will make the simplifying and perhaps correct

assumption that the grammar need only say that the choice between Direct and Indirect Relative in this circumstance is free, and that the question of exactly what considerations affect the choice in practice is a matter for a theory of performance. This is a useful assumption, but it should be pointed out that it leaves unanswered and unasked a number of very interesting questions.

To summarize then, the position in simplex relative clauses is that if the relativized position is the subject of the clause, then the gap-producing Direct Relative must be used; if the relativized position is the direct object of the clause, then either the Direct Relative or the pronoun-retaining Indirect Relative may be used; for all the more remote positions on the Accessibility Hierarchy of Keenan and Comrie (1977) (prepositional object, possessive NP, object of comparison), the pronoun-retaining Indirect Relative must be used.[4]

Before proceeding to an analysis of the data presented so far, it is probably in order to say something about the particle *a* which introduces the relative clauses in examples (1)–(6). The particle in both the Direct and Indirect types is a stressless, caseless particle, pronounced [ə], which deletes very freely. Although it looks at first sight as if the same particle introduces both Direct and Indirect Relatives, the two are probably best regarded as distinct items, despite the fact that in the examples considered so far, they show identical phonetic realizations. There are several reasons why they should be kept distinct: firstly, they show different morphological variants under certain conditions. This matter is discussed in Section 2.2 below. Secondly, they induce different mutations of the initial segment of the following word. Irish, like all the surviving Celtic languages, has a complex system of initial mutations. Irish has two mutations – Lenition and Nasalization. These are complex sets of phonological changes in the initial segment of a word, induced usually by a preceding word or morpheme on the basis of such grammatical features as gender and case. Often the mutations carry semantic information in that they distinguish what would otherwise be homophones. For example, the 3rd person possessive pronoun in Irish always has the form **a**, whether it means 'his', 'her' or 'their'. But the three forms are in fact distinguished by the fact that **a** ('his') causes Lenition of a following segment; **a** ('their') causes Nasalization and **a** ('her') induces no mutation. So an important part of the account of any morpheme in the language is an account of its mutation effect. In the case of the two relative particles, the mutations are different – the Direct Relative particle lenites a following verb, while the Indirect Relative particle nasalizes it. Since the phonetic

and morphological realizations of Lenition and Nasalization are very complicated matters, I will represent the difference between the two relative
particles by writing the **a** of the Direct Relative as **aL**, and the **a** of the Indirect Relative as **aN**. As a general convention, I will use **L** to mark an element that induces Lenition on a following element, and **N** to mark an element
that induces Nasalization.[5]

There is a further reason for distinguishing **aL** from **aN**. Northern and
Western dialects preserve, as an optional variant, special 'relative' forms of the
verb in the 3rd person singular forms of present and future tenses (the forms
in Ulster are **-(e)as** and **-f(e)as** respectively). These forms have been lost
(fairly recently, it seems) in Munster (O Rahilly, 1932, pp 219–220;
Ó Cadhlaigh, 1940, pp 361–363). Thus in Ulster we have both (12a) and
(12b) as optional variants:

(12a)   **an t-iascaire a dhíolas   a   bhád**
        the fisherman sells(+rel) his boat

(b)   **an t-iascaire a dhíolann   a bhád**
                         sells(−rel)

        'the fisherman who sells his boat'

The simplest and most general statement that I know of that will account for
the distribution of these forms, is to say that they occur after **aL**, but in no
other situation – in particular, not after **aN**. Both **aL** and **aN** occur in a wide
variety of clause-types apart from relative clauses, and in every clause-type
which contains **aL**, the 'relative' forms may occur. For example, the conjunction **nuair** ('when') requires an **aL**-clause, and in such clauses one may find
the 'relative' forms.

(13a)   **Nuair a thiocfas   sé 'na bhaile**
        when   will come(+rel) he home

(b)   **Nuair a thiocfaidh   sé 'na bhaile**
                 will come(−rel) he home

        'when he comes home'

In none of the clauses introduced by **aN** can one find the 'relative' form:

(14)   ***an fear a dtabharfas   tú   an t-airgead dó**
        the man   will give(+rel) you the money   to-him

        'the man that you will give the money to'

The conjunction **sul** ('before') requires an **aN**-clause, and here again, 'relative' endings are impossible:

(15a)   *sul   aN dtiocfas   sé 'na bhaile
        before   *will come(+rel)* *he home*

(b)   sul   aN dtiocfaidh·   sé 'na bhaile
                 will come(−rel)

        'before he comes home'

These factors in combination suggest, I think, rather strongly that we should distinguish two separate items – **aL** and **aN** – and take the fact that they show identical phonetic realizations under certain circumstances, to be a case of partial homophony.

To summarize the material presented so far then, we might diagram the essential features of the structure of relative clauses as in (16):

(16)   *Direct*   [(Det) Nom [$_S$**aL** ... _ ... $_S$]]

        Indirect [(Det) Nom [$_S$**aN** ... Pro ... $_S$]]

where '_' is to be understood as indicating a missing constituent (a 'gap'), and where the choice between the Direct and Indirect strategies is understood to be governed by a language-particular realization of the Accessibility Hierarchy of Keenan and Comrie (1977).

2.2. MOVEMENT OR DELETION?

Generative Grammar has traditionally provided two ways of accounting for the gap that appears in such structures as the Direct Relative – by movement of some constituent out of the clause or by deletion of some constituent in the clause. In the following section I weigh the relative merits of deletion and movement analyses.

The most obvious way in which to go about formulating a movement analysis for Irish relatives would be to take the particle **aL** of the Direct Relative to be a preposed relative pronoun – fronted to sentence-initial position by a rule much like English WH-Movement. Thus example (1) might be derived as in (17):

(17)   [$_{NP}$ an fear [$_{\bar{S}}$ COMP [$_S$ dhíol aL an domhan]]]
            the man   *sold rel. the world*

        'the man who sold the world'

(Assuming the analysis of WH-Movement which moves WH-phrases into COMP-position; see Bresnan 1972.) On this account, the derivation of Indirect Relatives would presumably involve no transformational rule at all – that is, the pronouns would simply be generated in place at the relativization site and **aN** would be generated in clause-initial position by the rules of the base. This analysis, however, suffers from a rather fundamental weakness. The trouble with it lies in its essential part – namely the identification of **aL** as a pronoun. Actually there is a sizeable body of evidence to suggest that neither **aL** nor **aN** should be taken as pronouns, but rather as complementizers.

Firstly, neither particle has any of the characteristics one might expect a pronoun to have. Unlike relative pronouns in English, they contain no indication of case, animateness, number or gender. All other pronouns in Irish show variants along one or more of these parameters. The two particles are subject to systematic variation of form, but this variation is entirely independent of any semantic or syntactic characteristics of the relativized constituent. Rather it is conditioned by the tense of the verb in the relative clause, and by the presence or absence of negation in the relative clause. This is hardly the sort of variation one expects to find in the form of a pronoun.

It is, however, exactly the kind of variation one finds in other elements of the language which are clearly complementizers. The particle **go**, for instance, which is the Irish equivalent of clause-initial *that* in English, participates in just this sort of variation. Consider the table in (18):

(18)

		Non-Past	*Past*
go			
	Affirmative	**goN**	**gurL**
	Negative	**nachN**	**nárL**
aN			
	Affirmative	**aN**	**arL**
	Negative	**nachN**	**nárL**
aL			
	Affirmative	**aL**	**aL**
	Negative	**nachN**	**nárL**

(where, as before, **L** and **N** mark elements that induce Lenition and Nasalization respectively)

Notice in particular that all three elements share identical negative variants.

The variation is illustrated in (19)–(21):

(19)
$$
\text{Deir sé} \left\{ \begin{array}{l} \textbf{goN dtuigeann} \\ \textbf{nachN dtuigeann} \\ \textbf{gurL thuig} \\ \textbf{nárL thuig} \end{array} \right\} \text{sé an scéal}
$$

Deir sé goN dtuigeann / nachN dtuigeann / gurL thuig / nárL thuig sé an scéal
says he *he the story*

'He says that he $\left\{ \begin{array}{l} \text{understands} \\ \text{doesn't understand} \\ \text{understood} \\ \text{didn't understand} \end{array} \right\}$ the story'

(20)
an fear aL thuigeann / nachN dtuigeann / aL thuig / nárL thuig — an scéal
the man *the story*

'The man that $\left\{ \begin{array}{l} \text{understands} \\ \text{doesn't understand} \\ \text{understood} \\ \text{didn't understand} \end{array} \right\}$ the story'

(21)
an fear aN n-insíonn / nachN n-insíonn / arL inis / nárL inis tú an scéal dó
the man *you the story to him*

'the man that you $\left\{ \begin{array}{l} \text{tell} \\ \text{do not tell} \\ \text{told} \\ \text{did not tell} \end{array} \right\}$ the story to'

These data indicate that at a superficial level both the Direct Relative particle **aL** and the Indirect particle **aN** belong in a class with the other complementizer in the language. It is of course perfectly compatible with an analysis that places preposed relative pronouns under a COMP node, thus making them subject to any late syntactic rule or morphological rule that applied to complementizers. A more important source of evidence that suggests that **aL** and **aN** are base-generated complementizers is the following.

Both **aL** and **aN** serve to introduce many other clause-types besides relative clauses. Some of these, like clefts, constituent questions, comparative clauses and so on clearly involve extraction rules, in that they contain a gap as do Direct relative clauses. Many of the clauses headed by **aL** or **aN**, however, contain no gap, and apparently involve no extraction. If the **aL** particle of Direct Relative clauses really were a preposed pronoun, then we would expect it to head only clauses which contained a gap – marking the site from which it had been fronted. Consider the following cases:

(i) **Amhlaidh.** The word **amhlaidh** is a (predicative) adjective which is usually glossed as English 'thus', 'so' or the like. One of the structures in which it appears is that diagrammed in (22):

(22)   Copula + **amhlaidh** + $\bar{S}$

Such a sentence means something like 'It is the case that S' or 'Actually, S'. The construction serves a variety of rhetorical functions (for a survey of these, see O'Nolan 1920, Vol. 1, pp. 79–81), but for our purposes the important point is that the complementizer of the $\bar{S}$-constituent is always the Direct Relative particle **aL**.

(23)   **Is   amhlaidh aL bhí neart   céad   fear ann**
         Cop.   was strength hundred men in him

         'It was a fact that he had the strength of a hundred men'.

(24)   **Ina ionad sin   is   amhlaidh aL d'fhill   siad 'na bhaile**
         instead of that Cop.   returned they home

         'Instead of that actually they returned home'.

This instance of **aL** too, is subject to the variation with respect to tense and negation documented in (18):

(25)   **Is   amhlaidh nárL thuig   na mná rialta an scéal**
         Cop.   understood the nuns   the story

         'The fact is, the nuns didn't understand the story'.

The embedded clauses headed by **aL** here are complete both syntactically and semantically and it clearly makes no sense to say that in these examples **aL** is a preposed WH-pronoun of any sort.

(ii) **Rud.** A very similar construction, serving very similar purposes, involves the dummy noun **rud**. The most literal translation of this construction goes 'It is a thing that S'. Again it means something like 'It is a fact that S' or 'Actually S'.

(26a)   **Is   é rud   aL gortaíodh é**
        Cop. it a thing   was hurt him

        'He was hurt'.

  (b)   **Is é rud aL thug siad scoláireacht dó**
                 gave they a scholarship to him

        'Actually, they gave him a scholarship'.

Notice that once again, although there is clearly no extraction from such clauses, they are introduced by **aL**.

(iii) *Alternative Questions*. One of the ways of forming Alternative Questions in Irish is by using the word **céacu** ('which of them') followed by a disjunction of clauses:

(27)   **[céacu $\bar{S}$ nó $\bar{S}$]**

(28)   **Níl fhios agam céacu   aL chuaigh sé go Doire nó aL**
        I don't know   which of them   went   he to Derry or

        d'fhán sé i Rann na Feirsde
        stayed he in Rannafast

        'I don't know whether he went to Derry or stayed in Rannafast'.

(29)   **Fiafróidh mé de   céacu   aL cheannaigh sé an**
        will ask I   of him which of them   bought   he the

        rothar nó aL ghoid sé é
        bicycle or   stole he it

        'I will ask him if he bought the bicycle or if he stole it.'

Here too the clauses are headed by the Direct Relative particle **aL**, but there is no reason to believe that any extraction rule operates into these clauses.

  What shall we say about these particles then? Their function seems to be to mark subordination in clauses, like clause-initial *that* in English, or *que* in French. Such particles have been known as 'complementizers' in generative grammar. The relative particles **aL** and **aN** pattern in several respects like one element in the language that is rather clearly a complementizer – namely the particle **goN** which introduces finite sentential complements. Apart from the morphological parallels already discussed, **aL**, **aN** and **goN** share certain distributional characteristics. For instance, the conjunctions that introduce adverbial clauses in the language (temporal, causal clauses etc.) appear in the structure diagrammed in (30):

(30)   [Conj $\bar{S}$]

Conjunctions are subcategorized in what seems to be a quite arbitrary way to take either a goN-clause, an aN-clause or an aL-clause. The conjunctions **cionn is** ('because') and **go dtí** ('until'), for instance, take **goN**:

(31)   **cionn is goN raibh na saighdiúirí sa   tóir   air**
        because   were the soldiers   in-the pursuit on-him
        'because the soldiers were after him'

(32)   **go dtí goN dtiocfaidh sé 'na bhaile**
        until   will-come he home
        'until he comes home'

Sul ('before') takes aN-clauses:

(33)   **sul   aN dtigeann an buíon ceoil**
        before   comes   the band
        'before the band comes'

Nuair ('when') takes aL-clauses:

(34)   **Nuair aL tháinig Mac Diarmada i   gcumhacht**
        when   came   MacDermot   into power
        'when MacDermot came to power'

One conjunction – **mar** – exhibits four different possibilities in this repect. With an aL-clause it means 'as'; with an aN-clause it means 'where'; with no particle, or with goN, it means 'because':

(35)   **D'inis sé an scéal mar aL chuala sé é**
        told he the story   heard he it
        'He told the story as he heard it'.

(36)   **ar an trá   mar aN mbíonn   sí   ag súgradh**
        on the beach   is (habitual) she at playing
        'on the beach where she plays'

(37)   **mar goN mbíonn   sé fliuch**
                is (habitual) it wet
        'because it is wet'

(38)   **mar bhíonn   sé fliuch**
         is(habitual) it wet
         'because it is wet'

All the complementizers in this construction are subject to the same variation of form with respect to tense and the presence or absence of negation, which is documented in (18)–(21). If any of the clauses in the examples above, for instance, had been negated, then the complementizer would appear either as **nachN** or **nárL**, depending on whether the tense of the verb was past or not.

Given these parallels, it seems reasonable to regard all these particles – **aL**, **aN** and **goN** – as belonging to the same syntactic category, the category of complementizers, which, following recent usage, I will represent as COMP. The treatment of complementizers that has become standard in recent years is that proposed originally by Joan Bresnan (1972), where COMP is introduced by the Phrase Structure rule (39):

(39) $\bar{S} \rightarrow$ COMP S

$\bar{S}$ in (39) I take to be the category of subordinate clauses. The initial symbol of the grammar I will take to be S – that is, I will assume that S is the category of main clauses, and that $\bar{S}$ is the category of subordinate (embedded) clauses.

To account for the facts about conjunctions, let us assume that the Phrase Structure rules of Irish include both the rules in (40):

(40a) $\bar{\bar{S}} \rightarrow$ CONJ $\bar{S}$

(b) $\bar{S} \rightarrow$ COMP S

where COMP can be realized lexically as **aL, aN** or **goN** and CONJ can be realized lexically as **cionn is, go dtí, sul, nuair, mar** and so on, along with certain other elements that we will have occasion to discuss later.[6]

The particles **aL** and **aN** share distributional characteristics with the complementizer **goN** in another respect as well.[7]

Consider what happens when the relativization-site is inside a clause embedded within the relative clause. That such is possible is illustrated by examples (42)a–d.

(42a)   **Thug sé léim   aL dúirt sé nárL   cheap   sé aL**
         took he a leap   said he that-NEG thought he

         thabharfadh sé choíche
         would take he ever
         'He took a leap that he said he didn't think he would ever take.'

(b)   **an t-Aire   aL deir siad aL dúirt __ goN raibh an cogadh thart**
       the minister   say they   said   was the war   over
       'The minister that they say said the war was over.'

(c)   **an t-úrscéal aL mheas   mé aL thuig   mé __**
       the novel   thought I   understood I
       'the novel that I thought I understood'

(d)   **an t-úrscéal aL mheas   mé aL dúirt sé aL thuig   sé __**
       the novel   thought I   said he   understood he
       'the novel that I thought he said he understood'

The facts that I want to draw attention to in this section have to do with
what happens to complementizers in such constructions. **GoN** is the complementizer which normally introduces sentential complements, as in (43) and
(44):

(43)   **Mheas   mé gurL thuig   mé an t-úrscéal**
        thought I   understood I   the novel
        'I thought that I understood the novel.'

(44)   **Mheas   mé gurL dhúirt sé gurL thuig   sé an t-úrscéal**
        thought I   said he   understood he the novel
        'I thought that he said that he understood the novel.'

However, if sentences such as (43) and (44) are embedded as relative clauses,
and the relativization site is inside a clause headed by **goN**, then the result is
as in (42c) and (42d) respectively – the complementizer **goN** is replaced by
the relative particle **aL**. Consider another example:

(45)   **Deir siad ⌐goN¬ síleann an t-athair ⌐goN¬ bpósfaidh Síle   é**
        say   they   thinks the father   will marry Sheila him
        'They say that the father thinks that Sheila will marry him.'

(46)   **an fear aL deir siad aL   shíleann an t-athair ⌐aL¬ phósfaidh**
        the man

        Síle __
        'the man that they say the father thinks Sheila will marry'

That is, in such complex relative clauses every complementizer that intervenes
between the head and the gap that marks the relativization site must be

realized as **aL**. How do these facts bear on the proposed rule of **aL**-movement? There are two distinct possibilities we must consider.

We could take the view, following the traditional analysis of WH-Movement, that **aL**-Movement is an unbounded leftward movement which moves **aL** from the relativization-site to a position right of the head in one operation. The data just cited are troublesome for this analysis because it is forced to distinguish between the various occurrences of **aL** in such clauses in a quite arbitrary way. The first occurrence of **aL** will be regarded as a preposed relative pronoun while all subsequent occurrences must be regarded as something quite different – presumably, complementizers. This artificial distinction is purely a consequence of taking **aL** in the simpler cases diagrammed in (41) to be a preposed relative pronoun.

But what if, following Chomsky (1973), we were to take **aL**-Movement to be a cyclic, clause-bound rule which moves a WH-pronoun up through successively higher COMP-nodes on successive cycles to its ultimate destination? If **aL**-Movement is a successive-cyclic COMP-hopping rule, then we would have to arrange for it to leave a copy, or at least a trace of its passing, at every COMP-node through which it passed. Now of course, such an analysis would be far from unheard of. It is in fact very reminiscent of certain proposals made within the framework of 'trace theory' – in some versions of which moved NP are thought to leave a trace at every COMP-node through which they pass between their original site and their ultimate destination (*cf.* Lightfoot, 1976). In the present instance we might propose that Modern Irish has a rule with the following effect:

(47)   COMP which dominates a relative pronoun or its trace is realized as **aL**.

The problem with such a proposal though is that exactly the same kind of complementizer-alternation is found in the case of the pronoun-retaining Indirect Relative. In this case, the $\bar{\text{S}}$-node which immediately dominates the pronoun which marks the relativization site is headed by the Indirect Particle **aN**; all complementizers to the left of that are realized as **aL**. Consider example (48).

(48)   **Measann sibh** |**goN**| **bhfuil an eochair insa   doras**
        think   you (pl)   *is   the key   in the door*
        'You think that the key is in the door'.

The embedded clause in (48) is marked by **goN**; when the sentence is embedded as a relative clause, however, **goN** is replaced by the Indirect Relative particle **aN** and the whole relative clause is headed by **aL**.

(49)   **an doras aL mheasann sibh aN bhfuil an eochair ann**
         the door   think   you   is   the key   in it

Example (50) has one more level of embedding than (48).

(50)   **Deir siad goN measann sibh goN bhfuil an eochair insa doras**
         say   they   you think   the key is in the door
         'They say that you think that the key is in the door'.

Again, when (50) is embedded within an NP as a relative clause, all the
complementizers appear as **aL** except that one which heads the $\bar{S}$ which
immediately dominates the retained pronoun:

(51)   **an doras aL deir siad aL mheasann sibh aN bhfuil an eochair ann**
         the door   they say   you think   the key is in it
         'the door that they say you think the key is in'

Now since relative clauses with retained pronouns, like (49) and (51) are
not subject to island constraints such as the Complex NP Constraint, as will
be demonstrated shortly, it cannot be the case that they are derived by the
same extraction rule that derives the Direct Relative forms. Therefore if we
attribute the substitution of **aL** for **goN** in examples such as (42a)–(42d),
(46) to the operation of a successive–cyclic rule of **aL**-Movement, that
explanation cannot in principle carry over to the substitution of **aL** and **aN**
for **goN** in pronoun-retaining cases such as (49) and (51). Yet it seems clear
that we are dealing with essentially the same phenomenon in both cases.
A unified account of these data, however, is ruled out in principle if the
successive-cyclic **aL**-Movement analysis is adopted. A unified analysis becomes possible only if we abandon the assumption that substitution of
relative complementizers for **goN** is an effect of a successive–cyclic rule of
WH-Movement.

There is another point to be made in connection with the data represented by examples (49) and (51). Notice that both of these examples involve
pronoun-retaining relatives and cannot, then, involve an extraction rule. Yet
both relative clauses are introduced by **aL**. (51), in fact, contains two occurrences of **aL** – one at the beginning of the relative clause and one at the
beginning of the second clause. So here we have yet more instances of the
particle **aL** in a relative clause which cannot be accounted for by the rule
of **aL**-Movement under consideration.[8]
What can we conclude from all this then?
The initial attractiveness of the **aL**-Movement analysis lies in its ability to

account for the correspondence between the presence of a gap and the presence of the clause-initial particle **aL** in the simplest kind of relative clause – those that do not involve embedding.

Against this, we set the evidence from other clause-types that **aL** should be regarded as a base-generated complementizer. Secondly when we look at the facts regarding the distribution of **aL** and **aN** in more complex kinds of relatives we find that the simple distributional pattern of (41) disappears and that, in fact, we lose more than we gain with the **aL**-Movement rule, because the correlation it predicts between the appearance of a gap in the relative clause and the appearance of the particle **aL** simply does not hold.

Suppose then that we take it as established that both **aL** and **aN** are complementizers whose distributions are not determined in any direct way by whatever rule produces the gaps in Direct Relative clauses. How then does this affect the possibility of defending a movement analysis for Irish relatives? It seems that one must propose the existence of an abstract WH-pronoun which is fronted to clause initial position (COMP-position) and is then oblig-atorily deleted in all contexts. There is no empirical evidence that I know of for the existence of such a morpheme or class of morphemes. As far as I can tell, such a move is required only by allegiance to the theoretical assump-tions of Chomsky (1973, 1975, 1976, 1977), Chomsky and Lasnik (1977), for in that theory the existence of unbounded deletions is denied, and one has available only the device of successive-cyclic movement rules to account for the unbounded dependencies between gaps and controlling expressions in examples like (42) and (46). Since I believe that that body of assumptions has been amply criticized elsewhere (*cf.* Bach and Horn, 1976; Bach, 1977; Brame, 1977; Bresnan, 1975, 1976b, 1977a; Bresnan and Grimshaw, 1978; Grimshaw, 1975; Maling, 1977, 1978; McCloskey, 1977a), this is not an alternative that I shall pursue here.

2.3. A DELETION ANALYSIS

I turn now from straw men to what seems to me to be the most coherent and natural account of the data – namely an analysis in which the gaps in the Direct Relative type result from the operation of a deletion rule. Given the examples in (42) and (46), this rule must be unbounded – that is, the target of the deletion (in the sense of Bresnan, 1976a) may be arbitrarily far from the controller. I shall call this rule Relative Deletion. This solution treats both **aL** and **aN** in the natural way – as complementizers – but avoids the *ad hoc* appeal to invisible and inaudible pronouns which are first preposed and then obligatorily deleted. The data can be most easily accounted for if we assume that Relative Deletion is a rule which deletes ordinary personal pronouns (as opposed to some specially marked relative pronoun) inside relative clauses. The pronoun-retaining Indirect type is then simply what surfaces if the deletion rule, for one reason or another, fails to operate. We can build the Accessibility Hierarchy into the rule by making it:

(52) (i) obligatory if the target pronoun is the subject of its clause.
    (ii) optional if the target pronoun is the direct object of its clause.
    (iii) block if the target pronoun bears any other grammatical relation in its clause.

All other things being equal then, pronouns will always be retained in the oblique cases, will sometimes be retained in direct object position, and never retained in subject position.

The statement of the accessibility conditions given here is meant as a temporary convenience only. As it stands, this treatment is both uneconomical and, as we will see, wrong. All these matters will be discussed in considerable detail later, but the statement given in (52) will serve our immediate purposes.

The remainder of this section will be given over to fleshing out and giving some substance to this analysis. I will begin by considering the question of the proper Phrase Structure source for NP containing relative clauses.

There are two conceptions of the constituent structure of such complex NP that are common in recent work – the 'NP S̄' analysis, as diagrammed in (53) and the 'Nom S̄' analysis, as diagrammed in (54).

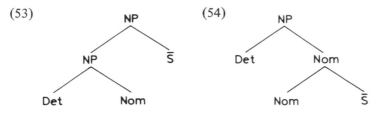

The relative clause construction in (55), for instance, would have the alternative structures (56) and (57) on the NP S̄ and Nom S̄ analyses respectively.

(55)   **an fear a   thit go talamh**
        the man COMP fell to earth

        'the man who fell to earth'

(56)

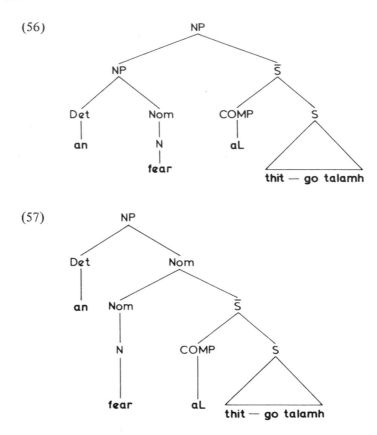

(57)

Those who have worked in the tradition of logical semantics have tended to work with (54) (or its equivalent in some different syntactic framework) and Barbara Partee (1976b) has in fact argued that semantic considerations decide the issue between (53) and (54), since only the Nom S̄ structure is compatible with the requirement that semantic interpretation be compositional. This, however, turns out not to be the case. Emmon Bach and Robin Cooper have shown how to define an adequate compositional semantics on the NP S̄ structure (53) (*cf.* Cooper, 1975; Bach and Cooper, 1978).

The issue may seem to be a small one, but for reasons that can only really become apparent later (when we come to consider the syntactic relationship between relative clauses and constituent questions), I must favour the NP S̄ structure. It is important then that Bach and Cooper have demonstrated that this syntactic choice is compatible with our fundamental semantic assumptions.

The following considerations can also, I think, be taken to support the NP $\bar{S}$ analysis over the Nom $\bar{S}$ proposal.

It is possible in Irish to get restrictive relative clauses on personal pronouns, as long as they are plural. Sentence (58) for instance has a preferred reading on which the relative clause is taken to be restrictive:

(58) **Sibh-se aL   tá _ tinn , gabhaigí   'na bhaile**
     you (pl) COMP are   sick   go (impv. pl.) home

'Those of you who are sick, go home.'

Some speakers find that (58) is ambiguous between appositive and restrictive readings of the relative clause, but all report that the restrictive interpretation is primary. Notice that on this reading, the semantic function served by the relative clause is exactly parallel to that served by obviously restrictive relatives. The pronoun head defines a domain of individuals (those being addressed) and the clause serves to restrict that domain, by specifying that the individuals under consideration must have some additional property (in this case, that of being ill). But there is no non-*ad hoc* way, that I can see, to analyze such examples as (58) in terms of the Nom $\bar{S}$ analysis. They are, however, natural candidates for the NP $\bar{S}$ analysis, given the assumption that pronouns are best analyzed as basic NP.

Consider also sentences such as (59).

(59) **Ní   chreidim iad   -seo   aL deir _ go   bhfuil an**
     NEG I believe them demon. ptc.   say   COMP is   the

cogadh thart
war   over

'I don't believe these people that say the war is over'.

Irish forms demonstrative pronouns by adding a demonstrative suffix – **seo** (proximate) or **sin** (distant) – to 3rd. person pronouns. Thus from **é** ('him, it') and **iad** ('them') we get:

é seo	'this'	iad seo	'these'
é sin	'that'	iad sin	'those'

As illustrated by (59), relative clauses can be attached to such demonstratives. Again, such examples seem to be, on the face of it, incompatible with the Nom $\bar{S}$ hypothesis, although it is perhaps less clear than in the case of examples like (58) that these are properly analysed as headed restrictive relatives.

A further difficulty must be faced in the case of relatives that happen to be inside interrogative phrases. Irish has two basic interrogative phrases – **cé** ('who') and **caidé** ('what') – both of which can serve as the head for a relative clause:[9]

> (60) **Tá mé faoi imní ó shin gan   a fhios   caidé aL**
> *am I   under worry since without knowledge what COMP*
>
> **dhéanfadh siad aL   chuirfeadh in áit a gcartaithe iad**
> *would do they COMP would put them in a terrible plight*
>
> 'I have been worried ever since, not knowing what they would do that would leave them in a terrible plight.'

If such structures are to be compatible with the Nom $\overline{S}$ analysis, we must derive the simple morphemes **cé** and **caidé** from some complex source containing a Nom-constituent. Since I know of no evidence for such a move, I will make the more straightforward assumption that such examples indicate that the correct constituent structure for relative constructions is as in (61):

(61)

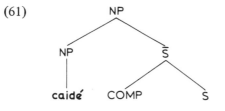

These arguments are of course only as strong as the assumption that the pronominal elements we have been discussing are to be taken as basic NP. Other positions are of course possible and have in fact been put forward. One might argue, for instance, that the elements in question are nouns subcategorized to take no determiners or adjectives. Alternatively one might take the position, following Postal (1966), that pronouns originate under Det and that their surface syntax results from transformational manipulation of one kind or another. Such proposals seem to me to be needlessly elaborate, but a detailed analysis of the internal structure of NP might well reveal that there are good reasons for favouring the elaboration. Until such evidence becomes available though, I will continue to make what seems to me to be the simplest assumption – namely, that **sibh, iad** and **caidé** are lexical members of the category NP.

We will assume that as well as the rules in (40), the Phrase Structure rules of Irish include (62).

(62)
$$NP \rightarrow \begin{Bmatrix} NP & \bar{S} \\ Det & Nom \end{Bmatrix}$$

This rule of course allows for iteration through the left branch NP-node, providing for 'stacking' of relatives. That such is required is indicated by the following examples.[10]

(63) **an fear seo aN   bhfuil mé ag caint   air   aL   bhí**
this man   COMP am   I   at talking about-him COMP was

ina   phaidléaraidhe
in-his pedlar

'the man that I was talking about that was a pedlar'

(64) **Ní   fhaca mé aon duine ariamh aL   bhí trom ar dhaoine**
NEG saw   I   any person ever   COMP was harsh on people

óga   nachN   raibh aithreachas ina dhiaidh air
young COMP+NEG was   regret   after it   on-him

'I have never seen anyone that was harsh with young people who didn't regret it afterwards.'

(65) **Tá mé cinnte nachN   bhfuil duine ar bith aN   bhfuil**
am I   certain COMP+NEG is   person any   COMP is

dúil   i   ngaisciúlacht aige   nachN   bhfuil cuimhne
liking in heroism   at-him COMP+NEG is   memory

aige   ar an bhuachaill seo ...
at-him on   this boy

'I am certain that there isn't anyone who likes heroism who does not remember this boy. . . .'

I propose also that attributive adjectives should be introduced by means of the rule in (66).

(66)

$$\text{Nom} \rightarrow \begin{Bmatrix} \text{N} \\ \text{Nom} \quad \text{Adj} \end{Bmatrix}$$

This rule, in combination with (62), predicts that if a complex NP contains both adjective and relative clause modifiers, then all the adjectives will precede all the relative clauses, as illustrated in (67).

(67)

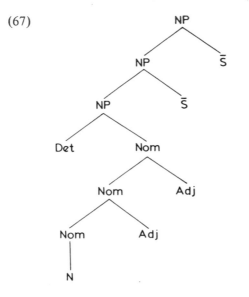

The rules will permit no other ordering of adjectives and relative clauses within the NP. The prediction turns out to be correct:

(68a) **an fear beag buí   aN   raibh mé ag caint   air**
       the man little yellow COMP was I   at talking about-him

       aL   bhí ina   phaidléaraidhe
       COMP was in-his pedlar

       'the little yellow man that I was talking about who was a pedlar'

(b) *an fear aN raibh mé ag caint air aL bhí ina phaidléaraidhe beag buí

(c) *an fear beag aN raibh mé ag caint air aL bhí ina phaidléaraidhe buí

(d)   *an fear beag aN raibh mé ag caint air buí aL bhí ina phaid-
       léaraidhe
(e)   *an fear aN raibh mé ag caint air beag buí aL bhí ina phaid-
       léaraidhe
(f)   *an fear aN raibh mé ag caint air beag aL bhí ina phaidléaraidhe
       buí

The most important decisions made so far then might be summarized as
follows. NP containing relative clauses have the structure (69):

(69)

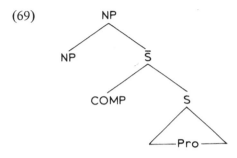

and are subject to a rule of Relative Deletion which deletes a personal pronoun inside the relative clause under the control of the head NP.

2.4. RELATIVE CLAUSE BINDING

In this section I will introduce and provide initial justification for an element
of the analysis that will turn out to be crucial for a number of different
purposes. This is a binding procedure that links the NP head of a relative
clause construction with a pronoun inside the clause.

One of the facts about relative clauses that we must account for is the
fact that a relative clause must contain either a gap in surface structure or a
resumptive pronoun – a pronoun, that is, which is obligatorily bound to the
head NP. We must account, in other words, for the deviance of examples
like (70).

(70)   *na daoine aL   léigh mé leabhar inné
        the people COMP read I   a-book yesterday
        *'the people that I read a book yesterday'

Such facts have been discussed by Akmajian and Kitagawa 1976. They propose in that paper a general principle that they call the Relative Clause Binding Convention (RCB) – "the universal well-formedness condition on relative clauses which stipulates that the relative clause must contain an NP which is coreferential with, or anaphorically related to, the head NP" (Akmajian and Kitagawa 1976 p. 66).[11] Akmajian and Kitagawa argue that this well-formedness condition is defined on deep structures and I will assume the correctness of that conclusion here. Let us assume that RCB takes the form of an indexing operation[12] on deep structure trees – an operation that inspects deep structure trees, looks for a pronoun in the clause, writes an arbitrary numeral which has not previously been used to the right of the Pro-node that immediately dominates the pronoun and then copies that numeral to the right of the head NP. I will give a formal statement of this procedure when more data has been presented and certain decisions made. The rule of Relative Deletion then operates on structures like (71):

(71)

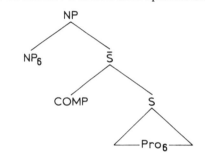

and can be stated as in (72):

(72)   SD: X $[NP_j$ Y Pro_k Z]   W
                 1   2   3   4   5   6

        SC: 1   2   3 $\emptyset$ 5   6

Conditions:
    (i)   obligatory if term 4 is subject in its clause
    (ii) optional if term 4 is direct object in its clause
    (iii) inapplicable if term 4 is neither subject nor object in
          its clause
    (iv) $j = k$

I will also assume that there exists a convention to the effect that co-indexed NP and pronouns must agree in the features of number and gender. This convention will block ungrammatical examples like (73):

(73a)   *an fear arL imigh a   bád go Gabhla
         the man   went her boat to Gola
         *'the man that her boat went to Gola'

(b)   *an fear arL briseadh   a   mbád i dToraigh
        the man   was wrecked their boat in Tory
        *'the man that their boat was wrecked in Tory'

If we further assume that co-indexed NP and pronouns must agree in the feature of person, and that all non-pronominal NP are by convention marked as 3rd person, then we solve the problem of ensuring that only 3rd person pronouns turn up as the bound pronouns in relatives with non-pronominal heads. That is, we will block examples like (74):

(74)   *an stiúrthóir scannán   arL thug an rialtas   deontas
         *the director films(gen)   gave the government grant

         duit
         to you

         *'the film-director that the government gave a grant to you'

The indexing procedure thus performs a variety of useful functions – it blocks examples like (75) where the relative clause contains no anaphor of the head:

(75)   *an rothar $\left\{ \begin{array}{l} \text{aL} \\ \text{aN} \end{array} \right\}$ tá Fionn Mac Cumhail ina chodladh
         the bicycle   is   asleep
         *'the bicycle that Finn McCool is asleep'

as well as all the examples (73)–(74). The indexing also performs useful semantic tasks as we will see when we come to define the semantics for relatives. In essence, it helps ensure that the NP head of a relative clause construction binds the appropriate position in the relative clause.

2.5. ISLAND CONSTRAINTS ON RELATIVE DELETION

Before going on to state the deletion rule more exactly, I need to broaden the notion of 'accessibility'. When the notion was introduced in Section 2.1 above with regard to the factors that govern the choice of one of the relative clause types over the other, we made reference only to the grammatical relation borne by the relativized constituent in the relative clause. But the notion of 'syntactic island' is also relevant to the choice. If the link between the head of the relative and its anaphor inside the relative clause has to be made across an island-boundary – that is, if the relativized constituent occurs inside a syntactic island which does not include the head of the relative – then the pronoun-retaining Indirect Relative must be used. To demonstrate this, we must first demonstrate the existence of certain syntactic islands in the language.

Consider first the Complex NP Constraint (CNPC) (discussed first by Ross (1967). CNPC blocks extraction from clauses with lexically-filled nominal heads. It is this constraint which is usually held to account for the fact that it is impossible, in English, to question or to relativize into relative clauses. Thus (76) and (77) are both ungrammatical:

(76)   *the man *who* I love [NP the woman [s̄ that márried _]]

(77)   **which man* do I love [NP the woman [s̄ that married _]]?

The same is true of the equivalent construction in Irish:

(78)   *an fear aL phóg mé an bhean aL phós _ _
         the man   kissed I   the woman   married
         *'the man who I kissed the woman who married'

(78) would have to derive from a structure like (79) in which the rule of Relative Deletion has already applied on the lower cycle:

(79)   [NP an fear₃ [s̄₁ COMP [s phóg mé [NP an bhean
         the man   kissed I   the woman

         [s̄₂ COMP [s phós   sé₃ _]]]]]]]
         married he

Here the rule of Relative Deletion would have to operate across an island-boundary in order to delete the pronoun (sé₃) coindexed to the head (an fear₃). The corresponding question is also ungrammatical:

(80)   *Cén fear aL phóg tú an bhean aL phós _ _
         which man   kissed you the woman   married
         *'which man did you kiss the woman who married?'

The constraint in question is not a general bounding condition. The extraction rule that derives both Direct Relatives and constituent questions can act over apparently arbitrary numbers of clause-boundaries, as long as those clauses do not have lexically-filled nominal heads, as illustrated by examples (42a)–(42d). It seems reasonable to suppose that the Complex NP Constraint must constrain the application of Relativization and Question-Formation rules in Irish.

The second island-constraint I will discuss here bears a close family resemblance to what has been called the WH-Island Constraint in English. The fact that this constraint holds for Irish and the form in which it holds seem to me to raise interesting questions about the proper formulation of that constraint, but to go in to those questions here would involve us in too much of a digression. For now, all I would like to do is demonstrate the validity of (81).

(81)   No item can be extracted from an embedded question.

The structure of questions in Irish will be gone into in some detail in a later section of the book; for now, let me just cite (82) and (83) as typical examples:

(82)   **An   bpósfadh   duine ar bith í   ?**
         Int. Part. would marry anyone   her
         'Would anyone marry her?'

(83)   **Cén bhean   aL phósfadh   sé _ ?**
         which woman   would marry he
         'Which woman would he marry?'

Yes/No questions are introduced by the particle **an**. Constituent questions have an interrogative phrase in initial position, followed by the complementizer **aL**, followed by a sentence with a 'gap' at the site questioned into. Neither type of question shows any change of structure when embedded:

(84)   **Níl fhios agam an bpósfadh duine ar bith í.**
         I don't know
         'I don't know if anyone would marry her'.

(85)   **Níl fhios agam cén   cineál mná   aL phósfadh   _ é**
         I don't know   what sort   woman (gen.)   would marry   him
         'I don't know what sort of a woman would marry him.'

To demonstrate the validity of (81), I cite (86) and (87), in which sentences (84) and (85) respectively have been embedded as relative clauses. In both cases, relativization by means of the Direct Relative produces thorough ungrammaticality:

(86)   *bean   nachN   bhfuil fhios agam an   bpósfadh
       a woman NEG–COMP I know   Int. Part. would marry

       duine ar bith __ __
       person any

       *'a woman who I don't know if anyone would marry'

(87)   *fear   nachN   bhfuil fhios agam cén cineál mná
       a man NEG–COMP I know   what sort of a woman

       aL phósfadh __ __
       would marry

       *'a man who I don't know what woman would marry'

Questioning into embedded questions is also hopeless:

(88)   *Cén   sagart nachN   bhfuil fhios agat caidé aL dúirt __ __
       which priest NEG–COMP you know   what   said

       *'which priest don't you know what said?'

(89)   *Cén   sagart aL d'fhiafraigh Seán díot   arL
       which priest   asked   John of you Int. Part.

       bhuail tú   __ ?
       hit   you

       *'Which priest did John ask you if you hit?'

Now we have formulated the relativization rule as a rule which deletes ordinary pronouns which are bound by indexing to an NP-head. But from this formulation and the fact that the rule is constrained by island constraints, and given the assumption that the rule is optional,[13] we derive an empirical prediction – namely that in all those cases where the deletion rule is blocked by an island constraint, there should be a corresponding grammatical example with a pronoun at the relativization site.

This prediction is in fact borne out. In each case where the CNPC or the Embedded Question Constraint prohibits relativization by deletion (i.e. prohibits the Direct Relative), the corresponding sentences with the pronoun-retaining Indirect Relative are perfectly grammatical. So, corresponding to (86) and (87), which violate the Embedded Question Constraint, we have the grammatical (90) and (91) with retained pronouns and the morphology of the Indirect Relative:

(90)   **Sin bean   nachN   bhfuil fhios agam an   bpósfadh**
        that a woman that not I know   Int. Part. would marry

        duine are bith í
        anyone   her

        ?'That's a woman that I don't know if anyone would marry her.'

(91)   **Sin fear   nachN   bhfuil fhios agam cén   cineál**
        that a-man NEG–COMP I know   which kind

        mná   aL   phósfadh   _ é
        woman (gen.sg.) COMP would-marry   him

        ?'That's a man that I don't know what kind of woman would
        marry him'.

I have noted the following examples in contemporary written sources, all of
which illustrate how a resumptive pronoun can save what would otherwise
have been a violation of the Embedded Question Constraint[14].

(92)   **Bhí sé fóinteach   . . . laoch a aimsiú, má ba laoch cineál**
        was it convenient   a-hero to find   if was a-hero sort-of

        corr   féin é nárbh fhios   cé   dar díobh é . . . .
        peculiar itself he that it wasn't known who that he was of them

        'It was convenient to find a hero, even if he was a fairly peculiar
        hero, that no-one knew who his people were . . . '.

(93)   **a   ghiolla feosaí   briotach nachN   feasach   sinn**
        his lackey wizened lisping   COMP+NEG knowledgable us

        an   Francach   nó Éireannach é
        Interr. Ptc. Frenchman or Irishman   he

        ' . . . his wizened, lisping little sidekick, that we don't know
        whether he's a Frenchman or an Irishman . . . '

(94)   **. . . íoróin den   chineál nachN   dtig linn a rá**
              irony of-the kind   COMP+NEG we-can to-say

        go baileach céacu   dáiríre aL   tá sé . . . nó an
        exactly   whether serious COMP is it   or Interr. Ptc.

        ag magadh   fúinn aL   tá sé . . .
        at making-fun of-us COMP is it

'... irony of that kind that we can't say exactly whether it's serious that it is, or if it's making fun of us that it is ...'.

Examples (95)–(99) demonstrate that it is possible to relativize into a Complex NP, as long as the relativization-site is marked by a resumptive pronoun. Examples (95) and (96) are my own inventions, checked against the intuitions of native speakers; examples (97)–(99) are taken from contemporary written sources.[15]

(95)   **Sin teanga   aN mbeadh   meas   agam ar duine ar bith aL**
         that a-language   would be respect at me on person   any

         tá ábalta í a labhairt
         is able   it to speak

         ??'That's a language that I would respect anyone who could speak it.'

(96)   **Sin madadh nachN   bhfaca mé ariamh asal   aL**
         that a dog   NEG–COMP saw   I   ever   a donkey

         bheadh   _ chomh mór leis
         would be   as   big with it

         ??'That's a dog that I have never seen a donkey that was as big as it.'

(97)   **fear   gurL mheas   an uile dhuine desna Fínínibh nárL**
         a man   thought everyone   of the Fenians NEG–COMP

         mháir an fear sin ariamh aL bhí níba dílse ná   é
         lived that man ever   was more loyal than him

         ??'a man that every member of the Fenians thought that the man never lived who was more loyal than he'

(98)   **amharc áilleachta ... nachN   bhfaca mé mórán riamh**
         a-sight of-beauty   COMP+NEG saw   I   much   ever

         aL   bhéarfadh bua   air
         COMP would-take victory on-it

         '... a sight of beauty that I have never seen much that would surpass it ...'

(99)   **daoine ... nárL   labhair éinne aL   bhain**
        people   COMP+NEG (Past) spoke anyone COMP took

leo   Gaeilge ... .
with-them Irish

' ... people that no-one who was connected with them ever spoke Irish ... '

The deletion analysis being defended here accounts for these data in a straight-forward way. The rule of Relative Deletion is an unbounded rule, and is therefore subject to island-constraints. Bound pronouns then will never be deleted if they occur inside a syntactic island which does not also contain the controller of the deletion – i.e. the head of the relative clause. It is some-what misleading then to talk, as I did in Section 2.1, about there being two different relative clause strategies. There is only one phrase-structure source for relatives and one deletion rule. The surface configuration known as the Indirect Relative is simply what surfaces if the rule of Relative Deletion, for one reason or another, fails to operate. This unification of both types of relative clause under a single analysis is one of the principal advantages of the deletion analysis. As we shall see later, a single rule of semantic interpretation also serves to interpret both types of relative.

This unification is something that is not possible under the WH-Movement analysis – for on that account some special WH-pronoun must be moved from the relativization site in the case of Direct Relatives while in the case of the Indirect Relative the relativization site is marked by an ordinary pronoun. The two kinds of relative clause thus have quite distinct sources and probably (although this is hard to determine in the absence of a detailed semantic analysis) must be interpreted in different ways. This extra apparatus requires empirical justification, which, as far as I can tell, is lacking.

2.6. AGAINST THE HEAD-RAISING ANALYSIS

There is another analysis of relative clauses that has led a sort of underground existence for several years, being proposed for the most part in oral presen-tations, footnotes and in unpublished work, and which has recently enjoyed a revival of interest. This is the so-called 'Head-Raising' or 'promotion' analysis (Brame, 1967, 1976; Chiba, 1972; Bresnan, 1973b; Chomsky, 1973 (fn 70); Schachter, 1973; Vergnaud, 1974; Carlson, 1977; Chomsky and Lasnik, 1977, notes 56, 76). The essence of such proposals is that the head of a relative clause originates inside the relative clause in underlying structure. The head NP-position is unfilled in underlying structure and a Raising rule promotes the relativized NP from inside the clause to fill the empty head position. Example (100) would be derived roughly as in (101).

(100)   The spy that came in from the cold

(101)

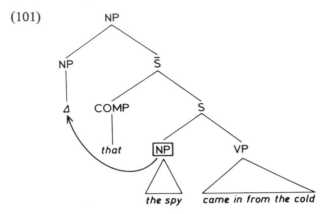

Given a framework that includes the Subjacency Condition, the analysis is necessarily a little more elaborate, since the Raising rule must operate over apparently unbounded contexts. Within the framework of Vergnaud 1974, for example, an example like (102) is derived as follows:

(102)   the spy who we thought came in from the cold

The NP *the spy* originates as subject of the lowest clause (*the spy came in from the cold*). Following placement of WH on [$_{NP}$ *the spy*] , WH-Movement moves the whole phrase successive-cyclically through the various intervening COMP-nodes to the COMP of the highest clause. This is followed by Raising of *the spy* to head-position, leaving *who* in the highest COMP.

The principal argument (in fact the only argument that I am aware of) that has been put forward in defence of this analysis has to do with the behaviour of idiom chunks like *make headway, pay homage to*, and so on. The argument starts from the premise that nouns like *headway* and *homage*, whose distribution is extremely limited, must be introduced by lexical insertion next to the verb that they must co-occur with. But this assumption is incompatible with the traditional analysis of Relative clauses, since in examples like (103) and (104), *headway* and *homage* will never be adjacent to the verbs that define their distribution.

(103)   The headway that we made at the meeting was amazing

(104)   The homage that the Spanish government now pays to Picasso is long overdue

But on the promotion analysis, these examples are quite consistent with the idea that *headway*, for instance, must be introduced in the frame $[_{VP} [_V make] \_]$.

Before going on to discuss the pros and cons of this proposal for Irish specifically, it is perhaps worth making some general points.

Firstly, as Joan Bresnan has pointed out (Bresnan, 1973b; Bresnan and Grimshaw, 1978), it is not clear that we can conclude anything at all from such arguments. This is because there are instances where *headway* and the like occur where it is well nigh impossible to come up with a syntactic analysis in which the NP and its verb are ever, at any stage of derivation, adjacent. Witness the examples in (105):

(105a)   We made what later seems to have been described as great headway on the problem
   (b)   *We provided what later seems to have been described as great headway on the problem
   (c)   We pay what the foreign press has seen fit to describe as insufficient homage to our dead comrades
   (d)   *We supply what the foreign press has seen fit to describe as insufficient homage to our dead comrades
   (e)   He took what was later described in the Press as great umbrage to the suggestion that he should attend Caroline's wedding
   (f)   *He got what was later described in the Press as great umbrage to the suggestion that he should attend Caroline's wedding
   (g)   We made what is known technically as a hames of the experiment
   (h)   *We did what is known technically as a hames of the experiment

What these examples suggest is that the general principle that idiom-chunks can be base-generated together is not tenable and therefore that arguments based on that conclusion cannot be viable. The historical precedent for such argumentation has been the use of arguments of exactly the same form to support the existence of a Passive transformation. But if Bresnan (1978) is right about the non-transformational nature of Passive (as seems likely) then in this case too the argument form has led to wrong conclusions.

Notice too that the idiom-chunk argument cuts both ways. Consider examples like those in (106):

(106a) The Spanish nation has never paid Picasso the homage that was due to him

   (b) He took a slash that later earned him a $100 fine for public indecency

(To 'take a slash', in my dialect at any rate, means to urinate. One can't do anything with a slash but take it.) In cases such as these it is the Head-Raising analysis that is incompatible with the view that idiom-chunks must be generated together, for on that analysis the heads of the relative clauses in (106) must be generated inside the relative clause, away from the verbs that define their distribution. (107a) and (107b) are of course bad:

(107a) *The homage was due to him

   (b) *A slash earned him a $100 fine for public indecency

What this means is that the treatment of idiom-chunks that we are lead to by the Head-Raising analysis is something like this: the co-occurrence restrictions on such items are such that they must occur adjacently at some point in a derivation. Whatever device checks such co-occurrence restrictions must be persuaded to ignore the ungrammaticality of (107) on the lowest cycle and then declare the sentence in which they occur OK because on the next cycle *slash* is the object of *take* and *homage* is the object of *pay*. So quite apart from the questions raised by examples like (105), the treatment of idioms that is compatible with the Head-Raising analysis is far from attractive, requiring as it does a device of essentially global power.

If we turn to facts from Irish, we find further reason for being suspicious of the claim that data on idiom-chunks provide evidence in favour of the Head Raising analysis.

In Irish we find relative clause constructions in which the head NP is part of an idiom-chunk, but in which the relativized position is marked by a resumptive pronoun. The noun **faopach**, for instance, has no independent meaning, but occurs only in the collocation (108):

(108)   **Tá X san   fhaopach**   =   'X is in a fix'
        is   in-the

Yet one finds examples like (109):[16]

UNIVERSITY OF WINNIPEG
& BALMORAL
WIN... R3B 2E9
DISCARDED

THE SYNTAX OF RELATIVE CLAUSES 39

(109) **Thuig   mé an t-am sin an fhaopach aN   mbeinn**
understood I   that time the fix   COMP I-would-be

ann dá mbínn   amuigh
in-it if I-were-to-be outside

'I understood then the fix I would be in if I were to be outside ... '.

Fassi Fehri (1978: note 31) has pointed out the existence of similar examples
in Moroccan Arabic.

It is surely the case that a derivation of these examples in terms of a rule
of WH-Movement is at best extremely implausible. But if this is the case, then
such idiom-chunks cannot be handled in the classical way, and arguments
based on that approach can have little force.

There is really no argument whatever from facts about items of limited
distribution in favour of the Head-Raising analysis. Given the elaborations
required by at least Vergnaud's version of this analysis (and, one imagines,
required by any theory which includes both Head-Raising and the Subjacency
Condition) it is difficult to see why one would prefer it over more traditional
approaches.

But if the two proposals (the Head Raising proposal and the more traditional approach on which the head NP is lexically-filled at deep structure
and the gaps are created by movement or deletion of some anaphoric element) are neutral with respect to the idiom chunk facts, there are certain
other empirical considerations that argue against the Head-Raising analysis.

There is in Irish, for instance, a Noun Phrase which is used *only* as the
head of relative clauses. This is the item **an té** ('the one who', 'he who'):

(110a) **an té aL   tá _ laidir**
       COMP is   strong

'he who is strong'

(b) **an té aN   bhfuil eagla air**
       COMP is   fear on him

'the one who is afraid'

(c) ****tá an té laidir**
(d) ****tá eagla ar an té**

This item has no other use in the language but to head relative clauses,
hence the ungrammaticality of (110c,d). There is a straightforward account

of these facts given the analysis of relatives assumed here: we enter **an té** in the lexicon as a complex item – an NP with the structure [$_{NP}$ [$_{Det}$ **an**] [$_{Nom}$ **té**]] – and give it the subcategorization feature [$_\_ \bar{S}$]. But on the Head-Raising analysis **an té** in an example like (110a) must originate in the relative clause – that is, we must generate the ungrammatical (110c). We will then need some device that checks post-transformational structures and says that **an té** is unacceptable in any position except the head of a relative clause construction. It is difficult to see how such a device could be formulated in any very economical way.

In general I think the Head-Raising analysis buys us nothing and costs us a good deal – both in terms of the elaborateness it requires (at least when embedded within a theory that includes Subjacency) and in bad empirical consequences.

2.7. CONCLUSION

The case in favour of the deletion analysis that I have sketched here is, I think, a strong one. It provides a unified account of both types of relative clause, it accounts for the retention or deletion of pronouns at the relativization site and how that relates to accessibility conditions and island constraints in a simple and direct way and it avoids the vacuity of 'invisible' WH-pronouns. I will therefore assume the correctness of this analysis from now on. It will be additionally supported when we come to consider how it copes with certain systematic parallels between the structure of relative constructions and that of constituent questions.

I will conclude this section by gathering here the rules that are made necessary by the decisions we have made so far. We need the following Phrase-Structure rules:

(111a) $S \rightarrow V$ NP   (NP)   (PP)

    (b) $PP \rightarrow Prep$ NP

    (c) $NP \rightarrow \begin{Bmatrix} NP & \bar{S} \\ Det & Nom \end{Bmatrix}$

    (d) $\bar{S} \rightarrow COMP$ S

    (e) $Nom \rightarrow \begin{Bmatrix} Nom & Adj \\ N & \end{Bmatrix}$

I will assume that pronouns belong to the category NP and that they are distinguished from other NP by the feature [+Pro].

We need also to allow for possessive pronouns. I will assume that these are introduced under Det:

(112)   **a   mac**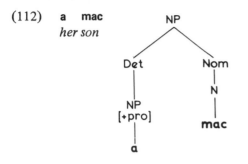
        her son

If NP in such constructions is not expanded as Pro, we will derive possessive nominals like:

(113)   **mac an fhir**
        son the man(gen.)

Example (113) will have the structure diagrammed in (114).

(114)

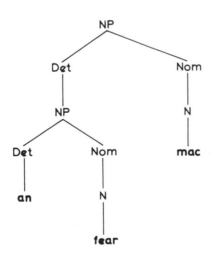

This analysis of possessive modifiers presupposes the existence of a rule postposing non-pronominal NP from the Det slot to post-nominal position. To defend this analysis in detail here would take us too far afield, since it is not crucial to our main concerns. It is discussed and defended in detail in some unpublished work (McCloskey 1978).

So to the PS-rules in (111), we add (115).

(115)   Det → NP

The category Det will also have as lexical realizations the definite article **an** and the zero indefinite article. The category COMP has the lexical realizations **aL**, **aN**, and **goN**.

The following transformational rule, to be known as Relative Deletion, has also been proposed:

$$(116) \quad SD: \quad X \quad [NP_j \quad Y \quad \begin{matrix} NP \\ [+Pro]_k \end{matrix} \quad Z] \quad W$$

$$ 1 \quad\quad 2 \quad\; 3 \quad\quad\quad 4 \quad\quad\; 5 \quad\; 6$$

$$ SC: \; 1 \quad\quad 2 \quad\; 3 \quad\quad\quad \emptyset \quad\quad 5 \quad\; 6$$

Conditions:

(i) $j = k$
(ii)   obligatory if term 4 is subject in its clause
(iii)   optional if term 4 is direct object in its clause
(iv)   blocks if term 4 is neither subject nor object in its clause

It remains for me to do three things to explicate the syntactic part of this analysis in proper detail – firstly, to give a more formal account of the accessibility conditions on Relative Deletion (i.e. conditions (ii)–(iv) of (116)); secondly, to give a formal account of the indexing procedure that binds the heads of relative clauses to pronouns inside the clauses; and thirdly, to give an account of the distribution of complementizers inside relatives.

All these matters will be taken up in due course. First though I want to finish this chapter by considering another type of relative clause which we have not yet discussed. In the following chapter we will then go on to consider the syntactic structure of questions, and the relationship between the syntax of relative clause constructions and that of constituent questions.

2.8. ANOTHER RELATIVE CLAUSE TYPE

There exists a third relative clause type which we have not yet discussed at all. This type can be used only when the relativized position is a prepositional object, and then only under certain rather limited circumstances. I will call this clause-type the 'Prepositional Relative'. The construction has the following general form:

> Head NP, followed by an amalgam of a preposition and a particle identical in form and morphology to the Indirect Relative Complementizer **aN**, followed by a clause with a PP-gap.

Typical examples are given in (117):

(117a) **an áit i-n-aN bhfuil muid inár   seasamh**
 the place   are   we   in-our standing
 'the place in which we are standing'

 (b) **an fear le-n-aN mbíonn   tú   ag caint**
 the man   are (habitual) you at talking
 'the man to whom you talk'

 (c) **an bord ar-aN bhfuil an bia**
 the table   is   the food
 'the table on which the food is'

The particle suffixed to the preposition in this construction has the same mutation-effect as the Indirect Relative Complementizer, and also shows the same past tense forms, as illustrated in (118).

(118a) **an áit   i-n-arL fhán siad**
 the place   stayed they
 'the place in which they stayed'

 (b) **an fear le-n-arL labhair tú**
 the man   spoke you
 'the man to whom you spoke'

This construction represents the productive way of relativizing prepositional objects in Old, Middle and Early Modern Irish, but in Modern Irish it is something of a relic. The Christian Brothers' Grammar (1960) gives the following comment (Section 671, p. 339):

Although such constructions are formally elegant, they are not much used in Modern Irish except in the written language .... . There is a strong tendency to use the (Indirect Relative) forms instead.   (My translation)

The construction is subject to a number of purely syntactic restrictions as well – firstly in that only a small subset of the prepositions may occur in the construction. The set of prepositions that may occur also varies considerably from dialect to dialect, but most commonly one finds **ar** (on), **as** (out of), **do** (to, for), **i** (in), **le** (with). A further syntactic restriction that the construction is subject to is that it may not be used if the relative clause is negated (Christian Brothers' Grammar, p. 339).

There is a certain amount of variation in how speakers react to examples in which the Prepositional Relative is used and in which the relativization-site is inside an embedded clause – examples corresponding to English 'the room in which you think they are'. Some speakers do not allow the prepositional relative under such circumstances at all, but grammars cite, and many speakers accept, examples like (119a) and (119b) as free variants.

(119a) **an seomra aL   mheasann sibh   inaN   bhfuil siad**
        the room   COMP think   you(pl) in + rel.ptc. are   they

(b)   **an seomra inaN   measann sibh   aN   bhfuil siad**
        the room   in + rel.ptc. think   you(pl) COMP are   they

        'the room in which you think they are'

Note that the relative prepositional phrase may appear either at the head of the embedded clause, or at the head of the entire relative clause. I should point out however that I have not managed to find any such examples in my reading of modern written sources, nor have I heard any such examples, as far as I can remember, in listening to ordinary conversation. Furthermore, even those speakers who accept such examples as (119a) and (119b) are uneasy about the matter, and report themselves as being unsure of their own intuitions.

Given the uncertainty and variability of the data, it is hard to know how this construction should be treated, and indeed I do not plan to attempt an analysis here. It does seem to me though that the Prepositonal Relative should be given a treatment separate from that given to the more productive relative clause types that we will be principally concerned with in this work. The syntactic properties of the Prepositional Relative seem to be quite different from those both of the Direct Relative and of the Indirect.[17]

There seem, on the face of it, to be two plausible approaches.

One could hold that the relative prepositional phrases arrive in clause-initial position as a result of the operation of a movement rule. Given the grammaticality of both (119a) and (119b) this would presumably need to be a 'successive–cyclic' movement rule in the sense of Chomsky 1973 – a rule, that is, that moves the relative phrase first to the nearest complementizer-position, then optionally to other complementizer-positions farther to the left. On this account, the examples (119) would be derived as diagrammed in (120). (119a) will be generated if only the first movement takes place; (119b) will be derived if both movements take place.

(120)

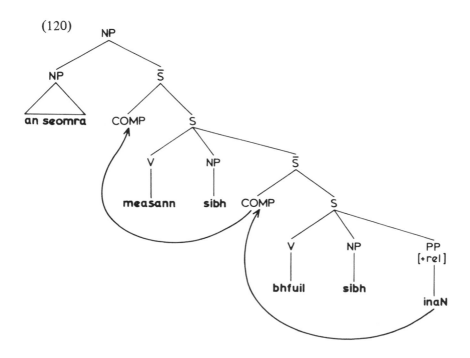

One might also propose a non-transformational solution, one that includes the Phrase Structure rule in (121):

(121) $\bar{\bar{S}} \rightarrow \underset{[+rel]}{PP}\ S$

where the category $\underset{[+rel]}{PP}$ is realized, by one means or another, as **inaN**, **araN**, **asaN**, **lenaN** and so on. This solution will assign to the two examples (119a) and (119b) the structures in (122a) and (122b) respectively.

(122a)

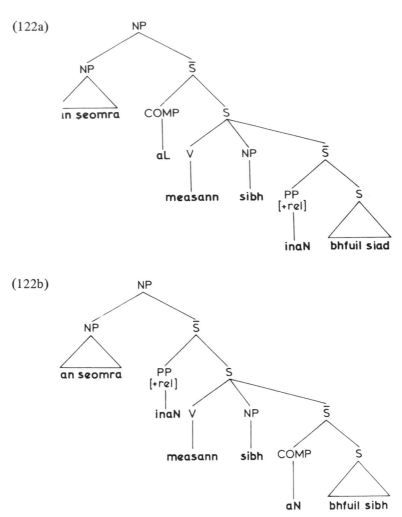

(122b)

This approach to the Prepositional Relative will require a certain amount of filtering to prevent S̄ being expanded as [PP S] in inappropriate positions – to prevent, for instance, the generation of (123).

(123)   *Deir siad araN   raibh an bia
          say they on + rel.ptc. was   the food
          *'They say on which was the food'

As it happens, if one adapts for the interpretation of such structures, the techniques of semantic interpretation developed by Robin Cooper (1977b, 1978) for the interpretation of English Wh-constructions, then the deviance of examples like (123) is predicted in a straightforward way.

But I would like to leave for future work the question of deciding which of these two approaches to the Prepositional Relative is the more adequate. As things stand, I know of no strong empirical grounds for favouring either approach.

NOTES

[1] There is, in fact, a third but less productive type which we will discuss shortly (Section 2.8 below).

[2] The presence of a resumptive pronoun in examples like (3) is obscured by one of the peculiarities of Irish morphology – namely that many prepositions are 'conjugated'; they form amalgams with pronominal objects whose form is largely unpredictable on the basis of the form of the preposition and that of the pronoun. Thus from the preposition **do** (to, for), for instance, we derive the paradigm **dom** (to me), **duit** (to you), **dó** (to him) **di** (to her), **dúinn** (to us), **daoibh** (to you(pl)), **dóibh** (to them). I will assume throughout that such amalgams derive from syntactic structures in which the preposition and the pronoun have a separate existence. The form **dó** (to him), for instance, will have the syntactic structure in (i):

(i)

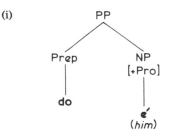

[3] Example (7) is from **An Druma Mór** by Seosamh MacGrianna (Oifig an tSoláthair, Dublin, 1969), p. 136. Examples (8)–(10) are from Ó Cadhlaigh 1940, p. 377. For the particle **gur** which introduces the relative clauses in (8) and (9), cf note 7.

[4] Use of the Indirect Relative is also obligatory when relativizing the object of comparison (again in accordance with the Accessibility Hierarchy of Keenan and Comrie (1977)).

(i)   **fear   aN   bhfuil mé níos mo ná   é**
      a-man COMP am   I   bigger   than him

'a man than whom I am bigger'

I will assume that in Irish at least this case is subsumed under the more general condition that forces retention of the pronoun following a preposition. I will assume, that
is, that the particle ná (than) is a preposition, at least in this construction.

[5] In the examples below and throughout the book, if a verb shows different forms
in Direct and Indirect Relative Clauses, this will be a reflection of the different mutation-
effects of **aL** and **aN**. The differences can be rather dramatic, since some verbs are
suppletive under nasalization or lenition. The verb **tá**, for instance, (one of the verbs
'to be') takes the form **bhfuil** in nasalizing environments.

[6] One might be tempted to regard such constructions as involving complex complementizers: [**nuairaL**], [**sulaN**] and so on. But this is made unlikely by the existence
of examples like the following:

(i)   **nuair aL   shroich sé an pháirc agus aL   chuala sé búireach an**
         when COMP reached he the field   and COMP heard   he roaring   the

         tslua
         crowd (gen.sg.)

         'when he reached the field and heard the roaring of the crowd'

The existence of such examples follows as an automatic consequence of the analysis
incorporating a rule like (40a), given that we have to allow for $\bar{S}$-Conjunction anyway
to generate examples like (ii):

(ii)   **Dúirt sé goN   raibh sé breoite agus goN   bhfanfadh sé sa bhaile**
         said   he COMP was   he ill   and COMP would stay he at home

         'He said that he was sick and that he would stay at home'.

A grammar incorporating these two rules will generate examples like (i) without further
fuss, and assign to them the structure diagrammed in (iii):

(iii)

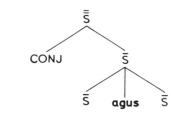

The existence of examples like (i) is unexpected given an analysis based on the assumption that **nuairaL** and the others are single complementizers.

   There is another prediction made by the combination of decisions we have made so
far, whose correctness I am far from convinced of, however. Presumably we must have a
rule of S-Conjunction, to provide for the conjunction of simple main clauses. Given that
rule though, and given our treatment of complementizers like **aL** and **aN** as arising from
an expansion of a category $\bar{S}$ distinct from S, then we predict the existence of examples
with the structure (iv):

(iv)

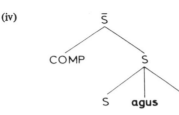

There may be instances of this structure, (v) for example (from **An Druma Mór**, Seosamh MacGrianna, Oifig an tSoláthair, 1969, p. 30);

(v) **Nuair aL   luigh dorchadas na h-oíche   go dlúth ar an tír   agus**
     when COMP lay   darkness   the night (gen) thickly on the land and

     lasadh na solais sna   tithe
     was lit the lights in-the houses

'when darkness lay thickly on the land and the lights were lit in the houses'

The trouble with judging the issue is that the particles we have been calling complementizers are stressless and extremely deletable. But when they delete, they normally leave their mutation-effect behind. Thus when **aL** fails to appear where we would normally expect it, we still find Lenition of the initial consonant of a following verb. The trouble with an example like (v) is that the complementizer in this case would have no mutation-effect anyway (because past impersonal forms, for some reason, can never be lenited). Therefore there is no way of telling whether (v) is an instance of S-Conjunction within S̄, or if it is an instance of S̄-Conjunction in which the second complementizer has been deleted. To confirm the prediction, one would need to find examples in which the initial of the verb was free of the mutation-effect of a putative deleted complementizer. I have not managed so far to find or compose any terribly convincing examples of this form.

⁷ Some dialects – particularly those of the southwest – permit or require the complementizer **goN** rather than **aN** in the Indirect Relative. See examples (8) and (9) above, for instance, both of which are taken from Ó Cadhlaigh (1940). Cf. also Ó Cuív (1944).
⁸ The force of these arguments is somewhat weakened by the fact that the datum upon which they are based – namely the possibility of having the relative particles substitute for the complementizer **goN** in clauses which contain a resumptive pronoun – is a little insecure. Although it is easy enough to find examples like (49) and (51) in grammars (cf. for instance Christian Brothers (1960) p. 344), many speakers are reluctant to accept them, or, more often, don't quite know if they should accept them or not. Inclusion of examples like (49) and (51) in the data base has two effects: it strengthens the case against a successive-cyclic movement analysis, and it complicates to a hideous degree the account of the complementizer substitutions. All these matters will be discussed in some detail in Chapter 5, after the proper range of the phenomenon and its interaction with other facts have been brought out. As it turns out, it is perfectly possible to give a good account of the complementizer substitutions without appeal to a successive-cyclic

movement analysis, even if we exclude examples like (49) and (51) from our data base.

The examples discussed in this section are treated in traditional grammars under the name of the 'Double Relative Construction'. The most thorough discussion of the facts that I know of appears in O'Nolan (1920, Vol. 1, pp. 114–134). The matter is also discussed in Ó Cadhlaigh (1940, Sections 484–487, pp. 406–409) and in the Christian Brothers' Grammar (1960, Sections 677–679, pp. 342–344). Eric Wheeler (1978) has analyzed the corresponding data from Scots Gaelic as being evidence for a successive-cyclic formulation of WH-movement.

⁹ Example (60) is from **Mo Bhealach Féin** by Seosamh MacGrianna, Oifig Dhíolta Foilseachán Rialtais (Government Publications Office), Dublin, (1965) p. 34.

¹⁰ Example (63) is from O'Neill (1975), (64) from **An Druma Mór**, Seosamh MacGrianna, Oifig an tSoláthair, Dublin, (1969) p. 146; and example (65) from **Mo Bhealach Féin**, p. 164.

¹¹ Akmajian and Kitagawa formulate the Relative Clause Binding Convention as a universal well-formedness condition on all relative clause structures, but as they point out, certain languages seem, at least on the face of it, to permit exceptions to the general principle (Japanese). Relative Clauses without anaphors of the head NP also seem to occur in Old Irish, particularly in the more archaic strata of the language. The Old Irish cases have recently been studied by Liam Breatnach (1979). I know of no such examples in Modern Irish.

¹² As we will see when we come to formulate the semantic rules which interpret relative clause structures, no actual statement of this well-formedness condition is needed. It falls out as a consequence of the interaction between the indexing procedure and the rules of interpretation that relative clause structures which do not contain an anaphoric element bound to the head NP will never receive an interpretation.

¹³ How the assumption of optionality is compatible with the apparent obligatoriness of the rule when it operates on unembedded subjects will be discussed in some detail in a later chapter.

¹⁴ (92) is from **Lig Sinn i gCathú** by Breandán Ó hEithir, Sáirséal agus Dill, Dublin (1976), p. 62; (93) is from the same book, p. 116; (94) is from the periodical **Feasta**, Samhain (1978) p. 11. My apologies to those with literary sensibilities for the Kiltartanese of the translation of (94), but it gives a better impression of the syntax of the original than would a more stylish translation. Similar comments apply to many of the examples to come.

¹⁵ (97) from **Mo Sgéal Féin**, (1915) by an t-Ath. Peadar Ó Laoghaire, p. 117; (98) from **Mo Bhealach Féin** by Seosamh MacGrianna, p. 145; (99) from 'News on Ghaeltacht', Gaeltarra Murphy, B. Comm., *Irish Times*, Nov. 15th., 1978.

¹⁶ Example (109) is from **Mo Bhealach Féin** by Seosamh MacGrianna, p. 119.

¹⁷ Note that there is no support in these data for deriving the Direct Relative by means of a rule of **aL**-Movement, as discussed in Section 2.2. There is no support, that is, for taking **aL** to be a preposed relative pronoun, because the element fronted in the Prepositional Relative along with the preposition is identical with the Indirect Relative particle **aN**, which cannot be taken to be a preposed relative pronoun.

CHAPTER 3

THE SYNTAX OF QUESTIONS

3.1. INTRODUCTION

I have gone to a lot of trouble in previous sections to defend what is perhaps not a particularly controversial proposal – namely that relativization strategies can involve unbounded deletions. Such proposals for relative clauses are by now common in the literature and have been made, for instance, for English (Morgan, 1972; Bresnan, 1972, for example), Middle English (Grimshaw, 1975), Albanian (Morgan, 1972), Basque (deRijk, 1972), and Old Icelandic (Maling, 1977).

I have gone to considerable trouble to defend this claim for Modern Irish, in order to prepare the ground for what probably is a more controversial claim, and one that, as far as I know, has not been made before – namely that the derivation of Constituent Questions can also involve unbounded deletion. The central contention of the following sections is that if one accepts the conclusion that relativization is an unbounded deletion rule in Modern Irish, one must also accept the conclusion that Constituent Questions are derived by means of an unbounded deletion – the same rule in fact, as is involved in the derivation of relative clauses.

3.2. THE RELATION BETWEEN RELATIVES AND CONSTITUENT QUESTIONS

Relative and Constituent Question structures are more similar in Irish than in many other languages. The situation is not as, for example, in English, where there are broad similarities of structure between WH-questions and WH-relatives but very messy differences in matters of detail. In Irish, relatives and Constituent Questions are similar in the smallest specifics. These similarities have lead Irish grammarians traditionally to the view that Constituent Questions are simply relative clauses adjoined to heads consisting of interrogative pronouns or interrogative phrases. A glance at examples (1)–(3) should suffice to indicate why this is such a natural view. (1)–(3a) are questions; (1)–(3b) are NP with relative clauses.

51

(1a)   **Cé   aL   dhíol an   domhan?**
        who COMP sold   the world
        'Who sold the world?'

(b)   **an fear aL   dhíol an domhan**
        the man COMP

        'the man who sold the world'

(2a)   **Cén   fear aN   bhfaigheann tú   an t-airgead uaidh**
        which man COMP get   you the money   from him

        'Which man do you get the money from?'

(b)   **an fear aN bhfaigheann tú an t-airgead uaidh**
        the man

        'the man from whom you get the money'

(3a)   **Cé   aL   mheas   tú   aL   chonaic tú**
        who COMP thought you COMP saw   you

        'Who did you think you saw?'

(b)   **an duine aL mheas tú aL chonaic tú**
        the person

        'the person that you thought you saw'

I believe that this traditional view is in essence correct, and that the derivation
of constituent questions in Irish involves no rule analogous to WH-Movement
in English, but involves rather the deletion rule that I have called Relative
Deletion.

Just as the basic surface pattern for relative clauses is as in (4):

(4) NP_j $[_{\bar{s}}$ COMP $[_{s} \ldots -_j \ldots]]$

        NP_j $[_{\bar{s}}$ COMP $[_{s} \ldots Pro_j \ldots]]$

so the surface pattern for nominal constituent questions is as in (5):

(5) QNP_j $[_{\bar{s}}$ COMP $[_{s} \ldots -_j \ldots]]$

        QNP_j $[_{\bar{s}}$ COMP $[_{s} \ldots Pro_j \ldots]]$

where QNP is the category of nominal interrogative phrases which includes
the basic members **cé** ('who') and **caidé** ('what') and more complex members
like **cén teach mór** ('which big house') and so on. The syntactic unit formed

by an interrogative phrase with its associated clause (let us call this the 'questioned clause') is syntactically indistinguishable from the unit formed by a head NP with its relative clause, as far as their internal properties are concerned. Given any relative clause, it is possible to form the corresponding constituent question by replacing the head NP with the appropriate interrogative phrase (see examples (1)–(3) above). Let us consider the parallels in more detail.

(i) Both constructions are subject to the same accessibility constraints – that is, pronouns are deleted or retained at the site questioned or relativized into under the same conditions – the conditions being those of the Accessibility Hierarchy and the island constraints.

Deletion is obligatory in subject position:

(6)

$\left\{ \begin{array}{l} \textbf{an fear} \\ \textit{the man} \\ \textbf{cén fear} \\ \textit{which man} \end{array} \right\}$ $\begin{array}{lll} \textbf{aL} & \textbf{thiteann \_ go talamh} \\ \textit{COMP falls} & \textit{to earth} \end{array}$

$\left\{ \begin{array}{l} \textbf{*an fear} \\ \textit{the man} \\ \textbf{*cén fear} \\ \textit{which man} \end{array} \right\}$ $\begin{array}{lll} \textbf{aN} & \textbf{dtiteann sé go talamh} \\ \textit{COMP falls} & \textit{he to earth} \end{array}$

$\left\{ \begin{array}{l} \text{'the man who falls to earth'} \\ \text{'which man falls to earth?'} \end{array} \right\}$

Deletion is optional in direct object position:

(7)

$\left\{ \begin{array}{l} \textbf{an t-údar} \\ \textit{the author} \\ \textbf{cén t-údar} \\ \textit{which author} \end{array} \right\}$ $\begin{array}{lll} \textbf{aL} & \textbf{mholann na léirmheastóirí} \\ \textit{COMP praise} & \textit{the critics} \end{array}$

$\left\{ \begin{array}{l} \textbf{an t-údar} \\ \textit{the author} \\ \textbf{cén t-údar} \\ \textit{which author} \end{array} \right\}$ $\begin{array}{llll} \textbf{aN} & \textbf{molann na léirmheastóirí é} \\ \textit{COMP praise} & \textit{the critics} & \textit{him} \end{array}$

$\left\{ \begin{array}{l} \text{'the author that the critics praise'} \\ \text{'which author do the critics praise?'} \end{array} \right\}$

In any other position retention of the pronoun is obligatory:

(8)   ⎧ **an píobaire** ⎫
      ⎪ *the piper*   ⎪   **arL briseadh   a   mhéar**
      ⎨   ⎬   *was broken his finger*
      ⎪ **cén   píobaire**⎪
      ⎩ *which piper*   ⎭

      ⎧ 'the piper whose finger was broken' ⎫
      ⎨ 'which piper's finger was broken?' ⎬
      ⎩   ⎭

And finally island constraints force the retention of pronouns in both constructions.

(9)   ⎧ **an píobaire** ⎫ **aN mbíonn fhios agat i gcónaí**
      ⎪ *the piper*   ⎪   *you know   always*
      ⎨   ⎬
      ⎪ **cén   píobaire**⎪ **caidé aL bhuailfidh sé**
      ⎩ *which piper*   ⎭   *what   will play   he*

      ?'the piper that you always know what he's going to play'
      ?'which piper do you always know what he's going to play'

(ii) One finds identical patterns of complementizer distribution in the two constructions. In simple one-clause questions, **aL** is the complementizer just in case the position relativized or questioned is marked by a gap and **aN** is the complementizer just in case the bound pronoun is retained. See examples (1)–(3) above.

The complex patterns of complementizer substitution in relative clauses, which we discussed in Section 2.2. of Chapter Two are also found in constituent questions. I repeat here the crucial examples from our earlier discussion and below each one I place the corresponding constituent question:

(10)   **an t-úrscéal** ⎡aL⎤ **mheas mé** ⎡aL⎤ **dúirt sé** ⎡aL⎤ **thuig   sé**
       the novel   *thought I*   *said he*   *understood he*
       'the novel that I thought he said he understood'

       cén   t-úrscéal ⎡aL⎤ **mheas mé** ⎡aL⎤ **dúirt sé** ⎡aL⎤ **thuig   sé**
       which novel   *thought I*   *said he*   *understood he*
       'which novel did I think he said he understood?'

(11) **an fear** $\boxed{\text{aL}}$ **deir siad** $\boxed{\text{aL}}$ **shíleann an t-athair** $\boxed{\text{aL}}$
  the man   say they   thinks   the father

phósfaidh Síle
will marry

'the man that they say the father thinks Sheila will marry'

cén   fear $\boxed{\text{aL}}$ **deir siad** $\boxed{\text{aL}}$ **shíleann an t-athair** $\boxed{\text{aL}}$
which

phósfaidh Síle?

'which man do they say the father thinks Sheila will marry?'

(12) **an doras** $\boxed{\text{aL}}$ **mheasann sibh** $\boxed{\text{aN}}$ **bhfuil an eochair ann**
  the door   think   you (pl)   is   the key   in it

'the door that you think the key is in'

cén   doras aL mheasann sibh aN bhfuil an eochair ann
which

'which door do you think the key is in?'

3.3. A DELETION ANALYSIS

These data all but require that we carry over to constituent questions the deletion analysis already proposed in the case of relatives. Notice that given the data summarized in (i) and (ii) above we could repeat verbatim all the arguments gone through in Chapter 2 against various movement analyses and in favour of the deletion analysis. We need only substitute QNP for NP-head throughout. It is also necessary, clearly, to capture in a systematic way the parallels between the structure of nominal constituent questions and the structure of relatives. The most natural way in which to do this is to derive both from similar underlying structures by means of the same transformational rule.

Such an analysis might be set up as follows. To the PS-rules in (111) of Chapter Two, add rule (13):

(13)   Q → QNP $\overline{\text{S}}$

Q is to be understood as the category of questions (of all types), QNP as the category of nominal interrogative phrases (**cé** ('who'), **caidé** ('what'), **cén**

sagart ('which priest') etc.). The internal structure of phrases of this category and its relation to the category NP will be gone into in detail shortly. If we assume that the same indexing procedure as in the case of relatives binds QNP to some pronoun in the questioned clause, and if we adjust the rule of Relative Deletion as in (14):

$$(14) \quad \text{SD:} \quad \text{X} \left[\left\{ \begin{matrix} \text{QNP}_j \\ \text{NP}_j \end{matrix} \right\} \text{Y} \underset{[+\text{pro}]^k}{\text{NP}} \text{Z} \right] \text{W}$$

$$\begin{matrix} 1 & 2 & 3 & 4 & 5 & 6 \\ 1 & 2 & 3 & \emptyset & 5 & 6 \end{matrix}$$

Conditions as in (116) of Chapter Two.

then all of the facts about pronoun deletion and retention will fall out identically in both relatives and questions. To the extent that the distribution of complementizers depends on the phrase structure configurations in which they find themselves and on the application or non-application of the deletion rule, those facts too will fall out identically in both cases. This claim will be given substance below.

On this account then, a question like (15) will derive from an underlying structure like (16) by deletion of the bound pronoun:

(15)   **Cén   rothar aL ghoid an garda**
        which bicycle   stole the policeman

        'Which bicycle did the policeman steal?'

(16)

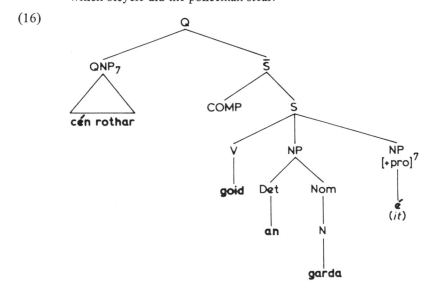

And a question like (17) will derive from (18), where in this case deletion of
the bound pronoun is blocked by the accessibility constraints, and it appears
on the surface incorporated in its preposition.

(17)   **Cén   garda   aN dtabharann tú   an rothar dó**
        which policeman   give   you (sg) the bicycle to him

        'Which policeman do you give the bicycle to?'

(18)

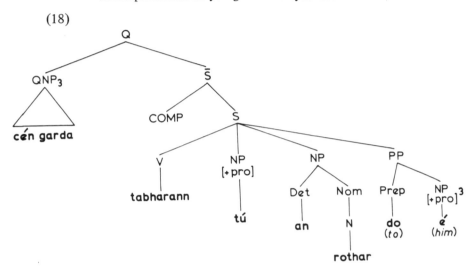

This proposal regarding the phrase-structure source of relative clauses and
questions is designed to allow certain rules and processes to apply identically
in both constructions. The rule of Relative Deletion, the indexing procedure
that binds a pronoun inside a relative clause or questioned clause, and certain
rules which will be discussed later that determine the distribution of complementizers inside relative clauses and questioned clauses, all apply identically
in the two structures because we leave unspecified in their structural descriptions whether the rules apply in the domain of NP or Q. In this way we capture important generalizations about the structural parallels between the two
constructions. It is important to note however that the proposal does not
predict that NP with relative clauses, and constituent questions with interrogative NP's will behave identically in all respects.

One respect in which the two constructions differ is that in the relative
clause structure, the NP in pre-COMP position is the head of the larger NP,
while in the case of constituent questions it is not. One way in which this

difference is reflected is in the fact that the pre-COMP NP of a relative clause construction will trigger number agreement on the verb if it is the subject of its clause but the pre-COMP NP of a question is irrelevant for purposes of number agreement. This is so presumably because the head of an NP and the NP-node which immediately dominates it must agree in the feature of plurality. The definiteness of a NP is also determined by the definiteness of its head.

Within the terms of the $\bar{X}$ Theory of phrase structure, (Chomsky, 1970; Bresnan, 1976a; Jackendoff, 1977; Hornstein, 1977) the notion of head is defined as that category-node which agrees in major syntactic features with the category-node which immediately dominates it. Given the definition of the present fragment in terms of the $\bar{X}$ framework to be presented in a later chapter, this definition will define the pre-COMP NP of a relative clause, but not that of a constituent question, as the head of its constituent thus making it available for the statement of rules of number agreement and the like. Certain other respects in which the two categories differ will be discussed shortly.

3.4. IN DEFENCE OF THE DELETION ANALYSIS

There are several respects in which the analysis proposed here departs from what have become widely-accepted assumptions within the paradigm of generative syntax about the proper analysis of constituent questions. Firstly, it recognizes the existence of a distinct syntactic category of questions – the category Q. This assumption will be defended in some detail at a later point in the chapter, when some more relevant data have been presented.

Secondly, the treatment of the positioning of interrogative phrases at the head of their clause is rather different from that which is usually assumed. Since the appearance of some important work by C. L. Baker and Emmon Bach (Baker, 1968, 1970; Bach, 1971) it has been widely assumed that there is a universally available rule of Wh-Fronting which is made use of by those languages that have clause-initial interrogative phrases. On the other hand, I propose that in Irish the interrogative phrases appear in clause-initial position because they are placed there by a Phrase Structure rule (namely (13)) and that the gaps which the interrogative phrases bind result from the operation of a deletion rule rather than a movement rule.

Consider first the question of base-generating the interrogative phrase in clause-initial position. An assumption that I have been guided by in all this work is that we would do well to deny to transformations the power of creating or inserting morphological material. Certain analyses are then ruled out in principle – in particular, it follows that transformations should not be able to leave pronominal copies of moved constituents. Given this working assumption, which I think is a fairly common one in recent work, it cannot be the case that examples like (2), (8) or (9), in which the interrogative NP binds a resumptive pronoun rather than a gap, are derived by means of any transformational rule at all. This means then that at least some questions must be derived by base-generating the interrogative NP in pre-COMP position. This much, I think, will be common to all approaches which do not allow rules which leave 'real' pronominal traces.

Given though that we allow a Phrase Structure rule like (13), then we must also allow some device like the Relative Clause Binding procedure discussed in section 2.4 of the previous chapter. This will be necessary to account for the deviance of such examples as (19).

(19) *Cén rothar $\begin{smallmatrix}aN\\aL\end{smallmatrix}$ bhí Fionn Mac Cumhail ina chodladh
      which bicycle *was Finn MacCool* *asleep*
      'Which bicycle was Finn MacCool asleep?'

But then in turn, given the independent need for this much apparatus, it seems perverse to prevent the rule of Relative Deletion, as defined and justified already on the basis of evidence from relative clause structures, from applying in constituent questions. By allowing the rule to apply in such structures, we predict that the same configuration of data with respect to accessibility and island constraints should turn up in constituent questions as in relative clauses – as indeed it does.

Consider also the following fact. Questions and relative clauses are parallel in another way that we have not yet discussed. In the final section of the previous chapter we discussed a relative clause type whose status is slightly marginal and which lies largely outside the ambit of the present work – a type that I named the Prepositional Relative. Examples (20)–(22) are typical.

(20) an fear le-n-arL labhair tú
      the man with+rel. ptc. spoke you
      'the man to whom you spoke'

(21) an bocsa i-n-arL chuir tú an leabhar
      the box in+rel. ptc. put you the book
      'the box into which you put the book'

(22) an seomra i-n-arL chodail Seoirse Washington
      the room in+rel. ptc. slept
      'the room in which George Washington slept'

I suggested at the end of the previous chapter that there were two approaches to the syntax of these constructions that seemed a priori to be plausible. One would place the amalgam of preposition and relative particle in clause-initial position by means of a movement rule whose domain was $\bar{S}$. Alternatively one could introduce the relative prepositional phrase into its position by means of a Phrase Structure rule expanding $\bar{S}$ as [PP S]. Now I have been arguing here that relative clauses and constituent questions are parallel in a particular way – namely, that they derive from the parallel structures (23) and (24) respectively:

(23)

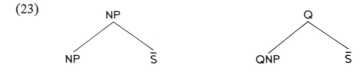

Given either of the alternative analyses of the Prepositional Relative we have been considering, we would expect the same phenomenon to turn up in constituent questions. Whether we treat the construction as involving a movement within the domain of $\bar{S}$ in (23), or as a result of a Phrase Structure expansion of $\bar{S}$, if (24) is the correct constituent structure for constituent questions in Irish, then we would also expect structures like (25) to be generated:

(25)

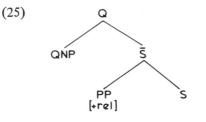

Such structures in fact exist:[1]

(26)   **Níor   dheacair a dhéanamh amach cé   araN   raibh sé**
        was-not difficult to make   out   who on + rel.ptc. was   he

        féin . . . ag smaoineamh
        self   at thinking

        'It was not hard to make out who he himself . . . was thinking about.'

(27)   **Níl a fhios agam cén   seomra inarL   chodail sé**
        I don't know   which room   in + rel.ptc. slept   he
        'I don't know which room he slept in.'

These examples fit rather easily into the general scheme being developed here, because that scheme has been designed to give formal expression to the intuition that in Irish the relationship between a relative clause and its head NP is in essential respects the same as that which holds between a questioned clause and its associated interrogative NP. They appear, however, rather unnatural in the context of the classical analysis of constituent questions. At the very least, examples like (26) and (27) suggest that, if there is a movement rule involved in their derivation, then what is moved is not the interrogative phrase itself (no more than it is the head NP that is fronted in a relative clause structure), but some anaphoric element from inside the questioned clause.

No doubt a movement rule could be formulated that will account for the data we have considered so far – particularly if we are willing to say that what is fronted by the rule is some abstract WH-pronoun which is obligatorily deleted following the movement. But the striking differences between the Irish construction and the corresponding English construction remain, and I am inclined to believe that any notion of 'movement rule' that will be sufficiently general to be applicable to both the Irish and the English cases will be a very harmless one indeed.

One consideration that might tempt one into proposing a movement analysis, even in the absence of overt evidence, is that the general account of the phenomenon of island constraints that is at the heart of recent work by Chomsky and his co-workers, depends on all rules which obey island constraints being construed as (successive–cyclic) movement rules. This is an extremely interesting position as long as the notion of 'movement rule' with which one works has substance – that is, that it predict some of the syntactic properties of the constructions in which movement rules apply. It seems to me though that the notion of 'movement rule' that we are left with if we attempt to use it to analyze the Irish data is little more than a metaphor for an indexing procedure that serves to invoke the various constraints on syntactic binding that in combination account for the facts about syntactic islands. To say that any construction which obeys island constraints will show the properties associated with a movement rule, when 'movement rule' is construed in the way that the Irish data seem to make necessary, is to take very little predictive risk. For my own part, I do not find the account of the island facts made available within this theory so compelling (in part for reasons that will be discussed in a later section) that I would feel tempted for its sake to assume the existence of WH-pronouns subject to obligatory deletion – an assumption for which, as far as I know, there is no evidence.

Further arguments that favour the base-generation and deletion analysis over its more traditional rivals will be considered as more data are brought to light. First I would like to consider the matter of the internal structure of interrogative NP; following that there will be a brief investigation of the syntax of another type of constituent question – those with adjectival or adverbial rather than nominal interrogative phrases.

3.5. THE INTERNAL STRUCTURE OF QNP

Nominal interrogative phrases can be divided into three classes depending on the complexity of their internal structure.

(i) They may consist of a single word – cé ('who') or caidé ('what'), for instance:

(28a)   [$_{QNP}$ Cé] [$_{\bar{S}}$ aL tháinig _ isteach]
              who   came   in

          'Who came in?'

(b)   [$_{QNP}$ Caidé] [$_{\bar{S}}$ aL thug tú   _ dó]
              what   give you   to him

          'What did you give him?'

(ii) They may take the form: Interrogative Determiner + Nom:

(29a)   **Cén   stócach**   'which youth'
          which youth

(b)   **Cén   fear mór**   'which big man'
          which man big

(c)   **Céna   fir   mhóra**   'which big men'
          which (pl) men big (pl)

(iii) QNP of both the above types may also contain what look like relative clauses. Questions containing such QNP always have the surface form [QNP $\bar{S}$ $\bar{S}$]. One of the curiosities of such questions is that they are always ambiguous in that, since relative clauses and questioned clauses are virtually identically syntactically, there is in general no way to tell which $\bar{S}$ is the relative clause and which is the questioned clause. Thus the questions in (30) and (31) below can be glossed by either of the associated English questions:

(30)   [_QNP Cé] [_s̄ aL bhí _ clúiteach] [_s̄ aL chonaic tú _]
        who   that   _ was famous   that you saw _

   a. 'Who did you see that was famous?'
   b. 'Who that you saw was famous?'

(31)   [_QNP Cén leabhar] [_s̄ aL cheannaigh tú _] [_s̄ aL bhí aige]
        which book   that you bought _   that he had _

   a. 'Which book that you bought did he have?'
   b. 'Which book did you buy that he had?'

I will assume that the ambiguity in question arises from the application or non-application of a rule that extraposes a relative clause to sentence-final position from inside an interrogative phrase. This of course is the familiar rule of Extraposition from NP (Ross, 1967). It applies to non-interrogative NP in exactly the same way as it does to interrogative NP, as illustrated by (32):

(32)   Chonaic mé fear   ar an bhóthar aréir   [_s̄ nachN
        saw   I a man on the road   last night   NEG+COMP

        bhfaca mé ariamh roimhe]
        saw   I   ever   before

   'I saw a man on the road last night that I have never seen before.'

Example (32) presumably derives by extraposition of the relative clause **nachN bhfaca mé ariamh roimhe** from a position immediately to the right of the head NP **fear** ('a man'). Given these assumptions, example (30) on its (a) reading derives from an underlying structure like (33):

(33)

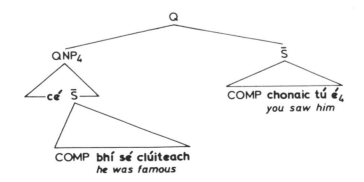

while on its (b) reading on the other hand, it derives from (34):

(34)

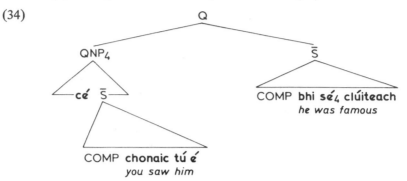

From now on I shall, for the sake of simplicity, ignore such ambiguities and treat all such sentences as if they had only the non-extraposed reading – the reading, that is, on which the clause immediately to the right of the QNP is the relative clause and the rightmost clause is the questioned clause.

How are these three types of QNP best analysed? Let us begin by making the natural assumption that QNP of type (i) – the single word type that includes **cé** ('who') and **caidé** ('what') – are best analysed as basic lexical items of the category QNP and so appear in deep structures dominated simply by the node QNP.

Consider now the case of non-lexical members of the category. Interrogative noun phrases of what we have called the second type have the form:

Interrogative Determiner + Nominal

Let us assume that these phrases are introduced by the PS rule in (35):

(35)   QNP → QDet Nom

The examples in (29) will on this account have the structures in (36):[2]

(36a)

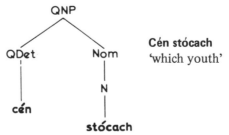

(b)

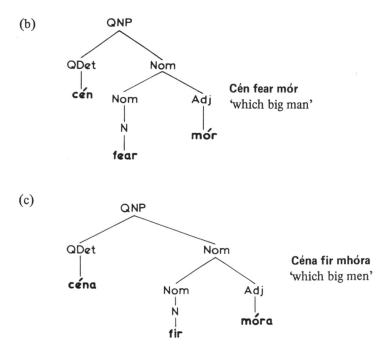

Cén fear mór
'which big man'

(c)

Céna fir mhóra
'which big men'

The category QDet will have other members as well. Certain abstract nouns, for instance, are subcategorized to take an interrogative determiner **cá**:

(37a)   **Cá mhinice aL bhí tú ann?**
       frequency were you there
       'How often were you there?'

(b)   **Cá mhéad úll   aL d'ith sé?**
       amount apples (gen)   ate he
       'How many apples did he eat?'

It seems natural to regard this particle as a lexical member of the category QDet.

Consider now the third and most complex type of interrogative noun phrase – those which contain a relative clause. Since one finds such relative clauses on un-analyzable QNP like **cé** and **caidé**, as in examples like (30), it seems we must postulate a PS-rule like (38):

(38)   QNP → QNP S̄

The interrogative phrases of examples (30) and (31) will then have the structures (39) and (40) respectively:

(39)   [QNP Cé   aL bhí _ clúiteach]
              who   was famous

'Who that was famous'

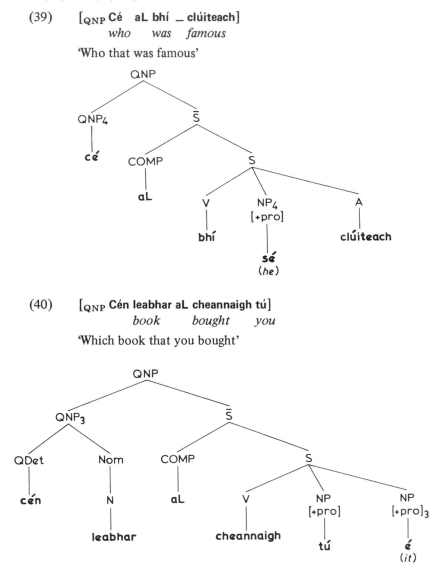

(40)   [QNP Cén leabhar aL cheannaigh tú]
                 book   bought   you

'Which book that you bought'

This analysis assumes, of course, that the indexing procedure that binds pronouns to relative clause heads treats such complex QNP exactly as if they were 'ordinary' NP. So too the rule of Relative Deletion, which deletes these bound pronouns, behaves exactly as if these QNP were 'ordinary' non-interrogative NP. These are only the first of many parallels between the structure of NP on the one hand and QNP on the other, that remain so far unaccounted for in this analysis. Notice that NP and QNP are expanded by PS-rules that parallel one another exactly:

(41)
$$NP \to \begin{Bmatrix} Det & Nom \\ NP & \bar{\bar{S}} \end{Bmatrix}$$

$$QNP \to \begin{Bmatrix} QDet & Nom \\ QNP & \bar{\bar{S}} \end{Bmatrix}$$

When we come to define a semantics on this syntactic base, we shall see also that NP and QNP correspond to the same type in intensional logic, and further that the translation rules that build up the translations of noun phrases treat NP and QNP identically.

We can account for these parallels in a systematic way if we assume, with many workers within the interpretivist tradition (see for instance Chomsky, 1970; Bresnan, 1976a), that category-labels are not unanalyzable wholes but are rather bundles of features. Let us assume that one of these features is $[\pm Q]$. Interrogative noun phrases will then differ from non-interrogative noun phrases only in being marked $[+ Q]$, where 'ordinary' NP are marked $[- Q]$. For convenience let us use 'np' to refer to the supercategory that embraces both NP and QNP – the category, that is, that has all the features shared by both NP and QNP, but which is unspecified for $[Q]$.

Let us also assume that it is this same feature $[Q]$ which distinguishes interrogative from non-interrogative determiners and introduce the lable 'det' for the supercategory that subsumes both types. We have thus three sub-categories of determiners – $\begin{bmatrix} det \\ + Q \end{bmatrix}$, $\begin{bmatrix} det \\ - Q \\ + def \end{bmatrix}$, $\begin{bmatrix} det \\ - Q \\ - def \end{bmatrix}$ – for the interrogative, definite and indefinite determiners respectively.[3] This system yields the following set of informal correspondences:

$$\begin{bmatrix} np \\ + Q \end{bmatrix} = QNP \qquad \begin{bmatrix} np \\ - Q \end{bmatrix} = NP \qquad \begin{bmatrix} det \\ + Q \end{bmatrix} = QDet \qquad \begin{bmatrix} det \\ - Q \end{bmatrix} = Det$$

We are now in a position to write a single PS-rule for the expansion of both NP and QNP, as in (42):

(42)

$$\begin{bmatrix} np \\ \alpha Q \end{bmatrix} \rightarrow \left\{ \begin{matrix} \begin{bmatrix} det \\ \alpha Q \end{bmatrix} \; Nom \\[2ex] \begin{bmatrix} np \\ \alpha Q \end{bmatrix} \; \bar{S} \end{matrix} \right\}$$

We are also in a position to get rid of the embarassing disjunction in the formulation of the rule of Relative Deletion given in (14), relying instead on (43):

(43)   SD: X [np_j Y $\underset{[+pro]^k}{NP}$ Z] W

                1   2 3   4   5 6

        SC: 1   2 3 $\emptyset$ 5 6

Conditions as in (14)

The procedure that assigns indices in relative clause and constituent question
configurations and the semantic rules that map QNP and NP onto expressions
of intensional logic will also now be stated in terms of the supercategories np
and det.

Feature-systems have classically been used to account for partial similarities
and differences in the structure and distribution of linguistic units. In the
present case, the analysis in terms of features allows us to present a unified
analysis of the syntax of relative and constituent question constructions, and
of the internal structural similarities between NP and QNP. The feature [Q]
will at the same time allow us to state what is different about the two
categories, in defining the limited distribution of interrogative noun phrases
and in triggering the occurrence of the appropriate determiners. [Q] actually
is not the only feature which filters down from np to det. I have argued elsewhere (McCloskey, 1978) that noun phrases (in Irish at least) must be specified for definiteness to account for certain syntactic facts that depend on the
distinction (the class of definite noun phrases, of course, includes pronouns
and proper names as well as noun phrases with definite determiners). The distinction is made necessary, for instance, by the fact that definite and indefinite NP trigger different word orders in copular sentences. The rule for
expanding np then will actually be as in (44):

(44)

$$\begin{bmatrix} np \\ \alpha Q \\ \beta def \end{bmatrix} \rightarrow \left\{ \begin{matrix} \begin{bmatrix} det \\ \alpha Q \\ \beta def \end{bmatrix} \; Nom \\[3ex] \begin{bmatrix} np \\ \alpha Q \\ \beta def \end{bmatrix} \; \bar{S} \end{matrix} \right\}$$

and the three samples in (45) will be assigned the structures in (46):

(45a)   **cén rothar**   'which bicycle'

(b)   **an rothar**   'the bicycle'

(c)   **rothar**   'a bicycle'

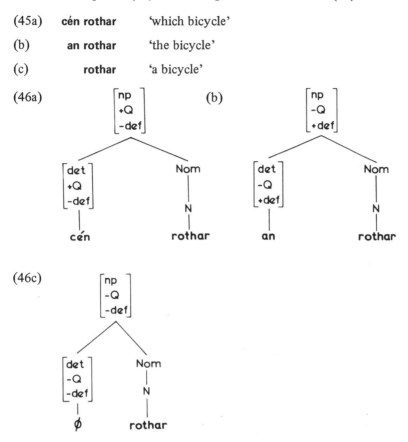

Notice finally that this material provides another argument in favour of the NP S̄ analysis of the relative clause construction over the Nom S̄ analysis – in that the NP S̄ configuration allows us to capture the fact that the deletion operations in both relative and questioned clauses are identical, in a way that the Nom S̄ configuration does not. Given the NP S̄ analysis we can write the single rule given in (43). If we were to work within the Nom S̄ framework, presumably the indexing procedure would be defined in terms of Nom and Pro and the controller in the rule of relative deletion would be the indexed Nom-node:

(47)

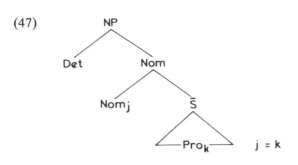

$$j = k$$

In this case, term 2 of the generalized rule would have to be the rather awkward and counter-intuitive disjunction: $\left\{ \begin{matrix} \text{Nom}_j \\ \text{QNP}_j \end{matrix} \right\}$, since there is no motivation for analyzing single word interrogative phrases like **cé** ('who') and **caidé** ('what') as being anything other than unanalyzable members of the category QNP. This hardly does justice to the intuition that the same rule is involved in both the relative clause and constituent question cases, since absolutely any pair of categories could appear inside the curly brackets, no matter how unrelated they were. The NP $\bar{\text{S}}$ analysis of relatives in combination with the strategy of decomposing syntactic categories into bundles of features allows us to preserve the economical and intuitively satisfying statement in (43).

I will propose one further elaboration of the system as so far developed. Let us assume, as seems natural, that the marked value of the feature [Q] is [+ Q]. Further assume that rules mention the feature only in order to give it its marked value, and that in all cases where a feature is not specifically mentioned it is given its unmarked value – in this case, [− Q]. This set of conventions, in combination with our proposal that interrogative phrases be generated in the base in pre-COMP position by means of the revised rule (48):

(48) $Q \rightarrow \underset{[mQ]}{np} \; \bar{S}$

predicts that Multiple WH-Questions should be ungrammatical. This prediction seems to be an accurate one. I have never come across such examples in reading or conversation and speakers judge examples that I have constructed to be ungrammatical, whether the second interrogative phrase is preposed or left inside the questioned clause:

(49a)   *Cé aL   rinne caidé?
         who COMP did   what
                                    'Who did what?'
         Cé caidé aL rinne?

(b)   *Caidé aL   thug sé do cé?
         what COMP gave he to who
                                    'What did he give to whom?'
         Caidé cé aL thug sé dó?
                      to-him

(c)   *Cé aL   bhí ag caint le   cé?
         who COMP was at talking with who

         'Who was talking to who(m)?'

Such examples will not be generated because interrogative phrases will be generated only in pre-COMP position by the rules of the base.[4]

3.6. ADJECTIVAL AND ADVERBIAL QUESTIONS

In this section I will look very briefly at a type of constituent question that has not so far been considered in this study – namely adjectival and adverbial questions. By these I mean the Irish equivalent of such English questions as 'How adequate is syntax?', 'How often are swindlers caught?' and so on. On a matter of terminology to begin with, the syntactic differences between adverbs and adjectives in Irish being minimal, let us agree to call these questions AP-Questions – where AP is meant to designate a category including both adjectives and adverbs. With respect to this interrogative construction in particular, the two behave identically.

I wish to demonstrate here that AP-Questions are very different in syntactic structure from nominal constituent questions, and that they too support a base-generation and deletion analysis, though of a different kind than in the case of nominal questions. I will argue that just as the rule that derives nominal questions is the same as the rule of Relative Deletion, so the rule that creates the gaps in AP-Questions is the same as the rule of Comparative Deletion. My purpose in this is not to present a detailed analysis – such an enterprise would take me deeper into the syntax and semantics of comparative and equative clauses than I can go at present. Rather I want simply to demonstrate the plausibility of a particular approach and the implausibility of another.

There are in fact two different ways of forming such questions in Irish.

First, many adjectives and adverbs have associated with them a special abstract noun known as the 'abstract noun of degree'. When preceded by the interrogative determiner **cá** these nouns form questions which translate English AP-Questions:

(50a)   **Cá mhinice   aL thigeann sé**
          frequency   comes   he

          'How often does he come?'

(b)   **Cá fhad   aL bhí   tú   i   mBaile Átha Cliath**
          length   were you in Dublin

          'How long were you in Dublin?'

The second possibility is the construction that will interest us here. This construction is parallel in many ways to comparative and equative clauses. Two typical examples are given in (51):

(51a)   **cé chomh minic agus   aL   thigeann sé?**
          as, so often CONJ COMP comes   he

          'How often does he come?'

(b)   **cé chomh dona agus aL bhí sé?**
          bad   was it

          'How bad was it?'

Compare the examples in (51) with the corresponding equative clauses in (52):

(52a)   **Imíonn sé [$_{AP}$ chomh minic agus aL thigeann sé]**
          leaves he

          'He leaves as often as he comes'

(b)   **An bhfuil sé [$_{AP}$ chomh dona agus aL bhí sé]**
          Int is   it

          'Is it as bad as it was?

Consider first how the equative clauses in (52) are best analyzed. These complex AP clearly have much in common with English '**as-Adj-as-S**' constructions, so let us carry over to these Irish facts the best-known and best-supported analysis of these clause-types in English – namely that presented in Bresnan (1973a, 1975).[5]

We already have a rule: $\overline{\overline{S}} \rightarrow$ CONJ $\overline{S}$ (see Chapter 2, Section 2.2 above) so let us assume that **agus** in these examples is a member of the category of conjunctions,[6] along with **nuair** ('when'), **sul** ('before') and so on.[7] Let us further assume the existence of a rule:

$$AP \rightarrow AP\ \overline{\overline{S}}$$

The S-constituent of such a structure must contain an occurrence of the special terminal element Δ dominated by a measure phrase[8] which is itself a constituent of AP.[9] This Δ will be bound to the AP head of the construction and will be deleted by the rule of Comparative Deletion. The AP of example (52a) for instance will have the structure (53) on this account:

(53)

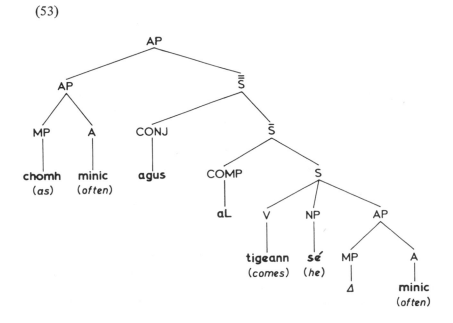

The AP of (54) will have the structure shown in (55):

(54)   **Tá sé chomh te   inniu agus aL   bhí sé fuar inné**
          is it as   hot today CONJ COMP was it cold yesterday

          'It is as hot today as it was cold yesterday'.

(55)

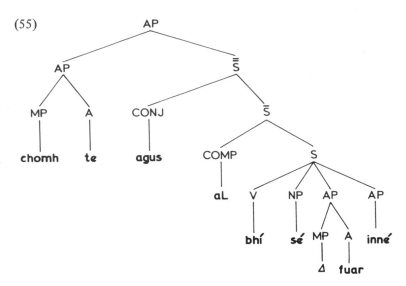

With different choices of conjunction and of measure phrase in the head AP, these structures and the rule of Comparative Deletion will also derive true comparatives:

(56)   **Tá sé** [_{AP} **níos ceolmhaire**   [$_{\bar{\bar{S}}}$ **ná**   [$_{\bar{S}}$ **aL**
        is he   more musical (comp)   than

        [_S **bhí sé** [_{AP} Δ]]]]]
            was he

'He is more musical than he used to be.'

Clearly it would take more than these few paragraphs to properly motivate and defend this analysis; I merely want to point out that this is a plausible direction in which to proceed and that these structures and the rule of Comparative Deletion can be motivated on much the same grounds in Irish as in English.

To return to the central topic however, it is clear that these decisions also provide us with an analysis of AP-Questions if we make certain assumptions – specifically if we assume that in these questions too the interrogative phrase is base-generated at the position in which it appears on the surface and that AP-Questions stand in roughly the same relation to the comparative construction as do nominal constituent questions to the relative construction. Let us assume, that is, that AP-Questions are introduced by the following PS-rule:

$$Q \rightarrow QAP \; \bar{\bar{S}}$$

where QAP is the class of interrogative APs. Suppose further that QAP stands in the same relation to AP as does QNP to NP – that is, that they are distinguished only by being marked [+ Q] and [− Q] respectively and that it is the feature [+ Q] that triggers the occurrence of the interrogative particle **cé**. Again let us use ap to refer to the supercategory that contains both QAP and AP. Given these assumptions, a question like (51a) will have the underlying structure sketched in (57):

(57)

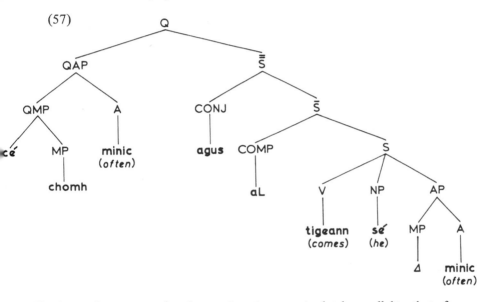

The internal structure of such questions is now completely parallel to that of equative clauses and the rule of Comparative Deletion, as independently motivated and formulated for comparative clauses, will apply identically in both structures. The situation here is quite parallel to the case of nominal constituent questions – by generating interrogative phrases in place we can let an extraction rule originally motivated for non-interrogative structures carry over to questions, thus capturing in a systematic way the similarities between these question-types and their non-interrogative counterparts.

These constructions pose what seem to me to be very serious problems for the 'classical' analysis of constituent questions, incorporating a universal rule of WH-movement. Such an analysis misses the point of the parallelism between AP-Questions and equative clauses – in the framework of the classical analysis, these similarities must be regarded as accidental. Consider for instance the problem of ensuring that the conjunction **agus** occurs in both AP-Questions and equative clauses. In the case of the questions, the occurrence of **agus** would have to be determined by the occurrence of a constituent down inside the clause with which it is associated – namely, an interrogative AP waiting to be preposed. This is, as far as I know, a completely unparalleled kind of sub-categorizational restriction. The occurrence of **agus** in equative clauses must be triggered in a completely different way – like the element *as* in the equivalent English constructions, its occurrence is triggered by the AP immediately to its left. On the analysis proposed here of course, only this second statement is necessary to ensure the occurrence of **agus** in both questions and equative clauses.

I do not want to understate the difficulties involved in the approach to AP-questions sketched here. The parallel with equative clauses is incomplete in two respects – firstly, in that equative clauses exhibit Subdeletion phenomena (as in example (54)), whereas AP-Questions do not:

(58)   *Cé   chomh fuar agus aL bhí sé te   anuraidh
          how cold   *was it warm last year*

Secondly, not all the dialects show the presence of the conjunction **agus** in AP-Questions – I believe that the correct approach in these dialects also is to assimilate AP-Questions to the rule of Comparative Deletion, but clearly the case in these dialects for that analysis will be weaker. The most serious reservation I have though is in the lack of a semantic interpretation for these structures. Until I can provide that, I regard these proposals as very tentative. Nevertheless the syntax proposed here is as likely to support an adequate semantics as the rivals I have been considering, and when the two are weighed on their syntactic merits alone, the Comparative Deletion analysis seems to me to emerge a clear favourite.

3.7. ON THE STATUS OF THE CATEGORY Q

The second major respect in which the analysis proposed here departs from traditional analyses of questions is in the recognition of a distinct syntactic category of questions – the category Q. This category is meant to embrace questions of all kinds – yes/no questions, alternative questions, constituent questions and so on. This is one of the things that the semantic analysis to be proposed here requires. Questions of all kinds are made to denote sets of true propositions – specifically, a question denotes that set of true propositions whose members jointly make up a true and complete answer to that question. Questions will thus correspond to expressions of intensional logic that have the denotation type $\langle\langle s, t \rangle, t \rangle$. One of the requirements of Montague's general theory of semantic interpretation is that expressions of natural language which belong to the same syntactic category must always correspond to expressions of the same denotation-type in intensional logic. Therefore one of the decisions that our semantic analysis dictates to us is that we distinguish two independent syntactic categories – one for interrogative clauses and one for declarative clauses, since declaratives presumably should not be made to denote sets of propositions, but rather truth values of propositions.

One of the things that an analysis of questions must do is provide us with a means of describing the distribution of questions. Their distribution is not the same as that of declarative clauses – there are many predicates which embed declarative clauses but not questions and *vice versa*. However all types of question share the same distribution – if a predicate can embed a yes/no question, then it can also embed a constituent question and so on. For discussion of these matters, see Baker (1968) and Karttunen (1977a).[10]

What we need then is a device that distinguishes questions of all types from all other categories. The category Q obviously fulfills that function. Verbs like **fiafraigh** ('ask'), **inis** ('tell') or **fógraigh** ('announce') will be lexically marked + [_Q]. Some (**inis, fógraigh** for instance) will also be marked + [_$\bar{S}$].

Traditional analyses have provided a less direct solution to this problem. Questions are assigned to the category S (or more recently $\bar{S}$) and are distinguished from other clause-types in that they contain an abstract question marker Q. Q has yes/no particles as its lexical realizations and also serves to 'attract' WH-phrases moved by the rule of WH-Movement, which is presumed to be universal. This analysis was first proposed by Baker (1968, 1970) building on earlier work of Katz and Postal (1964). Baker gives the following essential bits of evidence:

(i) only languages which have clause-initial interrogative particles have an obligatory rule of WH-fronting. If Q is thought of as both the category of interrogative particles and the target for WH-fronting, then this fact is predicted.

(ii) fronted WH-phrases do not co-occur with interrogative particles. This fact is explained under the assumption that WH-fronting is given a universal formulation in which WH-phrases replace Q-nodes.

(iii) languages front only one WH-phrase. Any others are left where they are placed by the base rules. This too is explained on the assumption that fronted

WH-phrases replace the Q marker, thus destroying the environment for the rule and preventing further application.

Bresnan (1972) elaborated on this analysis by identifying Q as a complementizer. Two of the principal pieces of evidence for this view are (i) the fact that in English WH-phrases, the interrogative particles and complementizers are all in complementary distribution, and (ii) the fact that this hypothesis provides an explanation for the fact that languages that have WH-fronting in questions also seem to have it in relative clauses. This fact is predicted if both rules are formulated as 'COMP-attraction' rules – rules that move material into complementizer position.

This analysis has been widely accepted and much has been built on it. Much of Chomsky's recent work on the explanation of island constraints, for instance (Chomsky, 1973, 1977), rests crucially on the assumption of a universal formulation of WH-movement which moves WH-phrases into COMP-position. This is true despite the fact that the original empirical base of support for these proposals has been seriously eroded in the years since they were first proposed. Many languages for instance, allow complementizers to co-occur with WH-phrases (Middle English (Grimshaw, 1977), Irish, Duala (Épée, 1976), Thai (Sornhiran, 1978)) and in Chomsky's recent work WH-phrases no longer replace complementizers but rather move into COMP-position alongside complementizers.

There are also now in the literature several counterexamples to the putative universals that originally motivated Baker's proposals. Tagalog (Kuno, 1974, note 19) allows yes/no particles and WH-phrases to co-occur, as does Duala (Épée, 1976). Krystyna Wachowicz (1976, 1978) has also presented a variety of counter-examples to this set of hypotheses. In particular she notes that several languages (among them Polish, Russian and Hungarian) permit the fronting of more than one interrogative phrase. Frantz (1973) presents data from the Peruvian language Sharanahua which is also troublesome for the Q-Morpheme Hypothesis. Sharanahua is a regular SOV language with a clause-right, post-verbal interrogative particle (-mun) but counter to what we might expect given the Q-Morpheme Hypothesis, it has leftward WH-Movement, and further the interrogative particle and the fronted interrogative phrase co-occur.

The data from Irish presented here casts further doubt on the Q-Morpheme or Q-COMP hypothesis. The essential empirical claim of the Q-Morpheme hypothesis is that Yes/No Interrogative particles and WH-phrases will all occur at the same phrase-structure positions. But this is not the case in Irish. We have not yet discussed Yes/No Questions in detail, but we can anticipate a little by noting that they are introduced by a particle **anN** (where, as before, **N** indicates that the item induces the nasalization mutation) and that this particle shows the positional and morphological characteristics of a complementizer:

(59)   **AnN bpósfaidh tú mé**
       Int   will marry you me
       'Will you marry me?'

The essential structure of Yes/No Questions is then as in (60a):

(60a)   COMP
        [+ Q]   S

But as we have seen, the structure of nominal Constituent Questions is as in (60b):

(60b)   NP
        [+ Q]   COMP S

And, as we have seen in the previous section, the structure of adjectival Constituent Questions is as in (60c):

(60c)   AP
        [+ Q]   CONJ COMP S

That is, interrogative elements appear at three different pre-sentential positions. There is no one element – Q-Morpheme or Q-COMP – which can plausibly be maintained to dominate all occurrences of interrogative elements.

In the light of these considerations, the idea that a Q-Morpheme or Q-COMP is a characteristic constituent of all kinds of questions seems to be a very questionable one, and the idea of using such a constituent to define the distribution of questions must be equally questionable.

But paralleling the distributional differences between interrogative and declarative clauses, there are a number of subtle but telling differences in syntactic behaviour as between the two types. The essential empirical prediction made by the theoretical requirement that there be a single denotation-type for every syntactic category is that category-distinctions forced on us by the semantics will have syntactic consequences – that is, that they will prove useful in stating syntactic generalizations. To the extent that we can motivate a syntactic distinction between interrogative and declarative clauses, our general hypothesis about the interpretability of syntactic structures will be supported. The following differences betweeen the two clause-types are well-known.

It has often been noted (Ross (1973) for instance) that in English, interrogative but not declarative clauses can be governed by a preposition

(61a)   We decided on who we should invite.
(b)   We decided (*on) that we should invite the Kissingers.

(62a)   We can't agree on whether we should annex Italy or not.
(b)   We can't agree (*on) that we should annex Italy.

(63a)   Some people are not certain about whether there are unbounded deletion rules or not.
(b)   Some people are certain (*about) that there are no unbounded deletion rules.

(64a)   We have an idea about who got the job, but we're not sure.
(b)   We have an idea (*about) that it was Henry who got the job.

(65a)   You shouldn't bet on who will succeed to the Papacy.
(b)   You shouldn't bet (*on) that an Italian will succeed to the Papacy.

This fact is accounted for in a perfectly straightforward way given a distinction between $\bar{S}$ and Q. We can for instance include a PS-rule $PP \rightarrow Prep\ Q$, but not $PP \rightarrow Prep\ \bar{S}$. A verb like *decide* will then have the subcategorization frames $[\_[_{PP}\ on\ Q]]$ and $[\_\bar{S}]$.

Here we have the predicted syntactic distinction between $\bar{S}$ and Q. There is at least one other account of these data though that would not make such a distinction. We could generate all complements of such verbs as prepositional objects. That is, we could generate examples like (70):

(70)   We decided on that we should leave

and propose a rule that deleted Prep before a *that*-complementizer. This rule would be formulated approximately as in (71):

(71)   Prep [*that* S]
         1   2 3 ⇒ ∅ 2 3

There seems to be no reason a priori to prefer this solution to one that recognizes a syntactic distinction between $\bar{S}$ and Q. But there are empirical reasons to prefer the solution that does distinguish the two categories syntactically. English (but not Irish) has a class of infinitival questions like (72):

(72a)   What to do?
(b)   He taught me how to tie knots
(c)   He told me which producers to talk to.

By the same criteria that make us assign tensed questions to the category Q, we must assign these phrases to the same category. Therefore the analysis of the facts in (61)–(69) which makes use of the category Q predicts that these constructions should behave identically with respect to the preposition facts. This is in fact the case:

(73a)   We couldn't agree on which set of parents to spend Christmas with.

We couldn't agree (*on) to spend Christmas with my parents.

(b)   We couldn't decide on which state to visit.

We couldn't decide (*on) to visit Kansas.

These facts follow as a straightforward prediction of the analysis which distinguishes Q from $\bar{S}$, but not from the Prep-Deletion analysis.

Ross has also noted (again in Ross, 1973) that declarative and interrogative clauses behave differently with respect to the constraint known variously as the Internal-NP-over-S Constraint (Ross, 1967; Kuno, 1973) or the Island-Internal Sentential NP Constraint (Ross, 1973). Declarative clauses give rise to more serious violations of the constraint than do interrogatives. Judgments in these matters are delicate, and many other factors seem to interfere in determining the acceptability or unacceptability of such sentences, so I leave the following examples without notation to let the reader decide on their status for him or herself. The claim is that the examples with clause-internal Q's are significantly better than those with clause-internal $\bar{S}$'s.

(74a)

It was
{
that you betrayed us that was hard to accept.
that you were a Provo spy that we thought
which side he was supporting that was hard to determine.
whether there had actually been a murder or not that Poirot was unsure of.
}

(b)   Does who will win the F.A. Cup depend on who wins the League?

Does that his serve was broken mean that he will lose the set?

(c)   Has {who got the government grant / that Pascal and Assumpta got the government grant} been announced yet?

(d)   Has {whether he will go to UCLA or MIT / that he will go to UCLA and MIT} been determined yet?

The Internal NP over S Constraint is, to say the least, a poorly understood phenomenon, but it seems that it does require that a distinction be drawn between declarative and interrogative clauses. An obvious way to make the necessary distinction is to distinguish two syntactic categories – Q and $\bar{S}$.

Finally, there is at least one more dramatic difference between interrogative clauses and declaratives. In many languages, among them Irish and English, questions are islands while declarative clauses are not (recall the discussion in Section 2.5 of the previous chapter). The problem of stating the Embedded Question Constraint and of the treatment of island-constraints in general will be gone into in some detail in the next chapter. I propose to take a rather simple-minded approach – that is, I shall simply stipulate that Q (but not $\bar{S}$) is a 'bounding node' in Irish. By saying that Q is a bounding node, I mean that the relation of syntactic binding that holds between a controller phrase and a gap cannot be made across a Q-boundary. Clearly if this approach to the formalization of the Embedded Question Constraint can be defended against alternatives, then we can take the proposed distinction between $\bar{S}$ and Q to be supported since obviously the proposal depends crucially on being able to draw just that distinction.

But these considerations aside, if we return to the Irish evidence, there is really very little reason why we would want to regard constituent questions as members of the same syntactic category as declarative clauses – the distribution of the two is quite different, the internal structure is quite different, as I have been at some pains to argue, and the semantic properties are quite different.

Why then, received assumptions aside, should we regard them as belonging to the same syntactic category? One might argue that they occupy the same phrase structure positions, and that to account for this in a principled way, one should assign them to the same category. But the observation on which the argument is built is only partly true to begin with – as has just been noted, interrogatives but not declaratives can occur as prepositional objects. To the extent that the observation *is* correct, I think it reflects only the fact that both $\bar{S}$ and Q can serve as arguments to certain predicates. Notice that whatever Q shares with $\bar{S}$ in this respect, it also shares with NP (Q and NP are in fact more closely related than Q and $\bar{S}$ in this respect, since both can be prepositional objects while $\bar{S}$ cannot.). The fact that NP, $\bar{S}$ and Q all occur in essentially the same phrase structure positions means only that these are the categories that typically occur as arguments to a predicate, and that languages have systematic ways of coding argument positions syntactically. So the fact that NP, $\bar{S}$ and Q can all occur, for instance, in subject position means only that all these categories can fill the first argument position of some predicate.

Now whatever account of these facts is to be given, it clearly will not do simply to demand that every kind of phrase that can appear at a particular set of phrase structure positions be regarded as belonging to the same syntactic category. To do this, we would have to give up the distinction between NP and $\bar{S}$. In short there is no more reason to conclude from this kind of data that declarative and interrogative clauses belong to the same category than there is to conclude that NP and declarative clauses belong to the same category.

An argument that might be made (and in fact has been made by Boër to appear) for the identification of $\bar{S}$ and Q is that they can be conjoined:

(75)   He told me that he was a seeker and what he was looking for.

The implicit assumption in this argument is that only like categories can be conjoined. But whatever form the requirement of parallelism on conjoined structures takes, it cannot be anything as simple or as straightforward as a requirement that the two conjuncts be of the same syntactic category. Note first that there are examples like (76) (pointed out to me by Lauri Karttunen):

(76)   I knew Mr. Colson but not that he worked at the White House.

Secondly, notice that it is possible to conjoin 'concealed questions' (Baker, 1968; Grimshaw, 1977) and overt questions. The following example is from Conan Doyle, via Jespersen (1909–49; III, 76) and Baker (1968):

(77)   . . . showing what kind of men they were and the sort of warfare that they waged

Now whatever about the semantics of these constructions, Jane Grimshaw (1977) has shown that syntactically there is no reason to regard them as being anything other than NP. This indicates that a restriction to the effect that only identical categories can be conjoined is simply wrong and there can be no argument here for the syntactic identity of declarative and interrogative clauses.

What if we were to say though that Constituent Questions in Irish were not to be identified with $\bar{S}$ but rather that they were simply NP? The fact that they can be governed by prepositions might suggest this conclusion. We might also point to the fact that many (though by no means all) predicates that take questions also take NP objects. Finally we might add that in Irish nominal Constituent Questions have very much the look of complex NP.

But there is no argument here either. Firstly, as Ray Jackendoff has pointed out (Jackendoff, 1973, 1977), the structure of Prepositional Phrases is not so simple that we can assume that a phrase-type is a NP just because it can be the object of a preposition.

Secondly, while it is true that the distribution of NP and the distribution of nominal Constituent Questions partially overlap, the distribution of adjectival Constituent Questions, adverbial Constituent Questions, Yes/No Questions and Alternative Questions are all *identical* to that of nominal Questions – that is, the class of predicates that take nominal Constituent Questions is identical to the class of predicates that take the other types. All this of course falls out as a consequence of the recognition of a syntactic category Q. How will the alternative being considered here handle these facts?

Consider the case of Adjectival and Adverbial Questions. As we have seen in the previous section, these questions in Irish stand in the same syntactic relation to AP's as do nominal questions to NPs – that is, syntactically they look just like complex AP with an interrogative determiner or measure phrase instead of a non-interrogative one. By the same kind of reasoning that leads us to call nominal questions NP, we would be led then to call adjectival questions AP. But there is, of course, no overlap at all between the class of predicates that take adjectival complements and those that take adjectival questions – the class of predicates that take adjectival questions – is simply the class that take questions of all kinds, as we would expect on the approach being advocated here. If we were to take adjectival questions to be AP, we would be as far wrong as we possibly could be in predicting their distribution.

But if this strategy fails in the case of adjectival questions, what merit is there in applying it in the case of nominal questions? The prediction of this kind of analysis is that nominal questions and adjectival questions should have the same distribution as NP and AP respectively (or at the very least that they should have similar distributions). That is, it predicts differences in the distribution of the three question-types that simply do not exist.

It seems to me that there is little more to object to in the proposal to draw a syntactic distinction between $\bar{S}$ and Q than its lack of orthodoxy. The distributional differences and the differences in syntactic behaviour between the two clause-types make the distinction a well-motivated one. But we must not ignore the fact that the two categories are also related. One respect, for instance, in which they behave similarly is in the fact that both are subject to Extraposition:

(78a)   That Carter will run for office again is quite clear.

(b)   It is quite clear that Carter will run for office again.

(79a)   Whether or not Carter will run for office is not clear.

(b)   It is not clear whether or not Carter will run for office.

(80a)   Who will win the Democratic nomination is not yet clear.

(b)   It is not yet clear who will win the Democratic nomination.

Similar facts hold for Irish, except that Extraposition is obligatory unless the clause is already in sentence-final position:

(81)   **Tá sé soiléir goN   dtoghfar   Breathnach**
       is it clear COMP will be elected Walsh

       'It is clear that Walsh will be elected'.

(82)   **Níl   sé soiléir anN dtoghfar   é**
       is not it clear Int will be elected him

       'It is not clear whether or not he will be elected.'

(83)   **Níl   sé soiléir cén   fear aL   thoghfar   —**
       is not it clear which man COMP will be elected

       'It is not clear which man will be elected'.

This seems to be a general characteristic of clausal as opposed to headed categories (*cf.* Grimshaw, 1977; Bresnan and Grimshaw, 1978).

Clearly what we must do is propose a feature decomposition of the two categories which will allow us simultaneously to express what they have in common (extraposability) and what is different about them. We have already demonstrated the usefulness of the feature [Q] in distinguishing interrogative from non-interrogative noun phrases, APs and determiners, so it seems natural to extend its use to distinguish between interrogative and non-interrogative clauses. Let us assume then that $\bar{S}$ and Q have the feature specifications in (84):

$$(84)\qquad \bar{S} = \left\langle 1, \begin{bmatrix} + \text{ clause} \\ - Q \end{bmatrix} \right\rangle$$

$$Q = \left\langle 1, \begin{bmatrix} + \text{ clause} \\ + Q \end{bmatrix} \right\rangle$$

(for an explanation of the notation used here see Bresnan 1976a and Chapter 5 below). Extraposition will then be defined on the supercategory $\langle 1,$ [+ clause]$\rangle$[11] which embraces both $\bar{S}$ and Q, but the feature [Q] will still enable us to make the distinctions that we have argued in this section to be necessary.[12]

3.8. YES/NO QUESTIONS

The last matter I want to discuss in this chapter is the syntax of Yes/No Questions. My purpose here will be to show how we can analyze these constructions within the general framework of assumptions about questions already developed here and at the same time capture the necessary syntactic generalizations.

The syntactic facts regarding Yes/No questions are, on the face of it, rather simple. Yes/No questions are introduced by the particle **an**, which, since it induces nasalization on a following verb, I will write **anN**:

(85)   anN mbuaileann sé a   bhean?
              beats   he his wife
         'Does he beat his wife?'

The particle **anN** exhibits a number of the surface characteristics of a complementizer. It undergoes the same variation of form with respect to tense and negation as has already been discussed in connection with the complementizers **aL**, **aN** and **goN**. That is, it has a Past Tense form **arL** with the characteristic final **r** and the characteristic mutation effect – Lenition. It has the same two negative variants as complementizers – **nachN** in non-Past contexts, **nárL** in the Past. Compare the following data with that presented in (18) of Chapter 2:

(86a)   **AnN   mbuaileann sé a bhean**
          'Does he beat his wife?'

(b)   **NachN   mbuaileann sé a bhean**
          'Doesn't he beat his wife?'

(86c)   **ArL bhuail sé a bhean**
          'Did he beat his wife?'

(d)   **NárL   bhuail sé a bhean**
          'Didn't he beat his wife?'

The particle of course also appears in the pre-sentential position typical of complementizers. It is tempting, then, to take **anN** to be a complementizer and to assign an example such as (86a) the structure (87):

(87)

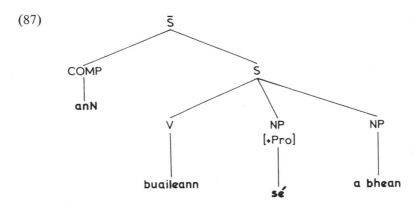

There are two problems with this proposal.

The first is that the distributional properties of **anN** are not at all like those of a declarative complementizer. In essence the situation is this. We must distinguish two pre-sentential positions in Irish – one that I will call COMP-position, and one that I will call pre-COMP position. In pre-COMP position are found interrogative noun phrases (**cén fear** ('which man'), **cé** ('who') etc.), adverbial conjunctions (**nuair** ('when'), **go dtí** ('until') etc.) and the heads of relative clauses. The point here is that all of the declarative complementizers (**aL, aN, goN**) can co-occur with elements in pre-COMP position.

(88)	pre-COMP	COMP	S
(a)	**nuair**	**aL**	**thigeann sé** ('*when he comes*')
(b)	**sul**	**aN**	**dtigeann sé** ('*before he comes*')
(c)	**go dtí**	**goN**	**dtigeann sé** ('*until he comes*')
(d)	**an fear**	**aL**	**thigeann** _ ('*the man who comes*')
(e)	**an fear**	**aN**	**n-éisteann tú leis** ('*the man that you listen to*')
(f)	**an fear**	**goN**	**n-éisteann tú leis**[13] ('*the man that you listen to*')

(g)   **cén fear**   **aL**   **thigeann** _
                                                        (*'which man comes?'*)

(h)   **cén fear**   **aN**   **n-éisteann tú leis**
                                                        (*'which man do you listen to?'*)

(i)   **cén fear**   **goN**   **n-éisteann tú leis**
                                                        (*'which man do you listen to?'*)

But the particle **anN** can never co-occur with any of the elements that appear in pre-COMP position. That is, the PS-rule presupposed by the structure in (87) over-generates wildly and will have to be supplemented with a set of conditions of one kind or another that prevent **anN** from occurring after any of the pre-COMP elements.

The second problem, of course, is that a structure like (87) is not compatible with our semantic proposals – in that $\bar{S}$ cannot plausibly be associated with the semantic type appropriate for questions.

These two problems are really two aspects of the same problem. Clearly constituents of the form **[anN S]** fail to show up in the wrong positions precisely because these are inappropriate contexts for a constituent with the semantic properties of a question. We solve both problems by letting Yes/No questions be dominated by Q. The question of blocking the occurrence of **anN** after the pre-COMP elements of (88) does not arise, because Q will not be generated after such elements. We also predict by this means that the distribution of Yes/No Questions will be the same as that of the other question types we have already studied – namely, nominal Constituent Questions and AP-Questions.

What then do we do about the syntactic intuition that **anN** is a complementizer, in a class with **goN**, **aL** and **aN**? Let us make the natural assumption that the feature [Q], as well as doing all the work we have already assigned to it, also serves to distinguish interrogative from declarative complementizers. That is, **goN**, **aL**, and **aN** will all belong to the category $\frac{\text{COMP}}{[-\text{Q}]}$, while **anN** will belong to the category $\frac{\text{COMP}}{[+\text{Q}]}$. We then write a PS-rule that requires that a clause agree with its complementizer in the value for the feature Q:

(89) $\left\langle 1, \begin{bmatrix} +\text{ clause} \\ \alpha Q \end{bmatrix} \right\rangle \rightarrow \frac{\text{COMP}}{[\alpha\,Q]}\, S$

The clauses in (90) will have the phrase structure sources diagrammed in (91):

(90a)   **anN mbuaileann sé a   bhean?**
            beats   he his wife

   'Does he beat his wife?'

(b)   **goN mbuaileann sé a bhean**
   'that he beats his wife'

(91a)

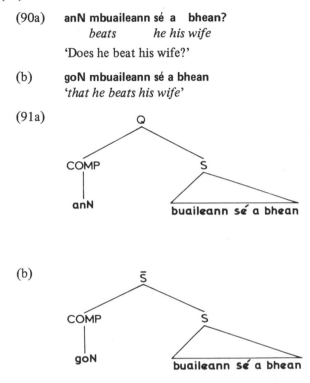

(b)

This account allows us to state in a maximally simple way the distributional constraints on Yes/No Questions – namely that their distribution is exactly like that of other question-types and quite unlike that of other declarative clause-types. But it also captures the necessary generalization that the particle **anN** is indeed a complementizer. Whatever morphological or late syntactic rules determine the different forms of the complementizers will apply to the interrogative complementizer in exactly the same way as to any other complementizer.

Given the decomposition of the clausal categories that we have been lead to in this section, the Phrase Structure rule for generating nominal constituent questions, which we have so far been writing as in (92), should more properly be written as in (93):

(92) $Q \rightarrow QNP \ \bar{S}$

(93) $\left\langle 1, \begin{bmatrix} + \text{clause} \\ + Q \end{bmatrix} \right\rangle \rightarrow \begin{bmatrix} np \\ + Q \end{bmatrix} \bar{S}$

The formulation (93) suggests a generalization of the rule using α-notation:

(94) $\left\langle 1, \begin{bmatrix} + \text{clause} \\ \alpha Q \end{bmatrix} \right\rangle \rightarrow \begin{matrix} np \\ [\alpha Q] \end{matrix} \bar{S}$

In the case where the feature [Q] has the negative value, rule (94) will give rise to structures like (95):

(95)

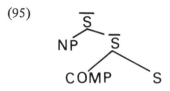

Such a structure might plausibly be used as the Phrase Structure source for a construction that I will call the 'reduced cleft' construction. Examples are given in (96):

(96a)   **Capall mór bán   aL   chonaic mé**
         a horse big white COMP saw   I

         'It was a big white horse that I saw'.

(b)   **Seán Bán aL   d'inis an scéal dom**
                            COMP told the story to-me

         'It was Sean Ban who told me the story'.

These are 'reduced' clefts in the sense that the constituent in focus-position is not preceded by the copula, as it is in the case of 'full' clefts. They are also 'reduced' in the sense that definite NP in focus-position are not preceded by the pronominal augments that normally appear before definite NP in copular sentences in general and in full clefts in particular. The full cleft version of (96b), for instance, would be (97):

(97)   **Is   é   Seán Bán aL d'inis an scéal dom**
        Copula him

        'It was Seán Bán who told me the story'.

(For a discussion of the phenomenon of pronominal augments in Irish, Manx
and Scottish Gaelic, see Ahlqvist (1978).)

One difference between full and reduced clefts is that indefinite NP may
not appear in the focus-position of full clefts, but may appear in the focus
position of reduced clefts. So (96a) is grammatical, but (98), which tries to be
the full cleft corresponding to (96a), is ungrammatical:

(98)   *Is   **capall mór bán aL chonaic mé**
        Copula

        'It was a big white horse that I saw'.

Rather than deriving reduced clefts from full clefts transformationally, we
might generate them directly in the base and give them the structure (95) by
means of the generalized expansion rule (94). Certain questions will then not
arise at all – the question, for instance, of how to persuade the reduction
transformation to delete both the copula and the pronominal augment in
cases like (97), and of how to persuade it to be obligatory in case the focus
NP is indefinite (to account for the ungrammaticality of (98)), but optional
otherwise (to allow for both (97) and (96b). Presumably we account for the
ungrammaticality of (98) on the base-generation approach by stipulating in
the Phrase Structure rule that gives rise to full clefts that if the focus constituent is a NP, then it must be [+ definite].

So far so good. There are certain difficulties with the proposal though. A
range of different constituent-types may appear in the focus-position of both
full and reduced clefts. At the very least, we must allow NP, AP and PP to be
the focus of both types of cleft. We have the following examples, for instance:

(99a)   **Dubh aL   bhí sé**
        black COMP was it

        ?'It's black that it was.'

(b)   **Ar an aonach aL   chonaic me é**
        on the market COMP saw   I   him

        'It was at the market that I saw him'.

In the case of reduced clefts, this will require a further generalization of rule
(94). If all the categories that may appear in the focus-position of clefts may

be abbreviated as $\bar{\bar{X}}$ (where this symbol is to be interpreted within the terms of the X-Bar theory of Phrase Structure, as discussed in Chomsky (1970). Bresnan (1976a), Jackendoff (1977), though whether all such categories can be plausibly so interpreted I am not sure), then the appropriate generalization might be as stated in (100):

(100) $$\left\langle 1, \begin{bmatrix} + \text{ clause} \\ \alpha Q \end{bmatrix} \right\rangle \rightarrow \underset{[\alpha Q]}{\bar{\bar{X}}} \, \bar{S}$$

This of course now raises the problem of how to prevent the appearance of categories other than np in the pre-COMP position of constituent questions. Why, that is, are there no questions corresponding to the reduced cleft examples of (99)? In the case of most of these categories (prepositional phrases, for instance), we might account for the absence of such examples by letting the corresponding interrogative categories be empty. So there will be no questions corresponding to clefts like (99b) because there are no interrogative PP's. This approach will not be possible, of course, in the case of AP's, because given the treatment of AP-Questions sketched in Section 3.6 above we do indeed need a non-empty category of interrogative ap's. We might then expect, given the approach being developed here, to find questions of the form in (101):

(101) $$\begin{bmatrix} \text{ap} & \bar{S} \\ _Q [+ Q] & _Q \end{bmatrix}$$

It is interesting to note then that such questions do in fact occur – but not in all dialects. That is, as was pointed out in Section 3.6, not all dialects require the appearance of the conjunction **agus** in AP-Questions. So besides examples like (51b) (repeated here), some dialects have (102):

(51b)   **Cé chomh dona agus   aL   bhí sé?**
          bad   CONJ COMP was it
         'How bad was it?'

(102)   **Cé chomh dona aL bhí sé?**

Notice that examples like (102) are exactly of the form (101) and are therefore of the form whose existence is predicted by the general approach under consideration here. But what exactly are we to make of the fact that they are dialectally limited?

The generalization of the base rule for nominal questions being considered here then may prove to be viable, and perhaps even useful, but the attempt to demonstrate that point in depth I think, would take us too far from our proper course, so for the purposes of this study, I will work with the narrower formulation (93).[14]

3.9. CONCLUSION

A lot of ground has been covered in this chapter and it would perhaps be as well at this point to summarize what conclusions we have come to and to lay out what remains to be done.

We have argued that in order to account for certain systematic regularities in the syntactic structures of relative clauses and nominal Constituent Questions, as well as to account for certain properties of Constituent Questions themselves, we must propose a rather unconventional analysis of such questions in Modern Irish – namely one in which the interrogative NP is generated in pre-COMP position by the rule (103):

$$(103) \quad Q \rightarrow \underset{[+Q]}{np} \ \bar{S}$$

We have argued further that the interrogative np is bound to some pronoun in $\bar{S}$ by the same indexing procedure that applies in relative clauses, and that the bound pronoun in both relative and questioned clauses can be deleted under certain conditions, in particular those of Island Constraints in the sense of Ross (1967) and the Accessibility Hierarchy of Keenan and Comrie (1977).

We have also defended the desirability of distinguishing a syntactic category Q for all kinds of questions and proposed a feature analysis of the categories $\bar{S}$ and Q that has them differ only in being $[-Q]$ and $[+Q]$ respectively. This allows us to state both what is different about the two categories and what they have in common. Finally we showed how this feature-analysis provides a simple analysis of Yes/No Questions that is consistent with our assumptions about questions in general and also incorporates the syntactically most natural account of the Yes/No interrogative particle **anN** – namely one that treats it as a complementizer.

To complete this syntactic analysis of relatives and questions it remains to us to do two things – to give a precise definition of the indexing procedure for relative clauses and questions and to do the same for the conditions on the rule of Relative Deletion.

Before moving on to these tasks and to a new chapter, I would like to end

this one by considering one respect in which the syntax of nominal questions
and that of relative clause structures is different.

3.10. POSTSCRIPT

There is, to my knowledge, just one major syntactic difference between relative clauses and constituent questions. In questions it is possible to front a
prepositional phrase containing a bound pronoun to a position immediately
to the right of the interrogative NP under certain conditions. That is, both
(104a) and (104b) are possible:

(104a) **Cé   aN   raibh tú   ag caint   leis?**
        who COMP were you at talking with-him

(b)   **Cé leis aN raibh tú ag caint?**
        '*Who were you talking to?*'

(For discussions of this pattern, see for instance Ó Cadhlaigh, 1940, pp. 422–
4, Sections 498–9; Ó Searcaigh, 1939, pp. 103–4, Sections 206–8; O'Nolan,
1920, p. 138.)

This construction is subject to a variety of rather idiosyncratic conditions.
It is only possible, for example, if the interrogative NP is a pronoun. So (105)
is ungrammatical:

(105)   *__*Cén fear leis   aN   raibh tú   ag caint?__
        which man with-him COMP were you at talking

        'Which man were you talking to?'

(106)   **Cén   fear aN   raibh tú   ag caint   leis?**
        which man COMP were you at talking with-him

        'Which man were you talking to?'

Not all interrogative pronouns however will allow the construction. It is
impossible with **caidé** (what), for instance.

(107a) *__*Caidé leis   aN   raibh tú   ag dúil?__
        what   with-it COMP were you at expecting

(b)   **Caidé aN raibh tú ag dúil leis?**
        'What were you expecting?'

With two prepositions (**ar** (on) and **le** (with)), one can use a special interrogative pronoun **cá** instead of **caidé** to form constructions like (108a):[15]

(108a)   **Cá leis   arL   bhris tú   an fhuinneog?**
         with-it COMP broke you the window
         'What did you break the window with?'

(b)   **Cá h-air aN   raibh sibh   ag caint?**
         on-it COMP were you(pl) at talking
         'What were you talking about?'

(c)   **Cá leis   aN   raibh tú   ag dúil?**
         with-it COMP were you at expecting
         'What were you expecting?'

Cá cannot normally be used to mean 'what' in such constructions. So there are no examples like (109).

(109a)   **Cá arL   bhris tú   an fhuinneog leis?**
         COMP broke you the window   with-it
         'What did you break the window with?'

(b)   **Cá aN   raibh sibh   ag caint   air?**
         COMP were you(pl) at talking on-it
         'What were you talking about?'

(c)   **Cá aN   raibh tú   ag dúil   leis?**
         COMP were you at expecting with-it
         'What were you expecting?'

Most, but not all, speakers allow the process over unbounded contexts, as in (110):

(110)   **Cé   leis   arL   shíl   tú   aL   bhí tú   ag caint?**
         who with-him COMP thought you COMP were you at talking
         'Who did you think you were talking to?'

The construction also seems to be subject to island-constraints, although plausible examples are a little difficult to construct and speakers are rather insecure in their intuitions in this respect. But all the speakers I have questioned judge (111) to be grammatical, while most of those who would venture an opinion at all judge (112) to be ungrammatical.

(111)   Cé   nachN   mbíonn fhios agat cén   teanga   aL
        who COMP+NEG you know   which language COMP

        ba chóir   a labhairt leis
        it-would-be-proper to speak   with-him

        'Who do you not know which language one should speak to him?'

(112)   *Cé leis nachN mbíonn fhios agat cén teanga aL ba chóir a
        labhairt?

        gloss as in (111)

This pattern is not now possible in relative clauses, although apparently it used to be. Ó Cadhlaigh (1940, Section 476, pp. 398–401) gives a collection of examples like (113):

(113)   an dream acu   aN   mbíonn meas   orthu féin
        the crowd at-them COMP is(habit) respect on-themselves

        'the crowd that respect themselves'

        (lit) the crowd at whom is respect on themselves

for the more expected (114):

(114)   an dream aN   mbíonn meas   acu   orthu féin
        the crowd COMP is(habit) respect at-them on-themselves

        'the crowd that respect themselves'

All such examples are from archaic sources though (the vast majority of them from a translation of the *Imitatio Christi* published in 1762) and they are clearly unacceptable for speakers of the modern language.

These considerations suggest a treatment along the following lines – suppose there is a transformational rule that fronts a prepositional phrase containing a bound pronoun to a position immediately to the right of an interrogative pronoun which binds the pronoun inside the PP. Such a rule is formulated in (115):

(115)   X QNP$_{[+Pro]}{}^{j}$ Y [$_{PP}$ Prep NP$_j$] Z
           1   2   3   4   5   6

        $\Rightarrow$ 1   2+ [4 5] 3 6

Given examples like (110), this must be an unbounded movement rule, and so we expect the ungrammaticality of (112). We may tentatively assume this to be a happy consequence. I trust that a suitable piece of ad hocery can be devised to account for the complementary distribution of **cá** and **caidé**.

As far as I can tell, these facts say nothing either for or against any of the analyses being considered here. They are equally awkward for all of them. The construction is vaguely reminiscent of Pied Piping, but the resemblance is in fact very superficial. Notice in particular that there is no reason to believe that the interrogative pronoun is or ever was the object of the fronted preposition, as would be the case in a traditional Wh-Movement analysis.

NOTES

[1] Example (26) is from **Lig Sinn i gCathú**, by Breandán Ó hEither, p. 147. (27) is from the Christian Brothers' Grammar, p. 339. For a collection of examples, see Ó Cadhlaigh 1940, p. 389.

[2] I assume here that the items **cén** and **céna** are to be taken as unanalyzable interrogative determiners. Historically they derive from an interrogative particle **cé** followed by the definite article (**an** in the singular, **na** in the plural). It is quite possible that they should also be analyzed synchronically as complex – that is as having the structure (i):

(i)

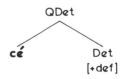

Nothing very crucial hangs on this choice as far as I can tell. The structure (i) is perfectly compatible with our general framework of assumptions, although the semantics turns out to be a little more complicated given this choice. I find it hard to imagine what empirical considerations would force a choice between these two alternatives, so I will work here with the one that seems to be most convenient semantically – namely, the analysis which takes **cén** and **céna** to be unanalyzable interrogative determiners.

[3] The only combination of determiner features that does not turn up is $[+ Q, + def]$. This combination will be generated by the PS rules but there will be no lexical items so marked in the lexicon. Therefore no lexical item can ever be inserted under a Det-node with this combination of features. If no lexical item is inserted under Det, the tranlation-rules, which work from bottom to top, will be unable to assign an interpretation to the sub-tree dominated by Det and therefore to any larger structure of which it is a part. For arguments to the effect that interrogative determiners should be marked $[- def]$ *cf*, for instance, Bach (1971). See also p. 236 below.

[4] I have come across one speaker who accepts Multiple Wh-Questions, and one speaker who, while not accepting them himself, reports having heard them, particular from those speakers and in those communities most susceptible to interference from English. This is the kind of datum that fits very uncomfortably into standard generative syntactic

frameworks. Fortunately or unfortunately, the general analysis being defended here is not as incompatible with the existence of Multiple Wh-Questions as I have claimed in previous incarnations of this work.

⁵ For an interesting discussion of the syntax of the comparative clause in Irish, see Stenson (1976).

⁶ The conjunction **agus** that appears in these examples also means 'and'. In this use and in its use in AP-Questions, it is frequently reduced (in both speech and writing) to the monosyllable **is**.

⁷ That the sequence **agusaL** is not a complex complementizer is demonstrated by the same kind of evidence that was presented in the case of the other conjunctions (Chapter 2, note 5). That is, there exist examples like (i):

(i)   **chomh luath agus aL thiocfaidh sé nó aL chuirfidh sé scéaʲ chugainn**
        as   soon   will come he or   will send he a story to us

        'as soon as he comes or sends us a message'

Once again the occurrence of such examples is predicted by the rule for $\bar{\bar{S}}$ given here, since we must allow for $\bar{S}$ conjunction anyway. An example like (i) will be assigned the structure (ii) by these rules:

(ii)

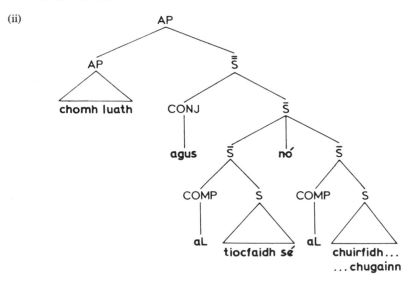

⁸ I use MP ('measure phrase') instead of Bresnan's QP to avoid confusion with QNP, QAP, QDet etc.

⁹ Perhaps we should let Δ in an example like (51) be dominated by the whole AP, rather than by MP. This will depend ultimately on the resolution of the vexed question of whether Comparative Deletion and Subdeletion are special cases of the same rule or

are independent rules. For a discussion of the issues involved, see the contributions of
Chomsky, Bresnan and Partee in Akmajian, Culicover and Wasow (1977).
[10] As noted by Karttunen, there are two troublesome exceptions to this generalization.
The verb *doubt* embeds *whether*-questions but not constituent questions:

(i)   I doubt whether he'll come.

(ii)   *I doubt which man will be elected.

Secondly, emotive factives like *be amazing, irritate, surprise* or *bother* take what look
like constituent questions but not *whether*-questions. This group might not constitute a
real exception since the complements of such verbs are perhaps susceptible to analysis as
embedded exclamatives as suggested by Jane Grimshaw (1977). The problem with this
idea is that such complements permit multiple WH-words (although judgments are a little
insecure on this):

(iii)   It is amazing who has married whom.

Matrix exclamatives of course do not permit this. The force of this objection is weakened
a little by the fact (observed by Grimshaw, 1977) that matrix and embedded exclamatives
differ in other respects as well. Perhaps what we are dealing with here is a special clause
type – that of embedded exclamatives. Irish yields direct evidence for the existence of
such a clause type. Emotive factives like *be amazing, irritate* and so on do not embed
questions in Irish. Rather they embed complements of the following form:

          [particle **a** + abstract noun of degree + **aL**-clause]

(iv)   **Goilleann sé orm   a mhinice   aL thigeann sé**
           irritates   it on me   frequency   comes   he

           'It irritates me how often he comes'

(v)   **Chuir sé iontas   orm   a fhad   aL bhí sé**
           put   it wonder on me   length   was it

           'It amazed me how long it was'

These constructions have the look of complex NP but it seems in fact that they must be
clauses rather than NP. This is shown by the fact that they can be extraposed (as in (iv)
and (v) above). This, if Grimshaw (1977) and Bresnan and Grimshaw (1978) are correct,
is a diagnostic for clausal categories as opposed to headed categories. If such phrases
were in fact complex NP then the extraposition pattern we would expect to find would
be that known as Extraposition from NP, as in (vi) and (vii). These patterns are however
ungrammatical:

(vi)   *Goilleann a mhinice   orm   aL thigeann sé**
           irritates   frequency on me   comes   he

(vii)   *Chuir a fhad   iontas   orm   aL bhí sé**
           put   length wonder on me   was it

Finally, note that such phrases cannot occur unembedded:

  (viii)   *A mhinice aL thigeann sé

  (ix)   *A fhad aL bhí sé

If there is indeed such a category as embedded exclamative, then perhaps the complements of English 'emotive factives' are instances of that category and need not stand as
exceptions to the generalization that questions of all types share the same distribution.
[11] This analysis assumes, contra Jackendoff (1977), that S and $\bar{\text{S}}$ are not verbal categories.
For arguments in support of this position, see Hornstein (1977). See also the discussion
in Chapter 5 below.
[12] Sue Schmerling, in some recent work on English (Schmerling, 1977), has argued on
syntactic grounds that we also need to distinguish a syntactic category of imperatives
distinct from both S and $\bar{\text{S}}$.
[13] The appearance of **goN** in relative clauses and constituent questions is dialectally
restricted. See note 7 of Chapter 2.
[14] There is another construction-type that might plausibly be taken to be an instantiation
of the non-interrogative expansion of (94), an instance, that is, of the structure in (95).
This is an emphatic negative construction in which an NP with an emphatic negative
quantifier like **dheamhan** (literally 'demon') appears in front of an **aL**-clause:

  (i)   **Dheamhan greim aL   fuair mé**
              bite   COMP got   I

              'Not a bite did I get'.

The syntax of such constructions is essentially like that of the reduced cleft construction,
but their semantic properties are evidently quite different. Since only NP may appear in
the pre-COMP position in examples like (i), this construction perhaps provides a better
parallel with nominal constituent questions than does the reduced cleft.
[15] These examples are from Ó Searcaigh (1939, p. 104). Ó Searcaigh cites the restriction
to **ar** and **le** in such cases without qualification, but some speakers at least, apparently
accept a wider range of prepositions in this construction. I have come across examples
with **roimh** (before) and **ó** (from), for instance, and the recent Irish-English dictionary
(**Foclóir Gaeilge – Béarla**, ed. Niall Ó Dónaill, Oifig an tSoláthair, Dublin 1977) cites the
following examples under **cá**:

  (i)   **Cá roimhe aN   raibh eagla ort?**
              before-it COMP was   fear on-you

              'What were you afraid of?'

  (ii)   **Cá uaidh   arL   tháinig sé   sin**
              from-it COMP came   that

              'From what did that come?'

CHAPTER 4

INDEXING AND THE FORMALIZATION OF
ACCESSIBILITY CONSTRAINTS

4.1. INTRODUCTION

In Chapter Two we discussed a series of alternations in the form of comp-lementizers that is characteristic of relative and questioned clauses. Essentially what happens is that any complementizer that is dominated by an S̄-node which contains the bound pronoun of a relative or questioned clause but which does not also contain the np-controller of that bound pronoun, can be realized as one of the relative complementizers **aL** or **aN**. So where one might expect to find the complementizer **goN**, which normally introduces the complements of *verba dicendi et sentiendi*, one may encounter either **aL** or **aN** instead. The situation is essentially as diagrammed in (1):

(1)

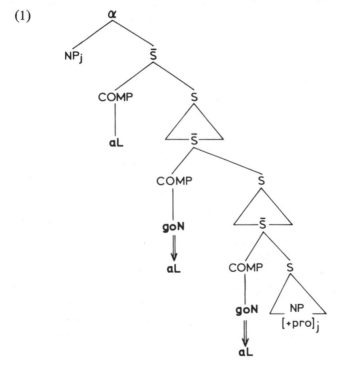

101

It turns out that this kind of alternation is characteristic of a whole series of constructions – Relative Clauses, Constituent Questions of all kinds, Clefts, Pseudo-clefts, Comparative and Equative Clauses. It is the purpose of the indexing procedure to characterize just this class of constructions and to account for some of their syntactic and semantic properties. We will begin by defining some of these rules and showing how they serve their basic purposes. In the second half of the chapter, we will show how to use the indexings to define the Accessibility Constraints and Island Constraints. Then in a later chapter we will show how to account for the complementizer alternations using the indices to trigger the rules.

It is fairly clear what all of these constructions have in common: they all involve the deletion of an anaphoric element across an unbounded context or the binding of an anaphoric element across an unbounded context. The function of the indexing procedure is to define this binding relation. Since unbounded deletions are triggered by the indices assigned by indexing rules, they delete only anaphoric elements that are bound to some phrasal head – their controller. It is also just this class of constructions, it seems, that are subject to island constraints. How the island constraints interact with this binding device will be considered shortly.

These constructions have certain other characteristics in common which are probably necessary concomitants of the binding relation – they are all, for instance, subject to a generalized version of what Akmajian and Kitagawa (1976) call the Relative Clause Binding Convention (RCB) – that is, in each case the subordinate clause ($\bar{S}$ or $\bar{\bar{S}}$) must contain an anaphoric element of the appropriate category (i.e. the same as the head). Brame (1979) has called this general property of constructions the *Filtering Property*.

We shall set the indexing rules up so as to ensure certain things – to ensure, for instance, that the head binds the appropriate argument position in the $\bar{S}$ or $\bar{\bar{S}}$ constituent, also to ensure that deletion rules (in those cases where a deletion operates) delete the appropriate element.

One of the consequences that falls out of the system is an account of this generalized RCB – in that if the subordinate clause does not contain an appropriate anaphor, the sentence is automatically denied a semantic interpretation. No statement of RCB itself is necessary.

All this will become clearer, I hope, as we discuss specific examples. The procedure will be discussed in detail for relative clauses and nominal constituent questions. A fairly detailed discussion of Cleft sentences will also be included and applications to some other construction types will be considered very briefly.

4.2. RELATIVE CLAUSES AND NOMINAL CONSTITUENT QUESTIONS

Consider first some facts about relative clauses and constituent questions. We have analyzed these constructions as having the structures (2) and (3) respectively.

(2)   NP   (3)   Q

       NP $\bar{\text{S}}$ QNP $\bar{\text{S}}$

In both cases the $\bar{\text{S}}$-constituent must contain an anaphoric element bound to the np-head. On the analysis defended here this anaphoric element will always be a personal pronoun. So examples like (4) are ill-formed:

(4)   *an rothar aL tháinig na Lochlannaigh go Béal Feirste
         the bicycle   *came*   *the Vikings*   *to Belfast*
         *'the bicycle that the Vikings came to Belfast'

This use of the pronoun is different from most in that the anaphoric relation between the np-head and the pronoun is obligatory – in that the pronoun cannot have a deictic interpretation (it is, in this sense, an exception to the 'anaporn' relation of Dougherty 1969). The pronoun (5) for instance, unlike most pronouns cannot refer freely to some individual identified in context.

(5) $\begin{Bmatrix} \text{cén} \\ \text{an} \end{Bmatrix}$ t-údar nár   tugadh   deontas dó
         author COMP-NEG was given a grant to him
         $\begin{Bmatrix} \text{'Which author was not given a grant?'} \\ \text{'the author to whom a grant was not given'} \end{Bmatrix}$

It must be interpreted as being bound to the np-head.

Note too that there must be only one such bound pronoun in a relative or questioned clause. If a clause contains two pronouns one will always be ambiguous between the deictic and bound interpretations:

(6)   an file arL thug a athair bocsa ceoil dó
         the poet   *gave his father an accordion to-him*

         'the poet whose father gave him an accordion'
         'the poet to whom his father gave an accordion'

Once we have fixed *one* of the pronouns in (6) as being the bound pronoun, the other will be ambiguous between readings on which it picks out the same individual as the bound pronoun and a reading on which it refers freely. It cannot be the case that both pronouns are interpreted as bound.

These facts are all to be accounted for in terms of an indexing operation that binds the head (interrogative or non-interrogative) of such a construction to a pronoun inside the relative or questioned clause, and in terms of how these indices interact with syntactic and semantic rules.

The rule is as follows:

(7)   In a configuration of the form:

where $\beta = $ NP and $\gamma = \bar{S}$,

(1)   Find a node-label $\dfrac{\text{NP}}{[+\text{Pro}]}$ which is dominated by γ and which has not previously been assigned an index and write a numeral n which has not previously been used in the indexing to the right of that node-label.

(2)   Copy the numeral n to the right of β.[1]

np, it will be remembered, is the cover symbol for the class of interrogative and non-interrogative noun phrases (QNP and NP). As we have set up the PS-rules, α must be either NP or Q.

The semantic function of the indexing mechanism is to ensure that the pronoun marking the relativization site receives only the bound interpretation and that the np-head of a relative clause or a question binds the appropriate argument-position in the relative or questioned clause. This is done by forming a lambda-abstract from the relative clause by binding the variable corresponding to the bound pronoun with a lambda-operator. The translation rules are then so set up that this variable will always be bound by whatever quantifier occurs in the determiner position of the head np. This lambda-abstract is formed when combining the translation of the np-head with the translation of the $\bar{S}$-constituent to derive the translation of the higher noun phrase or question. At this point the index on the np-head encodes the crucial information as to what variable in the translation of $\bar{S}$ should be bound by the lambda-operator.

Since the translation rule for these structures is defined on indexed trees, if β has no index then α will receive no interpretation. This situation will arise if the indexing procedure has failed to find an appropriate pronoun under S. Thus if a relative or questioned clause contains no pronoun, the larger NP or Q of which it is a part will not receive an interpretation. Examples like (4) then will be defined by the grammar as being syntactically well-formed but literally meaningless. In this way we deal with Brame's (1979) Filtering Property in the case of relative clauses and constituent questions.

To see how the facts discussed under example (6) above will be handled, we need to discuss the status and treatment of deictic pronouns, and to examine the question of how they differ from pronouns bound by the procedure in (7).

4.3. DEICTIC PRONOUNS

The indexing procedures under consideration in this chapter define relations of obligatory anaphora – cases where the pronoun corresponds to a bound variable in the semantics and where the 'anaporn' relation of Dougherty 1969 fails to hold. More specifically, the indexing procedures characterize that class of bound anaphora that Robin Cooper (1977b, 1978) has described as involving 'controlled quantification'. Such pronouns will be interpreted by a special convention which treats them like the pronouns of Montague 1974b (PTQ) by reading off the index of the NP-node:

(8)   NP

$[+ \text{pro}]_n$ translates to $\lambda PP (x_n)$
  |
  α

Translation rules are set up in such a way that in every instance the variables in these expressions will ultimately be bound by quantifiers.

I do not intend here to give a treatment of quantification, but to make available a reasonable class of example sentences, I do want to treat deictic pronouns. The essential difference between bound and deictic pronouns is that deictic pronouns will be unindexed. They will thus never trigger the syntactic effects that the binding relations between controllers and bound anaphors do (the complementizer alternations discussed in 4.1, for instance). Semantically, deictic pronouns will be treated in the standard way – that is, they will correspond to free variables which are assigned values with respect to a context of use (in Section 6 of Montague, 1974a (UG), a set of contexts of use in a given interpretation is defined as a set of assignments of values to free variables). To this end, we introduce a special translation convention for such unindexed pronouns:

(9)   NP

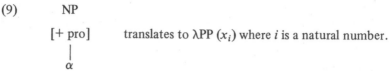

[+ pro]   translates to $\lambda PP\,(x_i)$ where i is a natural number.
|
α

Such a move is invalid within the context of Montague's general theory, because of the requirement that there be just one expression of intensional logic corresponding to each expression of natural language. However Robin Cooper (1975) has developed a theory of quantification and pronoun interpretation which eliminates the need for any syntactic or configurational representation of quantifier scope or variable-binding and which depends crucially on our being allowed to associate expressions of natural language with sequences of meanings (or equivalently with sequences of expressions of intensional logic). This requires a relatively minor adjustment to the general theory as presented in UG and has no very drastic semantic consequences – it remains possible to characterize precisely the notions of truth and entailment and the new system is equivalent to that of UG in the meanings it assigns. The necessary modifications to the theory of UG and the demonstrations of equivalence are given in detail in Cooper (1975) Chapter 4.

This system will work as follows. In the Irish equivalent of a sentence like (10):

(10)   John thinks he is late

the pronoun *he* will be unindexed and the interpretation convention (9) will assign an arbitrary index to the variable in its translation. So the final translation of (10) might be (11):

(11)   think $(j,\,{}^{\wedge}\text{late}(x_2))$

The variable x_2, being free, will be assigned different values in different contexts and so the truth of the sentence itself will vary from context to context. One of the values available for assignment to x_2 is, of course, the individual John. It is this assignment which gives rise to the 'coreferential' reading of (10). If x_2 is assigned any value other than John in a particular context of use, then we derive the 'noncoreferential' reading. Similarly a sentence like (12) has two different possibilities:

(12)   He thinks he is late

Either the indexing convention (9) can assign the same index to the two pronouns or it can assign different indices. In the first case the two pronouns are 'coreferential', they will be assigned the same value in every context. In the second case of course the two pronouns are noncoreferential.

There is a certain amount of redundancy in this system since a sentence can in general acquire a coreferential reading in two different ways. Consider (13):

(13)   The policeman thinks he is late

The pronoun *he* in (13) will receive a translation including an indexed variable as in (9). In some contexts of use this variable will be assigned as value the same individual picked out by the definite description *the policeman*, giving rise of course to the coreferential reading. But the coreferential reading of (13) can be arrived at in another way by quantifying in the NP *the policeman* over the variable corresponding to the pronoun *he*. In this case, the pronoun will correspond to a bound variable semantically and pragmatics will play no role in determining the coreference possibilities.

I am not sure whether or not this redundancy should be regarded with suspicion, but in any case it seems to be unavoidable since we must allow variables corresponding to personal pronouns to be bound in the course of quantifying in, in order to do semantic justice to an example like (14):

(14)   Every king believes that he has a divine right to rule

The reading where *he* refers freely will be derived pragmatically in the normal way, but the other reading must be derived by quantifying in and concomitant binding of the variable corresponding to *he*.

Consider now how this system will interact with the indexing procedure for relative and questioned clauses. An example like (15) can be interpreted in a number of different ways:

(15)   **fear   arL   thug a   athair scilling   dó**
         a man COMP gave his father a shilling to him

Firstly, the example is ambiguous as to which of the two pronouns in the relative clause is the bound pronoun. That is, (15) can be translated either as (16a) or (16b) in English:

(16a)   a man to whom his father gave a shilling

(b)   a man whose father gave him a shilling

This ambiguity in our system turns on which pronoun the indexing

procedure selects for binding to the head. The syntactic structure corresponding to reading (16a) is the tree in (17a); reading (16b) corresponds to the tree
in (17b).

Both (16a) and (16b) are of course in their turn ambiguous, or better,
perhaps, vague, in that the 'extra' pronoun in each (*his* in (16a), *him* in (16b))
can be taken either to pick out the same individual as the relative pronoun or
else can be taken to refer freely. On the reading where the relative pronoun
and the other pronoun are 'coreferential' (16a) and (16b) are indistinguishable. Our system assigns these readings in the following way.

(17a)

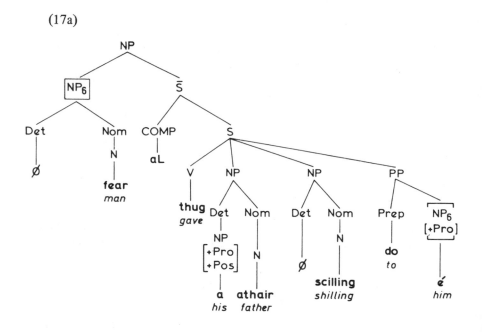

The translation convention in (9) will translate the unbound pronoun in (17a)
or (17b) (next page) either with the same index as the bound pronoun or
with a different one. If the same index is used, then both variables will be
bound by a lambda operator and the ultimate result will be an expression like
that represented (very) informally in (18).

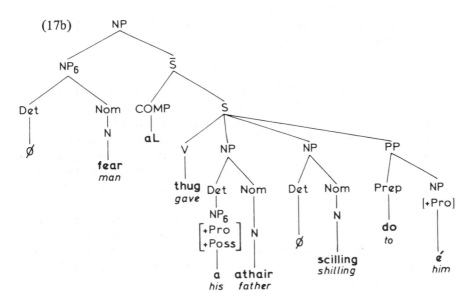

(18) $\lambda P \,\exists x \,[\text{man}(x) \wedge \text{give } x\text{'s father a shilling to } (x) \wedge P(x)]$

This of course is the interpretation on which (16a) and (16b) are indistinguishable.

If (9) translates the unbound pronoun with an index different from that assigned by the indexing procedure to the bound pronoun, then the result will be as in (19a) and (19b) respectively:

(19a) $\lambda P \,\exists z \,[\text{man}(z) \wedge \text{give } x_8\text{'s father a shilling to } z \wedge P(z)]$

(b) $\lambda P \,\exists z \,[\text{man}(z) \wedge \text{give } z\text{'s father a shilling to } x_8 \wedge P(z)]$

(19a) is the reading (16a); (19b) is the reading (16b). Both (19a) and (19b) permit an 'accidental' coreference reading in which the value assigned to x_8 is also that individual that validates the existential quantification in (19). This is again the 'coreferential' reading under which (16a) and (16b) are indistinguishable. The variable x_8 in (19a) and (19b) may of course be assigned any number of different values in different contexts of use and it is these assignments that give rise to the noncoreferential readings of (16a) and (16b).

One thing that is perhaps worth stressing at this point with regard to the indexing procedures defined in this chapter is that they are not to be identified with the logical device of variable-binding. We have already mentioned that an example like (20) must be analyzed as involving variable-binding in the semantics, on one of its readings:

(20)   Every politician says he is honest

But the relation between the NP and the pronoun in an example like (20) is quite different from that holding between a controller np and the pronoun bound to it in a relative or questioned clause. Notice that the anaphoric relation in (20) is not obligatory. The pronoun *he* can be interpreted either as bound or as referring freely. This is not the case in relative and questioned clauses. Syntactically whatever the relation between *every politician* and *he* is, it does not trigger the complementizer alternations which the relation between np-controllers and bound pronouns does.

We model this distinction in the system proposed here by defining a syntactically visible binding between controller np's and bound pronouns (by means of the indexing-rule (7)) and by writing translation rules in such a way that such pronouns always end up being interpreted as bound variables. We define no syntactic relation whatever between *every politician* and *he* in an example like (20).

The essential distinction here I think is between two kinds of quantification: obligatory quantification that has syntactic consequences (modeled by the indexing procedures) and optional quantification that has no syntactic consequences.

4.4. CLEFT SENTENCES

My purpose in discussing clefts here is not that of constructing a detailed or a complete analysis – I will be making many assumptions on a largely arbitrary basis – but rather to illustrate how the indexing procedure will work in a different case. Clefts in Modern Irish have a familiar structure. As already pointed out in Chapter 3, they exhibit the following surface configuration:

(21) $[_S \text{Cop } \bar{\bar{X}} \; [_{\bar{S}} \text{aL } [_S \ldots [_{\bar{\bar{X}}} e] \ldots]]]$

Let us call the $\bar{\bar{X}}$-constituent of the matrix the 'focus constituent'. NP, AP, and PP can all occur at this position. $[_{\bar{\bar{X}}} e]$ indicates a gap in the subordinate clause whose category matches that of the focus constituent. I give some examples in (22a–d).[2]

(22a)   **Is   é   Seán aL thigeann 'na bhaile**
        Cop him   comes home
        'It's John that comes home'.

(b)   **Is   le   Ciarán aL labhraíonn sé**
       Cop with   speaks   he
       'It's John that he speaks to'.

(c)   **NachN   ramhar aL d'éirigh sé**
       NEG INTERR. fat   became he
       'Didn't he get fat?' ('Isn't it fat that he got?')

(d)   **Is   leisan   chigire   aL shíl   sé aL labhair sé _**
       Cop with the Inspector   thought he   spoke he
       'It was the inspector that he thought he had spoken to.'

We face a series of problems here essentially similar to those we faced in the case of relative clauses and constituent questions – namely, to make sure that the clefted clause contains an appropriate anaphoric element (one that matches the focus constituent in category), to make sure that the clefted clause contains only one such element, and finally to make sure that it gets bound in the proper way. We must also cause the complementizer substitution rules to be triggered, as is illustrated by example (22d). Notice that in this example, the complement of **síl** is introduced by the relative complementizer **aL** rather than by **goN**, as complements of **síl** normally would be. We must also make sure that island constraints are invoked in this construction, as is illustrated by (23):

(23)   **Is le   Seán aL fuair mé amach cé   aL bhí ag labhairt*
        Cop with   found I   out   who   was at speaking
        *'It was John that I found out who was talking to.'

Again, the indexing mechanism will play a crucial role in bringing all this about.

Let us assume that the focus constituent is generated in place – that is, that clefts are introduced by means of the PS-rule (23):

(23) $S \to Cop \; \bar{\bar{X}} \; \bar{\bar{S}}$

where $\bar{\bar{X}}$ can be NP, PP, or AP. The next question that arises is the following: what is the anaphoric element in the clefted clause that is bound to the focused constituent and that appears as a gap on the surface?

It seems clear that, unlike the case of relatives and questions, the item in question cannot be a deleted personal pronoun. If it were, we would expect a resumptive pronoun to turn up in those cases where extraction is impossible for one reason or another. This is not the case. Thus, if extraction would violate the constraint against preposition stranding, we might expect examples like (24) to be grammatical. They are not.

(24)   *Is é   Seán aL d'iarr mé úll   air
         Cop him   *asked I   an apple on him*
        'It was John that I asked for an apple'.

Or, if extraction would violate an island constraint, we might expect a resumptive pronoun to save the day, as is the case with relatives and nominal constituent questions. Again, this is not the case:

(25)   *Is é   Seán aL fuair me amach cé   aL bhí ag labhairt
         Cop him   *found I   out   who   was at speaking*

        leis
        with him

        *'It was John that I found out who was talking to him'

Let us suppose, then, that the anaphoric element is simply a phrasal node (NP, PP or AP) that has no lexical content. That is, we let these three nodes dominate the empty string in deep structure trees. So example (22b) will derive from the deep structure tree in (26):

(26)

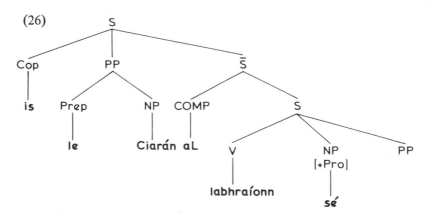

We can define the indexing procedure for clefts as in (27):

(27)   In a configuration of the form:

(where α does not dominate the empty string)

(1)   Find under $\bar{S}$ an occurrence of the category label α which dominates the empty string. Pick a numeral n which has not previously
been used in the indexing and write it to the right of that node-
label.

(2)   Copy the numeral n to the right of α.

Once again, if the procedure in (27) fails to find an appropriate anaphor under
$\bar{S}$, no index will be assigned to α. This in turn will have the effect that the
translation rule for clefts will not be able to process such examples, and they
will go uninterpreted.

So clefts without appropriate gaps in the clefted clause will never receive
an interpretation. Similarly we rule out examples where empty NP, PP or AP
nodes turn up where they are not supposed to. Such nodes will never receive
an interpretation because the contexts in which they occur will not satisfy
the structural condition of (27). The translation convention for interpreting
empty nodes is defined for indexed empty nodes, so unindexed empty nodes
will be uninterpretable and will make the sentences in which they occur
uninterpretable. Similar comments apply in cases where there are two or more
gaps of the appropriate category in the clefted clause. This amounts to a formal
version of the intuition that gaps can occur in a sentence only when they are
uniquely controlled by (bound to) some constituent with real content.

How will the semantics work? I will consider here only truth-conditional
aspects of the meaning of clefts. The discussion will draw heavily on the work
of Per-Kristian Halvorsen. For a treatment of the truth-conditional and non-
truth-conditional aspects of the semantics of cleft constructions, within the
framework of a transformational syntax, see Halvorsen (1978).

As far as truth-conditional semantics goes, we will assume that clefts mean
exactly the same as their non-clefted counterparts.[3] Our problem, then, is to
get (28a) to come out meaning the same thing as (28b).

(28a)   **Is   le   Ciarán aL imíonn Deirdre**
         Cop with   leaves

         'It is with Ciaran that Deirdre leaves.'

(b)   **Imíonn Deirdre le Ciarán**

We can make this come about in the following way.

We assume a general convention for the interpretation of indexed empty nodes as in (29):

(29) $\bar{\bar{X}}_n$

$\quad\quad\quad$ $\bar{\bar{X}}'_n = {}^\vee v_n^{\langle s, f(\bar{\bar{X}})\rangle}$

$\quad\;\;$ |
$\quad\;\;$ e

The notation used in (29) is interpreted as follows. For any category X, X' is the translation of a tree rooted by X. In PTQ, Montague defines a function f that is a mapping from the syntactic categories of natural language to the types of intensional logic. So for any syntactic category X, we can abbreviate the type of intensional logic that corresponds to X as $f(X)$, and the intensional type corresponding to the category as $\langle s, f(X)\rangle$. Further, for any type α, v_n^α is the n-th variable of type α. So what the convention (29) does is translate any empty node of category X indexed by n, as the extension of the n-th variable of the type of X-intensions.

The syntactic evidence that the null anaphoric element in clefts does not derive from an underlying personal pronoun has an interesting semantic correlation. The scope properties of a cleft sentence mirror those of the corresponding non-cleft sentence. So, for instance, an NP in focus-position can perfectly well be within the scope of an intensional verb in the clefted clause. Sentence (30a) for instance, has a de dicto interpretation exactly like that of its non-clefted counterpart (30b).[4]

(30a)   **Lúchorpán aL   bhí sé a chuartú**
         leprechaun COMP was he looking for

         'It was a leprechaun he was looking for.'

(b)   **Bhí sé ag cuartú   lúchorpán**
         was he   looking for a-leprechaun

         'He was looking for a leprechaun.'

We allow for this reading to be derived by using the high type variable in the translation convention for empty nodes (29). Empty NP-nodes translate not to sets of properties of individual variables as do pronouns, but rather to variables over NP-types. If it were the case that the syntactic evidence from clefts indicated that pronouns were the appropriate anaphoric elements for clefted clauses, then we would have to translate them as pronouns. With these variables of lower type, only the wide-scope or de re reading of a sentence like (30a) would be derivable.

The translation rule for clefts will be as in (31):

(31)

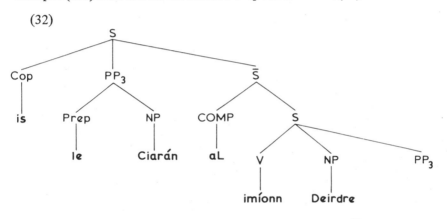

$$S' = \lambda v_n^{\langle s, f(\bar{\bar{X}}) \rangle} [\bar{S}'] (\hat{\bar{\bar{X}}}'_n)$$

The effect of this rule is probably best appreciated in working out a specific example. (28a) derives from the indexed deep structure tree (32):

(32)

By convention (29) and by rules which will be presented later, $\bar{S}$ will translate to (33):

(33) $\check{}v_n^{\langle s, f(PP) \rangle}$ ($\hat{}$leave (d))

The matrix PP **le Ciarán** translates as in (34).

(34)   with ($\hat{}$**Ciarán'**)

The translation rule (31) for Clefts binds the PP-variable in the translation of $\bar{S}$ (33) with a lambda operator and applies the resulting function to the translation of the focussed constituent. By lambda conversion the translation of the PP substitutes for the PP-variable in the translation of $\bar{S}$ and the result is (35):

(35)   with ($\hat{}$Ciarán') ($\hat{}$leave (d))

This is exactly the result that would have been obtained if we had built up the translation of (28b) directly in the normal way.

Example (36) works similarly:

(36a)   **Lúchorpán aL chuartaíonn Seán __**
         leprechaun   seeks   John

         'It's a leprechaun that John seeks'.

(b)   **Cuartaíonn Seán lúchorpán**
         seeks   John leprechaun

         'John seeks a leprechaun'.

(37)

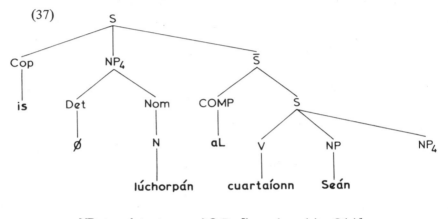

NP₄ translates to $\lambda Q \exists x \, [\text{leprechaun}(x) \wedge Q(x)]$

S̄   translates to $\text{seek}(s, \mathscr{P}_4)$

(where $\mathscr{P}_4$, as in PTQ is a variable over NP intensions, that is, a variable of type $\langle s, f(\text{NP}) \rangle$)

S translates to $\lambda \mathscr{P}_4 \, [\text{seek}(s, \mathscr{P}_4)] \, {}^\wedge \lambda Q \, \exists x \, [\text{leprechaun}(x) \wedge Q(x)])$

By lambda-conversion this expression is equivalent to (38), which is the translation of (36b) on its *de dicto* reading:

(38) $\text{seek} \, (s, {}^\wedge \lambda Q \, \exists x \, [\text{leprechaun}(x) \wedge Q(x)])$

Before leaving the subject of clefts, there is one further interesting and slightly bothersome datum that should be mentioned. This has to do with the interaction between clefts on the one hand and relative and questioned clauses on the other. Clefts occur quite freely as both relative and questioned clauses:

(39)   **an fear arL   dó   aL   thug mé an t-airgead**
         the man COMP+Copula to-him COMP gave I   the money

         ??'the man that it was (him) I gave the money to'

(40)   **Cén   fear arL   dó   aL   thug tú an t-airgead**
         which man COMP+Copula to-him COMP gave you the money

         'Which man was it you gave the money to?'

(41)   **an té   nachN   é   Dia aL   bhíonn**
         the person COMP+NEG+Copula him God COMP is

         os comhair a   shúl aige
         before   his eyes at-him

         ??'he who it isn't God that he has before his eyes'

(42)   **Cé   nachN é Dia aL bhíonn os comhair a shúl aige**
         who

         ??'Who is it not God that he has before his eyes?'

(43)   **rudaí arL   as   na nuachtáin is**
         things COMP+Copula from the papers   COMP+Copula

         dóiche aL   baineadh   iad
         probable COMP were-taken them

         ??'things that it was from the papers that it is probable they were
         taken'

(44)   **Cén   garda   arL   leis   aL   bhí tú ag**
         which policeman COMP+Copula with-him COMP were you at

         caint
         talking

         'Which policeman was it you were talking to?'

This is one other respect in which relatives and questions behave identically in
Irish but differently in English. English tolerates clefts easily in constituent
questions (subject to island constraints), but hardly at all in relative clauses
(witness the translations in (39)–(44)).

   The system as so far set up handles these facts without difficulty, as far as
I can see – how the rules of semantic interpretation handle such examples as
(39)–(44) will be demonstrated in a later chapter, but the Phrase Structure

rules and indexing rules already discussed will assign to (40) and (43), for instance, the indexed trees in (40′) and (43′) respectively. Details of how the complementizers and the Copula are handled are ignored in (40′) and (43′) (the Copula is one of those elements, like Negation, that fuses with complementizers), but this does not affect the points we want to make. All of the examples in (39)–(44) can be handled similarly.

(40′)

(43′)

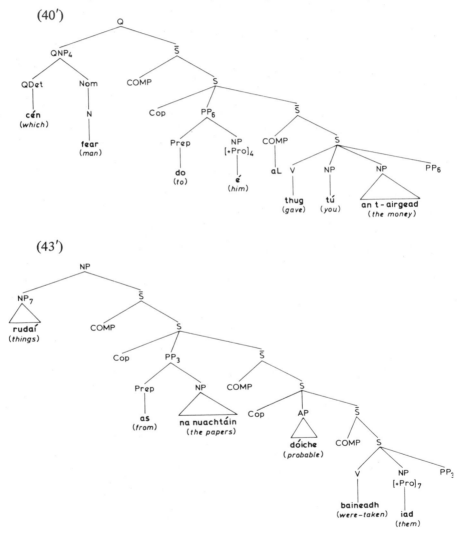

Notice though that in none of the examples in (39)–(44) is the focus of the cleft *identical* to the bound pronoun of the relative or questioned clause. Either the bound pronoun is contained within the focus (as in (39), (40) and (44)) or the bound pronoun and the focus are entirely distinct (as in (41), (42) and (43). However there are also grammatical examples in which the bound pronoun actually *is* the focus of the cleft, as in (45), and it is these examples that are troublesome.

(45)   **an fear arbh   é   aL   mharaigh mo mhadadh**
         the man COMP+Cop him COMP killed   my dog
         'the man that it was (he) who killed my dog'

If one examines carefully the binding rules as formulated, it turns out that they do indeed index such examples in the appropriate way. Notice that the indexing rule for relatives and nominal constituent questions, as stated in (7), is subject to a condition to the effect that only pronouns that have not already been assigned an index can be bound by the rule. This condition is needed to avoid the generation of examples like (46):

(46)   *****an fear nachN   bhfuil fhios agam cé   arL   phós**
         the man COMP+NEG I-know   who COMP married

         Bríd é
             him

         *'the man that I don't know who Brid married him'

In the absence of the prohibition on double-indexing of pronouns, example (46) would be indexed as in (47):

(47) $[_{NP}NP_j[_{\bar{S}} \ldots [_Q QNP_k \ldots Pro_{kj} \ldots]]]$

In the light of these considerations then, consider (45) again. Before indexing, (45) will have the structure (45′).

If the indexing rule for clefts should apply first, binding the pronoun in focus-position to the empty NP-node in the clefted clause, then the indexing rule (7), for relative and questioned clauses, will not be able to bind the pronoun to the head NP (**an fear**). (45) will not be interpreted under this indexing. However if the relative clause indexing rule should apply first, there is

(45′)

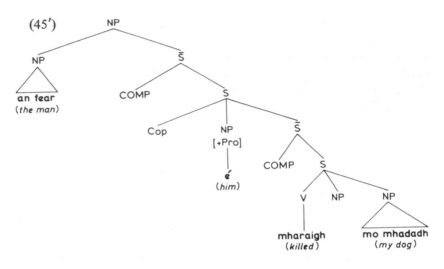

nothing in the cleft binding rule, as stated in (27), which would prevent it applying to bind the focussed pronoun to the empty NP position in the clefted clause. There is then a legal indexing of the tree (45′), as diagrammed in (48):

(48) $[_{NP} NP_j [_{\bar{S}} COMP [_S Cop \, Pro_{jk} [_{\bar{S}} \ldots -_k \ldots]]]]$

Clearly though, if the semantic rule for interpreting clefts, (31), is to handle such examples correctly, it must be adjusted in some way. One way to assure the right result would be to assume the existence of a convention saying that the rule for interpreting clefts (or perhaps any rule) looks only at the outermost of a series of subscript numerals. The prohibition against double-indexing of pronouns in the relative clause rule (7) assures that the order of indices on Pro of (48) is the only possible one. Therefore the outermost index will always be that one which binds the pronoun to the empty NP position in the clefted clause – that is, the binding relation defined by the outermost index will always be that one which is relevant for the correct operation of the semantic rule for clefts. So the meaning of the focus-constituent will eventually be substituted back into the appropriate position in the clefted clause – the position identified by the index k in (48). If we further assume that the translation-convention for interpreting bound pronouns ((8)) looks only at the innermost index in a series, then the interpretation-rule for relative clause constructions and constituent questions will work in the appropriate way in examples like (45). This should become clearer when these semantic rules have been presented and specific examples worked out.

I will not attempt a statement of the indexing rule for comparative and equative clauses here. I assume that it will be of essentially the same form as the rules we have looked at already, except that it will look for an AP-anaphor in the relevant clause. I further assume that the same rule will apply in AP-Questions as discussed in Section 3.6 of the last chapter. In this way we predict not only that these constructions will exhibit Brame's 'filtering property' (the generalized version of Akmajian and Kitagawa's RCB) but further that they will obey island-constraints and trigger the complementizer-alternations, which as we will show in a later chapter are diagnostic of this relation of syntactic binding in Irish.

In the second half of this chapter we move on to consider the treatment of accessibility constraints and island-constraints that we are led to given the decisions we have made so far.

4.5. ON FORMALIZING THE ACCESSIBILITY CONSTRAINTS[5]

The problem we will be concerned with in this section is the general one of giving a formal statement of the conditions that govern whether or not the rule of Relative Deletion applies to delete a bound pronoun in a questioned or relative clause. We will revise the treatment that has so far been assumed in several fundamental ways. Firstly, an attempt will be made to eliminate the appeal to rule-particular conditions. So far the accessibility constraints have been handled by tacking a list of conditions onto the statement of the rule itself; I will attempt to eliminate those conditions and analyze the facts that motivated them as being reflexes of more general conditions with a much wider range of applicability. Secondly, we have been assuming until now that the constraints are of two essentially different kinds – conditions having to do with the grammatical relation borne by the target pronoun in its clause on the one hand, and island constraints in the sense of Ross 1967 on the other hand. We shall end up by proposing (with a degree of reservation) a system that gives an essentially non-relational account of both sets of facts and treats them both as being reflections of the same condition-schema.

I will begin by repeating the statement that we have so far been working with.

(49)   *Relative Deletion*
        SD: X [np$_j$ Y $\underset{[+Pro]_k}{NP}$ Z] W

                1   2 3   4   5 6
                1   2 3 $\emptyset$ 5 6

Conditions:
(i)   obligatory if term 4 is subject in its clause
(ii)   optional if term 4 is direct object in its clause
(iii)   inapplicable if term 4 is neither subject nor direct object in its clause
(iv) $j = k$

There are several comments that are worth making about this formulation. The first is that it is wrong. Condition (i) stipulates that the rule must apply if the target pronoun is the subject of its clause. This is true given the range of data we have discussed so far, but we do not have to look very far to find counter-examples. In particular, subjects of embedded clauses may be retained:[6]

(50)   **Is   raiteas   é arL   cheart goN   gcuirfeadh**
        Cop a-statement it COMP+Copula right   COMP would-put

        sé iontas   orainn
        it wonder on-us

        'It is a statement that rightfully should amaze us'.

(literally – 'It is a statement that it is right that it should amaze us'.)

The constraint then is not one that holds of subjects in general, but rather only of subjects that are not in clauses embedded within the relative clause. This is a point that we shall return to in more detail shortly.

The formulation of (49) also presupposes a rather elaborate theory of what we may permit in the way of conditions appended to a rule. One of the central efforts in recent work in syntax has been the attempt to eliminate such rule-particular conditions in favour of more general conditions that affect the working of rules in a more indirect way. In particular, it seems excessive to allow a rule to be obligatory in some sets of circumstances but optional in others – particularly when the propriety of allowing a stipulated distinction between optional and obligatory rules at all has been much called into question by recent work. Apart from these general reservations, we have good reason to be unhappy, on the basis of Irish facts alone, with a situation in which the rule of Relative Deletion is sometimes obligatory. One of the boasts that we have been making on behalf of the analysis as formulated so far, is that it predicts the observed interaction between the deletion rule and island constraints. That is, it predicts that in any case where island-constraints block the application of Relative Deletion there should be a corresponding grammatical example with a resumptive pronoun (that is, an undeleted bound pronoun) in place of a deletion-site. This prediction holds, of course, only as long as the rule is taken to be optional. Failure of an obligatory rule to apply because of an island constraint should yield an ungrammatical output. So the system as it stands incorrectly predicts that an example like (51) should be ungrammatical:

(51)   **an píobaire nachN**   **mbíonn fhios agat in am   ar bith**
        the piper   COMP+NEG you-don't know   in time any

        caidé aL   tá sé ag dul   a bhualadh
        what COMP is he at going to play

        ?'the piper that you never know what he's going to play'

A final and most damaging criticism that might be made of a formulation such as (49) is that it is a paragon of the ad hoc, which does not relate the facts it is designed to deal with to any other facts in the language, and which takes little predictive risk. It represents a re-description rather than an account of the facts.

How can we improve on (49) then?

Let us begin with the assumption that Relative Deletion is an optional rule. By this means we eliminate the anomaly in the treatment of island constraints that is illustrated by (51). It may seem a little perverse, however, since in the data we began by looking at, the rule reveals its optionality in only one circumstance – namely, when the target pronoun is direct object in its clause. But when we look beyond one-clause relatives, of course, we find that there are many circumstances in which either a deletion-site or a resumptive pronoun can mark the relativization-site. Given the analysis presented here of course, these are cases in which the rule of Relative Deletion is free to apply or not apply.[7]

(52a)   **Bhí Gaeilge ag fear   arL   shíleamar   gurL**
        was Irish   at a-man COMP we-thought COMP+Copula

        Shasanach   é
        an-Englishman him

(b)   **Bhí Gaeilge ag fear   aL   shíleamar   ba**
            was Irish   at a-man COMP we-thought COMP+Copula

            Shasanach   —
            an-Englishman

            'A man that we thought was English spoke Irish'.

(53a)   **Bhí uaireadóirí aige   arbh   fhiú   a lán iad**
            was watches   at-him COMP+Copula worth a-lot them

(b)   **Bhí uaireadóirí aige   ab   fhiú   a lán —**
            was watches   at-him COMP+Copula worth a lot

            'He had watches that were worth a lot.'

(54a)   **an fear arL   theastaigh uaithi é   a phósadh**
            the man COMP she-wanted   him to-marry

(b)   **an fear aL   theastaigh uaithi — a phósadh**
            the man COMP she-wanted   to-marry

            'the man that she wanted to marry'

(55a)   **Is   gúna   é arL mhaith liom go mór é a cheannach**
            Cop a-dress it that I would like greatly it to buy

(b)   **Is   gúna   é aL ba mhaith liom go mór — a cheannach**
            Cop a-dress it that I would like   greatly   to buy

            'It is a dress that I would greatly like to buy.'

(56a)   **Daoine arL chuimhin liom iad   a bheith i láthair**
            people that I remembered them to be   present

(b)   **Daoine aL ba chuimhin liom — a bheith i láthair**
            people that I remembered   to be   present

            'people that I remembered being present'

The fundamental difference between the (a) and (b) examples in the pairs above is that the (a)-sentences have a resumptive pronoun while the (b)-sentences have a deletion-site – the other differences are reflexes of the fact that different complementizers appear in clauses with resumptive pronouns than appear in clauses with deletion-sites. The eccentricity of the ways in which the Copula combines with the two complementizers accounts for the remaining differences. The rule of Relative Deletion then applies optionally to subjects and objects of embedded clauses (both tensed and finite), to direct objects in un-embedded clauses and even to subjects of copular clauses (example (53a)), where grammatical relations are defined in quite different structural ways than in the case of non-copular sentences.

Granted then that it is reasonable to take the deletion rule to be optional, the task of defining the accessibility constraints then separates into two parts: to define the cases where the rule is blocked from applying, and resumptive pronouns must appear, and to define the circumstances where the rule must apply, and resumptive pronouns are ungrammatical.

Consider first those cases where the rule is blocked from applying. We will begin with the island constraints. Such constraints have often been taken to be conditions on proper analyses – in effect then, conditions on the applicability of transformational rules. Given the treatment of clefts sketched earlier in this chapter though, we must look at the constraints in a rather different way. Clefts *are* subject to island constraints (see example (23) above, and further examples below), but on the analysis sketched here, no transformational rule applies in such structures. If that analysis is to be maintained then, island constraints cannot be interpreted as conditions on proper analyses or on rule-applicability.

We will take the constraints to be conditions on the kind of structures that can intervene between an indexed empty node and the phrase to which it is bound by the indexing-procedures we have been discussing in this chapter. In the case of clefts we take these empty nodes to be generated in the base. In the case of relative clauses and constituent questions the constraints will be invoked if we assume that the elementary transformational operation of deletion is taken to delete only the lexical content of the category, leaving behind an empty node. In the case of controlled deletions like Relative Deletion, these will be indexed empty nodes (indices having been supplied by the procedure (7)) and the constraints will be invoked.

Some care must be taken in the matter of deciding at what level of a derivation these conditions hold. Clearly they must be checked after the application of rules like Relative Deletion. It cannot be the case though that they are checked after *all* transformations have applied. They must be checked before the application of certain rules, like Extraposition from NP, which destroy Complex NP configurations without making deletion of a bound pronoun in the extraposed relative clause any more grammatical. I assume that examples like (58) would derive from (57) by means of Extraposition from NP. But (58b) is every bit as ungrammatical as (57b), despite the fact that the clause into which the deletion rule has operated is no longer dominated by NP.

(57a) **teanga   nachN   raibh aithne   agam ariamh ar**
       a-language COMP+NEG was   acquaintance at-me ever   on

       aon duine aL   bhí _ ábalta í a labhairt
       anyone   COMP was   able   it to speak

(b)   ***teanga   nachN   raibh aithne   agam ariamh ar**
       a-language COMP+NEG was   acquaintance at-me ever   on

       aon duine aL   bhí _ ábalta _ a labhairt
       anyone   COMP was   able   to speak

       ?'a language that I have never known anyone who was able to
       speak it'

(58a) **teanga   nachN   raibh aithne   agam ar aon duine**
       a-language COMP+NEG was   acquaintance at-me on anyone

       ariamh aL   bhí ábalta í a labhairt
       ever   COMP was able   it to speak

(b)   ***teanga   nachN   raibh aithne   agam ar aon duine**
       a-language COMP+NEG was   acquaintance at-me on anyone

       ariamh aL   bhí ábalta _ a labhairt
       ever   COMP was able   to speak

       ?'a language that I have never known anyone who was able to
       speak it'

This is a question to which we will return.

Say we take it then that island constraints are well-formedness conditions
(non-local filters if you like) on the structures that form the output of rules
like Relative Deletion.

What then are the constraints? Let us begin by considering the Complex
NP Constraint. I propose that (59) be taken to be one of these well-formedness
conditions.[8]

(59) $\dots \bar{\bar{X}}_j \dots [_\alpha \dots [_{\bar{\bar{X}} - j}] \dots _\alpha] \dots$

          ungrammatical if $\alpha = NP$

I will use the notation $[_{\bar{\bar{X}} - j}]$ to denote an empty node of category $\bar{\bar{X}}$ indexed
by j.

This statement makes all NP islands. In the most obvious cases this will account for the Complex NP facts as discussed and illustrated in Chapter 2 above. That is, it will declare to be illegal any attempt to define a binding into a relative clause, if the controller of the binding is outside the NP of which the relative clause forms a part. This will account for the Complex NP facts discussed in Chapters 2 and 3 with respect to Relative Deletion. But since (59) is a general constraint on binding, rather than a condition peculiar to the rule of Relative Deletion, we expect to find the same phenomenon in the case of other constructions involving the binding we have been discussing in this chapter – clefts and equative clauses, for instance. This is in fact the case, as illustrated in (60) and (61).

(60)   *Is í an Ghaeilge aL   mholfainn   duine ar bith aL
        Cop it the Irish   COMP I-would-praise person any   COMP

        tá ábalta _ a labhairt
        is able   to speak

        *'It's Irish that I would praise anyone who is able to speak'.

(61)   *Tá sí   chomh dóighiúil agus aL   phós   bhur n-athair
        is she as   beautiful as   COMP married your father

        bean   aL   bhí
        a-woman COMP was

        *'She is as beautiful as your father married a woman who was'.

The rough syntactic structure of (60) and (61) is given in (60') and (61') respectively, where it is also illustrated how it is that they give rise to violations of (59).

But further predictions follow from (59) of course. Notice first that it accounts for the fact that possessive pronouns resist deletion. These modifiers will always be inside NP and therefore any attempt to delete such a pronoun will lead to a violation of (59). We therefore predict in the case of relatives and constituent questions that resumptive pronouns will be obligatory when the relativized or questioned constituent is a possessive modifier. That is, we achieve part of the effect of condition (iii) of (49). Once again, since (59) is a general constraint on binding, we expect to find parallel facts in the case of

(60')

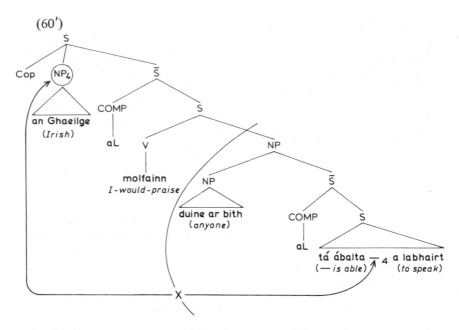

other binding constructions – clefts, for instance. NP can of course appear in the focus position of a cleft, as in (62) for instance:

(62)   **Máirtín aL   tá ＿ i   gceannas i   nDoire**
         Martin COMP is   in charge   in Derry

         'It's Martin that is in charge in Derry'.

When the focus is NP, then we would expect the associated gap to turn up in any NP-position in the clefted clause, including that of possessive modifier. Such examples are, however, hopeless:

(63)   ***Seán aL   cailleadh ＿ mac**
         John COMP was-lost   son

         *'It is John's that son died'.

(63') represents the rough syntactic structure of (63) and why it fails.

     Since the indexing rule for clefts requires not a pronoun in the clefted clause, but rather an empty node matching the category of the focussed con-stituent (see (27) above), there will be no corresponding grammatical examples

(61)

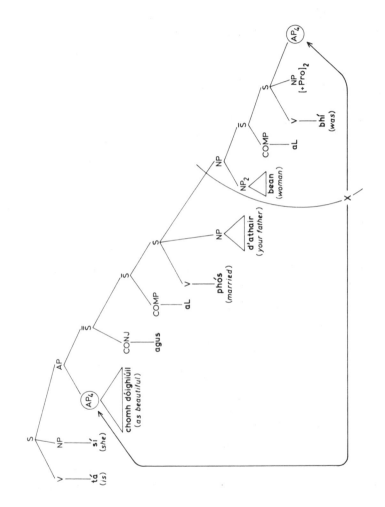

(63')

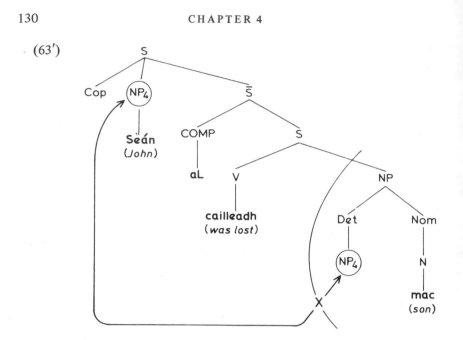

with resumptive pronouns. (64) is (correctly) predicted to be ungrammatical, because the requirements of the indexing rule (27) are not met:

(64)   *Seán aL   cailleadh a   mhac
         John COMP was-lost his son

        *'It was John that his son was lost'.

The only grammatical example like (63) or (64) in the relevant respects is (65):

(65)   Mac Sheáin   aL   cailleadh _
         son John(poss) COMP was-lost

        'It was John's son who died'.

There is at least one other correct prediction that follows from (59). Recall that it is possible to have adjectives and adjective-phrases (AP's) in the focus position of a cleft:

(66a)   Dubh aL   bhí sé
         black COMP was it

        ?'It was black that it was'.

(b)   **Marbh gan   anam aL   thit sé ar an fhód**
       dead   without soul COMP fell he on the sod
       'He fell dead and lifeless to the ground.'

(c)   **Chomh geal le   sneachta na   h-aon oíche   aL   bhí a**
       as   fair with snow   the(gen) one night(gen) COMP was her

       craiceann
       skin

       'It was as white as the snow of one night that her skin was'.

In all the examples in (66) the position bound in the clefted clause is that of predicative adjective. (59) will predict that it should be impossible to have attributive adjectives in focus position, since this will always involve the binding of an empty node inside an NP-node from without the NP. This prediction happens to be correct:

(67a)   *__*Dubh aL   tháinig an t-éan chugam__
        black COMP came   the bird to-me

        *'It was black that the bird _ came to me'.

(67b)   *__*Chomh geal le   sneachta na   h-aon oíche   aL   bhí__
        as   fair with snow   the(gen) one   night(gen) COMP was

        craiceann uirthi
        skin   on-her

        *'It was a fair as the snow of one night that she had _ skin'.

There are of course rules that move elements out of NP – Extraposition from NP is one such rule, and examples such as (68) are presumably derived by moving a prepositional phrase to the right out of the larger NP:

(68)   **Thug sé trí   chloch dom   den   choirce ab fhearr aL   bhí**
        gave he three stone to-me of-the oats   best   COMP was

        le fáil
        available

        'He gave me three stone of the best oats available'.

But since such rules do not involve syntactic binding in the sense in which we have defined it here, and since conditions like (59) are checked before such rules as Extraposition from NP apply, there is no reason to expect them to obey (59).

I propose to treat the Embedded Question Constraint in an equally simple-minded way. This constraint as we discussed it in Chapter 2, said simply that questions of all kinds were syntactic islands. Since we have been using a system that recognizes the existence of a distinct syntactic category of questions – the category Q – we can account for these facts quite straightforwardly by revising (59) as in (69):

(69) $\ldots \bar{\bar{X}}_j \ldots [_\alpha \ldots [\bar{\bar{x}} - j] \ldots _\alpha] \ldots$

ungrammatical if $\alpha = $ NP or Q

Consider next the question of how to avoid preposition-stranding in relatives and questions – why can prepositional objects not be deleted by the rule of Relative Deletion?

The first point to be made is that once again, the phenomenon is not restricted to relative or questioned clauses. Preposition-stranding is also prohibited in clefts.

(70)   **Ba   leis-an   ghirseach bheag rua   aL   bhí Tarlach**
         was with-the girl   little   red-haired COMP was Charlie

         de Brún ag caint
         Brown   at talking

'It was to the little red-haired girl that Charlie Brown was talking'.

(71)   ***Ba í   an ghirseach bheag rua   aN   raibh Tarlach**
         was her the girl   little   red-haired COMP was   Charlie

         de Brún ag caint   le   __.
         Brown   at talking with

'It was the little red-haired girl that Charlie Brown was talking to'.

Since NP can of course be clefted, some device is needed which will block cases like (71), where there is a NP in focus-position which binds a prepositional object in the clefted clause.

This much established, it is clearly wrong to deal with the relative clause and questioned clause facts by appeal to a condition particular to that rule, as is done in (49). One possible solution that would have sufficient generality to deal with all the data so far considered, would be to propose the existence of a surface filter banning preposition-stranding:

(72) $^*[[_{PP}\text{Prep}[_{NP}-]]$

Before committing ourselves to this solution however, we might explore a different approach – a more interesting one in the sense that it generalizes to a broader range of data and takes greater predictive risks than does (72). Several people have proposed recently that prepositional phrases should be regarded as islands (cf. Baltin 1978, Van Riemsdijk 1977, for example). We can incorporate this proposal in our framework by further revising (59) to (73).

(73) $\ldots \bar{\bar{X}}_j \ldots [_{\alpha} \ldots [\bar{\bar{x}}-_j] \ldots_{\alpha}] \ldots$

ungrammatical if $\alpha = $ NP, PP or Q

This formulation will deal in the obvious way with the data we have considered so far. Any attempt to bind an empty NP-node inside a PP from the outside will be declared ungrammatical, so the filter (72) falls out as a special case of (73). What then of the other predictions derivable from (73)?

One constituent-type that frequently functions as prepositional object is the class of infinitival clauses. Before we discuss the relevant examples, it will be useful to point out some of the syntactic differences that distinguish tensed clauses from infinitival clauses. First, in an infinitival clause the verb appears in a special form uninflected for tense, mood, voice or person and which exhibits noun-like morphology. Secondly, the order of major constituents in the two clause-types is different. In infinitival clauses the subject and object NP both precede the verb (in that order).[9]

(74a)   **D'iarr sé orm   úll   a   cheannach dó**
         asked he on-me an-apple ptc buy(VN)   to-him
         'He asked me to buy him an apple'.

(74b)   **Ba mhaith liom tú   a   bheith   i láthair**
         I   would like you ptc be(VN) present
         'I would like you to be present'.

(c)   **Tá mé ag feitheamh le   tú   na   deich bpunt   sin a**
         am I   at waiting   with you those ten   pounds   ptc

         thabhairt dom
         give(VN) to-me

         'I am waiting for you to give me those ten pounds'.

Such clauses are frequently governed by prepositions – for example after certain verbs:

(75a)   **Chrom siad ar an obair a   dhéanamh**
        bent   they on the work ptc do(VN)

        'They set themselves to do the work'.

(b)   **Ní   raibh mé ag dúil   le   tú   a   fheiceáil**
        NEG was I   at expecting with you ptc see(VN)

        'I wasn't expecting to see you'.

(c)   **Thug siad faoi   íde   a   thabhairt dom**
        took they under abuse ptc give(VN) to-me

        'They set about abusing me'.

I assume that such structures are generated by means of the expansion-rule (76).

(76)   PP → Prep $\underset{[-\text{fin}]}{S}$

and that a sentence like (75c), for instance, will have the structure sketched in (77).

(77)

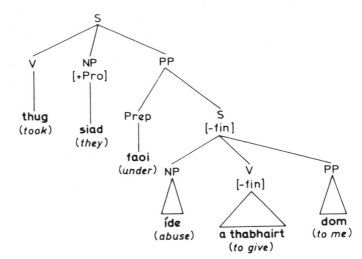

Given this kind of structure and the condition (73), we derive a rather obvious prediction – namely that it should be impossible to bind a position inside the prepositional phrase from the outside. This should mean that resumptive pronouns will be obligatory when one attempts to relativize or question into such a clause. In the case of other binding constructions, like clefts and comparative clauses, we should get ungrammaticality. These predictions seem to be borne out.

(78)   *Relatives and Questions*

(a)   *na daoine aL   bhí muid ag feitheamh le   _ a   theacht
        the people COMP were we   at waiting   with   ptc come(VN)

        na daoine aN   raibh muid ag feitheamh le   iad   a
        the people COMP were we   at waiting   with them ptc

        theacht
        come(VN)

        ?'the people that we were waiting for them to come'

(b)   *an t-airgead aL   bhí mé ag dúil   le   tú _ a
        the money   COMP was I   at expecting with you   ptc

        thabhairt dom
        give(VN) to-me

        an t-airgead aN   raibh mé ag dúil   le   tú é a
        the money   COMP was   I   at expecting with you it ptc

        thabhairt dom
        give(VN) to-me

        'the money that I was expecting you to give me'

(c)   *Cén obair aL   d'éirigh tú   as   _ a   dhéanamh
        what work COMP rose   you out-of   ptc do(VN)

        Cén obair arL   éirigh tú   as   í a   dhéanamh
        what work COMP rose   you out-of it ptc do(VN)

        'What work did you stop doing?'

The syntactic structure of (78c) is sketched in (78') for illustration.

(78′)

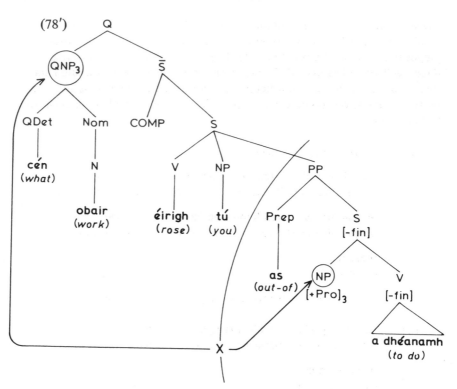

(79)   *Clefts*

(a)   *Is í mo mháthair nachN raibh mé ag dúil le
       Cop her my mother COMP+NEG was I at expecting with

       _ a fheiceáil
       ptc see(VN)

       'It was my mother that I wasn't expecting to see'.

(b)   *leabhar faoi theoiric na lorg aL tá mé ag
       a-book about theory the(gen pl) traces COMP am I at

       smaointeamh ar _ a scríobh
       thinking on ptc write(VN)

       'It's a book about trace-theory that I'm thinking of writing'.

(c)   *Deich bpunt aL   bhí mé ag feitheamh le   tú   _ a
       ten   *pounds COMP was I   at waiting   with you   ptc*

       thabhairt dom
       give(VN) to-me

       'It was ten pounds that I was waiting for you to give me'.

(80)   *Comparative Clauses*

(a)   *Tháinig sé ní ba luaithe ná   aL   bhí mé ag dúil   le
       came   he earlier   than COMP was I   at expecting with

       é   a   theacht
       him ptc come(VN)

       'He came earlier than I expected him to come'.

(b)   *D'éirigh léi   níos mó oibre   a   dhéanamh ná   aL
       she managed more   work(gen) ptc do(VN)   CONJ COMP

       d'fhéach mise ariamh le   _ a   dhéanamh
       tried   I   ever   with   ptc do(VN)

       'She managed to do more work than I ever tried to do'.

Another idiom in which constituents of the form

$$[_{PP} \text{Prep } \underset{[-\text{fin}]}{S}]$$

are put to use is in that described in (81):

(81a)   **Tá** NP $[_{PP}$ **le** $\underset{[-\text{fin}]}{S}]$ 'NP is to VP'.
         is   *with*

(b)   **Tá mé le   h-imeacht amárach**
       am I   with leave(VN) tomorrow

       'I am to leave tomorrow'.

(c)   **Tá mé le   sibh   a   fheiceáil amárach**
       am I   with you(pl) ptc see(VN) tomorrow

       'I am to see you tomorrow'.

These constructions too seem to be islands:

(82a)   *na daoine aL   bhí mé le   _ a   fheiceáil inniu
         the people COMP was I   with   ptc see(VN) today

(b)   na daoine aN   raibh mé le   h-iad a   fheiceáil inniu
         the people COMP was   I   with them ptc see(VN) today

'the people that I was to see today'

So far so good then. There is at least one kind of example however that con-
stitutes at least a *prima facie* counter-example to the general claim that PPs
are islands. The preposition **i ndiaidh** or **tar éis** (after) in combination with an
infinitival clause is used to form a perfective aspect:

(83)   Tá siad i ndiaidh na prátaí   a   bhaint
         are they after   the potatoes ptc dig(VN)

'They have just dug the potatoes'.
(literally 'They are after digging the potatoes'.)

There seems to be no less reason to take these examples as being PP's than
there is in the other cases we have been examining here. Yet it is possible to
delete bound pronouns inside the infinitival clause of such constructions:[10]

(84)   Thug siad leo   na prátaí   aL   bhí siad tar éis _ a
         took they with-them the potatoes COMP were they after   ptc

         bhaint
         dig(VN)

'They took with them the potatoes that they had just dug'.

Unless there turns out to be some plausible way of analyzing such constructions as being other than PPs, they must stand as exceptions to the generalized
condition.

But to serve our immediate purposes and with this reservation in mind, I
will continue to work with the condition-schema (73).

(73) will account for all the data we have considered with respect to the
appearance of resumptive pronouns in relative and questioned clauses, and it
predicts a fairly wide range of other facts as well.

So much for the circumstances under which the rule cannot apply. What
now shall we say about the circumstance in which the rule of Relative Deletion
must apply? This circumstance is really quite limited. We must account for
the ungrammaticality of (85):

(85)   *an garda   aN   dtáinig sé na bhaile
        the policeman COMP came   he home
        'the policeman that came home'

This case is in a sense the most troublesome we will have to deal with in that the attempt to construct an appropriate device to do what we want raises issues that go beyond what I can deal with here.[11]

I will begin with the assumption that having got this far with the strategy of removing special conditions from the statement of Relative Deletion itself and replacing them with independent surface filters, we should continue in the same vein. I will accordingly propose that we account for the obligatoriness of pronoun-deletion in subject position by writing a surface filter that bans resumptive pronouns from subject position. How this can be done we shall see in a moment. However it should be pointed out before we go any further that we cannot in this claim any independent motivation for the required device, as we have been able to do in the case of the other accessibility conditions. As far as I am aware, the filter we need here serves no other useful purpose than to force deletion of bound pronouns in subject position in relative and questioned clauses.

The filter is stated in (86):

(86) $*np_j$ COMP V $\underset{[+\text{Pro}]}{\text{NP}}{}^j$

To demonstrate how (86) will work, certain assumptions must be made explicit.

First, the statement of the filter in (86) assumes an interpretive convention to the effect that a term will not be interpreted as dominating no lexical material unless it is explicitly written in to the filter that it be so. That is, the fourth term of (86) will not be satisfied by an occurrence of NP that has been subject to deletion. So relative and questioned clauses will not be declared ungrammatical if they contain a deleted subject pronoun.

Secondly, the notion 'resumptive pronoun' is defined in terms of the indexing procedure that binds a pronoun in relative and questioned clauses to an np-head, as formulated in (7). The indexing procedure is useful to us in this regard, because essentially what it does is to provide us with a syntactically-visible way of identifying resumptive pronouns. Recall that the indexing procedure is used to define *only* the binding relation that holds between the controlling and the controlled constituent in a deletion process. No other constituents will be indexed. Indices will not be used to define pronominal coreference as they have frequently been used in transformational studies. So if a pronoun and a np are co-indexed it can only be because that pronoun is bound to the np-head. In other words, an indexed pronoun is a resumptive pronoun. This in turn means that the filter can distinguish correctly between the grammatical (87) and the ungrammatical (88):

(87)   an fear$_3$ aL   mharaigh sé __$_3$
        the man COMP killed   he

        'the man that he killed'

(88)   *an fear$_3$ arL   imigh sé$_3$
        the man COMP left   he

        'the man that left'

The subject pronoun of (87) is not indexed and therefore does not invoke the filter. In (88) the subject pronoun is indexed and does invoke the filter.

Thirdly, the filter as it stands will apply incorrectly to possessive pronouns, if they happen to be next to the verb – that is, if they modify the subject NP. An example like (89) will incorrectly be tagged ungrammatical by filter (86):

(89)   an bhean arL mharaigh a fear céile an t-Uachtarán

        'the woman whose husband killed the President'

One way out of this difficulty is to add another clause to (86):

(90)   *np$_j$ COMP V NP$_{[+Pro]}$^{j}

        if the fourth term is immediately dominated by S.

This is not beautiful and it may be symptomatic of a more fundamental problem with the whole approach to these facts embodied in the formulations of (86) and (90). What (90) attempts to do of course is to provide a structural definition of the notion 'subject' for Modern Irish. Both formulations ((86) and (90)) exploit what is an almost exceptionless generalization about word order in Modern Irish – namely that no constituent may intervene between the verb and the subject of its clause.[12] Given the extra clause in (90), the filter should pick out only subject NP.

There are at least two sorts of possible objection to this approach – one theoretical and one empirical. If it should turn out to be the case that the notion 'subject' is relevant to the description of other syntactic processes in the language, then clearly we should define that notion once and for all and let a filter like (90) refer directly to 'subject'. The question of the extent to which we need to let syntactic rules refer to grammatical relations is a very controversial one of course (*cf.* Postal 1976, Lasnik and Fiengo 1976).

A second possible objection is that (90) may be empirically inadequate. Irish has nothing resembling the Passive transformation, but it has got an Impersonal Passive construction. Impersonal Passive clauses differ from active clauses in that the verb of an Impersonal Passive has special morphology and also in that Impersonal Passives seem to lack subjects. There are no other differences between the two clause-types: in particular there are no differences in word order between the two clause-types and there is no apparent change in the grammatical relations involved. In (91) we have an active clause, and in (92) the corresponding Impersonal Passive:

(91)   **Bhuail sé go tobann é**
        struck he suddenly him
        'He suddenly struck him'.

(92)   **Buaileadh go tobann é**
        'He was suddenly struck'.

Note that in (92) the direct object **é** ('him') retains its non-subject case-marking; notice too that the adverb **go tobann** intervenes between the verb and **é**. These are both indications that **é** in (92) should not be taken to be a derived subject – rather it remains a direct object. But what if such an impersonal clause contained no adverb, as in (93):

(93)   **Buaileadh é**
        was struck him
        'He was struck'.

The pronoun in such a clause continues to act like a direct object with respect to the rule of Relative Deletion – that is, in a relative or questioned clause it can optionally be deleted or retained:

(94a)   **an fear arL   buaileadh é   i ndiaidh an Aifrinn**
        the man COMP was struck him after   the Mass

(b)   **an fear aL   buaileadh __ i ndiaidh an Aifrinn**
        the man COMP was struck   after   the Mass

        'the man who was struck after Mass'

Notice now that whether or not the non-relational statement of (90) can be maintained depends on how these Impersonal Passives are to be analyzed. To work correctly, the filter must recognize the pronoun é of an example like (92) or (93) as a direct object, even though it is apparently immediately to the right of the verb and subject to analysis by (90). This seems to presuppose an analysis of the Impersonal Passive in which some invisible dummy subject intervenes between the verb and the direct object and in which the surface filter can 'see' this dummy. Whether such an analysis can be maintained or not is unclear to me.

These issues seem to me to be quite open, but for the sake of concreteness and because I do not understand the proper role of grammatical relations within the kind of model I assume here, let us continue to use the filter as stated in (90) to do the work that needs to be done.

One other noteworthy characteristic of the filter (90) is that it is completely local – that is, it contains no variables. This is a useful characteristic, for it helps us to solve some of the problems associated with our original approach to the problem of accounting for the ungrammaticality of (85) – namely the condition on (49) that says Relative Deletion is obligatory in its application to subjects. In any case where any material intervenes between the head and the bound pronoun other than the topmost complementizer and the topmost verb of the relative clause, then bound pronoun subjects should appear quite freely. We predict for instance that when the bound pronoun is the subject of an embedded clause, then deletion or retention of the pronoun should be optional. As already mentioned, this is in fact the case:

(95a) **an fear aL   mheas mé aL   bhí _ ann**
        the man COMP thought I   COMP was   there

(b)   **an fear arL   mheas mé goN   raibh sé ann**
        the man COMP thought I   COMP was   he there

        'the man that I thought was there'

(96a) **Cé   aL   mheas tú aL   bhí _ ann**
        who COMP thought you COMP was   there

(b)   **Cé   arL   mheas tú goN   raibh sé ann**
        who COMP thought you COMP was   he there

        'Who did you think was there?'

It will also permit the generation of grammatical examples like (51), in which an island-condition forces the retention of a pronoun in subject-position, which were also anomalous for the original treatment. Another kind of example which is problematical for the original approach ((49)) is (97), in which the relative clause is a cleft and has a resumptive pronoun as its subject:

(97)   cuairteoirí arL   as   as   an Mhór Roinn aL   tháinig siad
         visitors   *COMP from from the Continent*   *COMP came*   *they*

?'visitors that it was from the Continent that they came'

Filter (90) will not of course apply in a case like (97), so there is no reason why it should not be grammatical.

One further advantage that (90) has over the simple relational approach embodied in condition (i) of (49), is that in those cases where grammatical relations are encoded in a different way than they are in ordinary clauses, the constraint doesn't seem to hold. The syntax of copular sentences in Irish, for instance, is quite different from the syntax of clauses that contain real verbs – the order of major constituents is quite different, for instance, and therefore the way that relations like *subject* are defined in the clause is quite different in the two cases. The matter is complicated to a terrifying degree, but consider just one case:

(98)   B'   fhiú   a lán na h-uaireadóirí
         Cop worth a lot the watches

'The watches were worth a lot'.

Notice that what seems to be the subject of a clause like (98) does not follow the copula. Therefore if the approach to this aspect of the accessibility problem embodied in filter (90) is right, if a clause like (98) were embedded as a relative clause, then (90) should not be invoked if the position relativized is that of **uaireadóirí** in (98) – simply because such structures would not meet the conditions of the filter. So, given (90) and the general assumption that Relative Deletion is optional, we would expect optional deletion or retention of the pronoun in a case like (98). This turns out to be the case, since both (99a) and (99b) are grammatical:

(99a)   Bhí uaireadóirí aige   arbh   fhiú   a lán iad
         was watches   at-him COMP+Cop worth a-lot them

(b)   Bhí uaireadóirí aige   ab   fhiú   a lán _
         was watches   at-him COMP+Cop worth a-lot

'He had some watches that were worth a lot'.

144 CHAPTER 4

I will end the discussion of accessibility constraints at this point. The condition-schema (73) accounts with very little fuss for what seems to me to be an interestingly broad range of data although, needless to point out, there is a great deal more to be said on the topic of island-constraints.[13] In particular, one would like to investigate the possibility of accounting in a general way for the fact that one binding relation cannot be defined into the scope of another – one cannot, for instance, topicalize out of a constituent question, or relativize into a comparative clause structure, and so on. As Michael Brame (1978, 1979) in particular has pointed out, this is an important general property of the binding-relation, and one would like to be able to capture that generalization. I am half-content to leave the topic here though, because it seems to me that such a statement would not render (73) unnecessary, but rather would supplement it. Something like (73) would remain, I think, at the core even of a revised system.[14] These are questions however that must be left for future work.

4.6. CONCLUSION

The indexing procedures we have been formulating and discussing in this chapter are essential mediators between syntax and semantics in the system being investigated here, and as such, serve a variety of purposes, both syntactic and semantic. It is the indexing for instance, which ensures that the variable bound by lambda-abstraction in the interpretation of relative and questioned clauses corresponds to that pronoun which is deleted by Relative Deletion rather than to some arbitrary pronoun in the clause.

The indexing also plays a crucial rôle, as we have just seen, in the proposed account of island-constraints. In this respect of course the procedures have much in common with the device of 'trace-binding' as developed by Chomsky and his co-workers in the past few years. One of the most important purposes served by traces is to invoke the general conditions on binding that in combination account for island-facts. One of the useful differences between the system described here and trace-theory though, is that, since we can index pronouns as well as empty nodes ('traces'), it also provides us with a way of defining the notion of 'resumptive pronoun' in such a way that syntactic rules can take account of it. This ability is put to crucial use at several points – in writing the filter (90), in stating the rule that fronts a prepositional phrase in a constituent question (we must make sure that not just any old PP is fronted, but rather that one which contains the resumptive pronoun, *cf.* Section 10 of Chapter 3), and, as we shall see, in stating the rules governing the distribution of the relative complementizers **aL** and **aN**.

NOTES

[1] To deal with conjoined relative clauses as in (i)

(i)   **an bhean aL   chuaigh go Nua Eabhrac agus aL   fuair bás   ansin**
        the woman COMP went   to New York   and COMP got   death there

      'the woman who went to New York and died there'

we would presumably add a clause to (7) stipulating that if γ consists of an $\bar{S}$-conjunction we must find a pronoun in each conjunct and assign the same index to each pronoun. This raises no semantic problems, but the syntactic problems – of ensuring the proper patterns of Across-the-Board-Deletion – strike me as being formidable. See Williams 1978 for some proposals.

[2] For an account of the 'extra' pronoun in examples like (22a) ('the pronominal augment'), see the discussion in Section 3.8. of Chapter 3 above and also Ahlqvist (1978).

[3] The *differences* between clefts and their non-clefted counterparts will be dealt with in a theory of conventional implicature (in the sense of Grice 1967), as formalized by Lauri Karttunen and Stanley Peters in a recent series of papers (Karttunen and Peters 1975, 1976, to appear; Karttunen and Karttunen 1976, 1977, Karttunen 1977c). Within that theory, rules of semantic interpretation build up in a compositional way two model-theoretic objects while processing a syntactic tree. One of these expresses the truth-conditional meaning of the sentence, the other expresses the conventional implicatures that a sentence gives rise to. For a specific set of proposals for the analysis of clefts and pseudoclefts within this framework, see Halvorsen 1978.

[4] (30a) has the particle **a** where (30b) has **ag** for the following reason. The progressive aspect in Irish is formed by combining a particle that is at least homophonous with the preposition **ag** (at), with the infinitival form of the verb (the 'verbal noun'). So (30b) is literally 'He is at seeking a leprechaun'. However, when the object of such a construction is bound in a relative clause, or question or cleft then the particle preceding the verbal noun is **a**.

[5] The discussion in this section owes a great deal to Ken Hale, and many of the proposals put forward here are originally his. See Hale (1978) for an alternative account of the facts addressed here.

[6] Example (50) is from the Christian Brothers' Grammar, p. 336, Section 665b.

[7] Examples (52a, b), (53a, b), (54a) and (55a) are from the Christian Brothers' Grammar, p. 336, Section 665b.

[8] Emmon Bach and George Horn have proposed a similar explanation for a range of facts from English. See Bach and Horn (1976), Horn (1974).

[9] Example (74c) is from **Mo Bhealach Féin**, by Seosamh Mac Grianna, p. 16. For a discussion of some of the syntactic and semantic properties of these constructions, and for a defence of some of the decisions about them made without support here, see McCloskey (1979), to appear.

[10] Example (84) is from **Is Glas na Cnoic** by Seán 'ac Fhionnlaoich, p. 240.

[11] Hale 1978 takes the ungrammaticality of examples like (85) to be an Irish reflex of the more general phenomenon of 'obviation'. For an account of this phenomenon, see Jeanne (1978).

[12] The generalization permits of the following exceptions. Corresponding to English *only*, Irish has a NEG . . . *but* construction, as illustrated in (i):

(i)   **Ní   fhaca mé ach Nollaig**
            NEG saw   I   but Noel

            'I saw only Noel'

When **ach** is prefixed to a subject NP, then it is possible to extrapose the whole unit to clause-final position:

(iia)   **Ní   raibh ach Nollaig sa   teach**
            NEG was   but Noel   in the house

            'There was only Noel in the house'.

(b)   **Ní raibh sa teach ach Nollaig**

            'There was only Noel in the house'.

(c)   ***Ní   raibh sa teach   Nollaig**
            NEG was   in the house Noel

            'Noel was in the house'.

Certain parenthetical interjections (**maise, leoga**) may also intervene between a verb and its subject. Such interjections seem to be restricted to main clauses and so may not cause a problem for (86).

A less ad hoc solution to the problem posed by examples like (89) might be to appeal to the A-over-A Condition. If it were a general property of filters such as (86) that they respect the A-over-A Condition in analyzing a tree, then one might claim that the fourth term of (86) would never be satisfied by a possessive pronoun, since a possessive pronoun is a NP within a larger NP. Such examples as (86) would not then be declared ungrammatical. The pronouns in examples like (88) however are not within larger NP and so would be analyzed by the filter. The structures containing them would then be marked ungrammatical. This approach however requires a rather unorthodox interpretation of the A-over-A Condition. This is normally invoked only when a rule can analyze a structure ambiguously, but this would not be the case when (86) applied to examples like (89).

[13] One interesting problem to be faced, for instance, is that Relative Deletion is subject to the Crossover Constraint (Postal 1971, Wasow 1972) – that is, in example (i)

(i)   **an file aL   shíl   sé aL   scríobh __ an dán**
            the poet COMP thought he COMP wrote   the poem

            'the poet that he thought wrote the poem'

and examples like it, the subject pronoun **sé** cannot be interpreted as being anaphorically related to the empty subject position in the embedded clause. This unfortunately is a reading that the system as presently set up will provide for an example like (i). It has been a matter of some dispute whether Crossover phenomena are diagnostic for movement rules or not (Bresnan 1975, Chomsky 1977). The fact that the constraint holds for Irish I take to be evidence in favour of Joan Bresnan's view that the phenomena are also characteristic of certain kinds of deletion.

[14] Notice that a constraint banning double extractions from a single clause (a constraint proposed informally as the 'double hole' constraint) is inadequate. Such a constraint accounts for the Complex NP facts by blocking double bindings like that in figure (i):

(i)

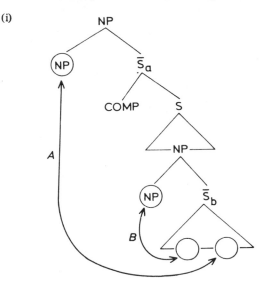

Now if the Complex NP Constraint is essentially a double-binding constraint prohibiting configurations like (i), then by filling *either* of the gaps in $\bar{S}_b$, we should save the structure. The relation between a head NP and a bound pronoun does not count as the kind of binding that invokes island-constraints, therefore no matter which gap is plugged with a pronoun, there will be only one binding.

The NP-Island approach advocated here makes a rather different prediction. Since what is illegal on this approach is binding into an NP, the only way that a structure like (i) can be saved is by filling the gap bound by the outermost binding A with a pronoun. Filling the gap bound by B with a pronoun should make no difference at all, since it is not this binding that is causing the trouble, but rather only the binding A. The prediction of the NP-Island analysis is borne out. In (ii) we have an example which is ungrammatical because it violates the Complex NP Constraint in the way diagrammed in (i) – it has two gaps bound outside the relative clause. In (iii) the gap bound by A is filled with a resumptive pronoun; in (iv) the gap bound by B is filled with a resumptive pronoun, but the gap bound by A is not. (iii) is fine; (iv) is unintelligible.

(ii)   *daoine nachN   bhfuil fhios agam teanga   ar bith aL labhraíonn _ _
         people COMP+NEG I don't know   language any   speak

(iii)   **daoine nachN bhfuil fhios agam teanga ar bith aL labhraíonn siad _**
                                                                             they

           ? 'people that I don't know of any language that they speak _'

(iv)   *__daoine nachN bhfuil fhios agam teanga ar bith aL labhraionn _ í__
                                                                             it

           *'people that I don't know of any language that _ speak it'

These considerations, along with the fact that the double-binding approach doesn't extend to the other cases here subsumed under the NP-Island condition, leave me fairly confident that however the double-binding constraint is to be formulated, it will not completely make redundant the schema (73).

CHAPTER 5

THE COMPLEMENTIZER SYSTEM*

5.1. INTRODUCTION

The focus of discussion in this chapter will be the distribution of those items that we have analyzed as being complementizers. It will be particularly concerned with the phenomenon known traditionally as the 'Double Relative' construction (see the references in note 8 of Chapter 2). This is the situation (already alluded to several times) in which we find a relative complementizer introducing a sentential complement where in the normal run of things we expect to find the non-relative complementizer **goN**. One of the interesting things about this phenomenon is that it seems to be a diagnostic in Irish for the relationship of syntactic binding. The central fact which we will attempt to document and analyze is that any clause into which the binding reaches (any clause, that is, that contains the bound anaphoric element but not the binder) is headed by a relative complementizer. I have left the matter till this late point because I wanted to approach the problem having discussed the indexing procedures of Chapter 4 in some detail. It is this set of rules which define formally the notion of syntactic binding in this model and that provide the basis on which the syntactic and semantic rules operate to account for the configuration of syntactic and semantic data that is associated with the binding relationship. It is the indexing rules then which provide a principled basis for distinguishing just the class of constructions of which the Double Relative phenomenon is characteristic. The claim is that the complementizer alternations show up in just those constructions that involve an obligatory anaphoric relationship of the sort that the indexing rules define, and further that the rules which account for the distribution of relative and non-relative complementizers in this construction make crucial reference to the indices assigned by rules like (7) and (27) of Chapter 4. What we are dealing with then is another of the ways in which the indexing rules, which were originally set up to facilitate the operation of rules of semantic interpretation turn out to have interesting syntactic uses as well.

Unfortunately we shall have to deal here not just with some rather complex data, but also with some very insecure data. The situation seems to be that there is a central core of hard fact – a range of examples and configurations where we find little or no disagreement among speakers about what the facts are. But then there is a further range of marginal cases, where we find firstly that there is a great deal of disagreement among speakers as to what the facts are, and secondly that speakers are themselves very insecure of their own intuitions. When speakers are asked for acceptability-judgments about such cases, one gets the response 'I'm not sure' more often than a decisive yes or no.

My strategy for approaching these problems will be to first present and discuss the facts that are not disputed, present an analysis that deals with them, and then go on to discuss those cases in which the facts are less clear.

5.2. THE DATA

We have isolated four elements that we have taken to be complementizers – the interrogative complementizer **anN** and three declarative complementizers **aL**, **aN** and **goN**. The correct distribution of the interrogative complementizer is determined entirely by the PS-rules already presented, so we will not discuss it any further here. The distribution of the three non-interrogative complementizers will be our concern in this chapter.

Recall that **goN** is the complementizer which normally introduces senten-tial complements:

(1)   **Chreid   siad   gurL briseadh   bád Fheidhlimidh i   dToraigh**
          believed they   was wrecked boat   in

          'They believed that Feidhlimidh's boat had been wrecked in Tory'.

However when the deletion rule is used to relativize a position inside such a sentential complement, we find the Direct Relative complementizer **aL** instead of **goN**:

(2a)   **Shíl   mé goN   mbeadh sé ann**
           thought I   COMP would-be he there

           'I thought that he would be there'.

(b)   **an fear aL   shíl   mé aL   bheadh   _ ann**
           the man COMP thought I   COMP would-be   there

           'the man that I thought would be there'

Every complementizer that intervenes between the head and the gap is subject to the alternation:

(3a)   **Dúirt mé gurL shíl   mé goN   mbeadh sé ann**
       said I   thought I   COMP would-be he there

       'I said that I thought that he would be there'.

(b)   **an fear aL   dúirt mé aL   shíl   mé aL**
       the man COMP said I   COMP thought I   COMP

       bheadh   _ ann
       would-be   there

       'the man that I said I thought would be there'.

Of course the **goN/aL** alternation is found only in those clauses into which
the binding actually reaches. Thus if the position relativized is in the matrix-
clause of an example like (2a) or either of the two higher clauses of an
example like (3a), then **goN** remains in the lowest clause:

(4a)   **an fear aL   shíl   _ goN   mbeadh sé ann**
       the man COMP thought   COMP would-be he there

       'the man that thought he would be there'

(b)   **an fear aL   dúirt _ gurL shíl   sé goN   mbeadh**
       the man COMP said   COMP thought he COMP would-be

       sé ann
       he there

       'the man that said he thought he would be there'

(c)   **an fear aL   dúirt sé aL   shíl   _ goN   mbeadh**
       the man COMP said he COMP thought   COMP would-be

       sé ann
       he there

       'the man that he said thought he would be there'

The following examples are given for illustration. In each case the (a) example
is from contemporary written sources;[1] the (b) example shows the form the
clause would have if it were not embedded as a relative clause.

(5a)   . . . **mar an mharcshlua aL**
                like the cavalry-host COMP

          mháiti   aL   bhí faoi
          claim (imperfect impersonal passive) COMP was

Aileach na Ri
Aileach of the Kings

' . . . like the cavalry-host that people used to claim was under Aileach of the Kings'

(b)   **Máití goN   raibh sé faoi Aileach na Rí**
           COMP was   it

'People used to claim that it was under Aileach of the Kings'.

(6a)   **. . . an leabhar aL   dúirt sé aL   chuirfeadh ar mo**
              the book   COMP said   he COMP would-put on my

chosa mé
feet   me

' . . . the book that he said would put me on my feet'

(b)   **Dúirt sé goN   gcuirfeadh sé ar mo chosa mé**
           COMP   he

'He said that it would put me on my feet'.

(7a)   **. . . na deich scillinge aL   gheall   an máta aL**
              the ten   shillings COMP promised the mate COMP

d'íocfadh sé le   Nadúr
would-pay he with Nature

' . . . the ten shillings that the mate promised he would pay Nature'

(b)   **Gheall an máta goN   n-íocfadh sé le Nadúr iad**
              COMP   them

'The mate promised that he would pay Nature them'.

(8a)   **. . . na cailíní agus an cóiriú   aL   shíl   siad aL**
              the girls   and the dressing COMP thought they COMP

bhí ceart orthu
was right on-them

' . . . the girls dressed as they thought was right'.

(b)   **Shíl siad goN   raibh sé ceart**
              COMP was   it

'They thought it was right'.

But the **goN/aL** alternation is characteristic of other constructions as well. Compare the examples in (a) and (b) of the following:[2]

Constituent Question

(9a)   **Cé aL   deir siad aL   chum   an t-amhrán sin**
        who COMP say they COMP composed that song

        'Who do they say wrote that song?'

(b)   **Deir siad gurL   chum sé an t-amhrán sin**
                COMP   he

        'They say he wrote that song'.

(10a)   **An bhfuil fhios agat caidé aL   ba mhaith liom aL**
                Do you know   what COMP I would like   COMP

        dhéanfadh Eithne?
        would do

        'Do you know what I would like Eithne to do?'

(b)   **Ba mhaith liom goN   ndéanfadh Eithne é**
                        COMP   it

        'I would like Eithne to do it'.

Comparative Clause

(11a)   **Tá an luach seo beagán níos airde ná mar aL**
        is this-value   a-little higher   than   COMP

        ceapadh   aL   bheadh sé
        think(past impersonal) COMP would-be it

        'This value is a little higher than it was thought it would be'.

(b)   **Ceapadh goN   mbeadh sé chomh h-ard sin**
                COMP   that high

        'It was thought that it would be that high'.

(12a)   **Ní   raibh na mná   chomh dána ... agus aL   mheas**
        NEG were the women as   bold   CONJ COMP thought

        mé féin   aL   bheadh   siad
        I reflex. COMP would-be they

        'The women were not as bold as I myself thought they would be'.

(b)   **Mheas mé féin goN   mbeadh siad chomh dána sin**
                     COMP   that bold

'I myself thought that they would be that bold'.

Cleft

(13a)   **I   mBetlehem aL   dúirt na targaireachtaí aL**
         in   COMP said   the prophecies   COMP

béarfaí   an Slánaitheoir
would-be-born the Saviour

'It was in Bethlehem that the prophecies said the Saviour would be born'.

(b)   **Dúirt na targaireachtaí goN   mbéarfaí an Slánaitheoir**
                                  COMP

i mBetlehem.

'The prophecies said that the Saviour would be born in Bethlehem'.

(14a)   **As   na nuachtáin is   dóiche   aL**
         out-of the newspapers COMP+Cop probable COMP

baineadh   iad
were-taken them

'It's out of the newspapers that it is probable they were taken'.

(b)   **Is dóiche gurL   baineadh as na nuachtáin iad**
                    COMP

'It is probable that they were taken from the newspapers'.

Pseudo-Cleft[3]

(15a)   **Is   é aL   shíl   mé aL   dhéanfadh sé imeacht go**
         Cop it COMP thought I   COMP would-do he to go   to

Meiriceá
America

'What I thought he would do was to go to America'.

(b)   Shíl mé goN   ndéanfadh sé é
          COMP   it
      'I thought he would do it'.

We must take account of one other datum. In those cases where we find
resumptive pronouns (i.e. relative clauses and nominal constituent questions), if the pronoun is not deleted we find another pattern, in which the
complementizer **goN** survives. That is, there exist examples like (16), with a
resumptive pronoun and the complementizer **goN** where we would normally
expect it to be:

(16a)   an t-úrscéal aL mheas mé aL thuig   mé _
        the novel   thought I   understood I

(b)   an t-úrscéal arL mheas mé gurL thuig   mé é
       the novel   thought I   understood I it

       'the novel that I thought I understood'

(c)   Cén   garda   arL shíl   sibh goN raibh saibhreas mór
       which policeman   thought you   was wealth   great

       aige ?
       at him

       'Which policeman did you think had great wealth?'

Notice that in these cases the whole relative clause is introduced by the Indirect Relative Complementizer **aN** (which appears in its past tense form in
(16b) and (16c). This pattern is only possible in clauses which have a resumptive pronoun. It can never occur in Comparative constructions, in Clefts or in
Pseudo-clefts, and in relatives and questions it can not occur if the bound
pronoun has been deleted by Relative Deletion. So examples like (17) are
ungrammatical:

(17a)   *an fear arL   mheas me goN   raibh _ tinn
        the man COMP thought I   COMP was   sick
        'the man that I thought was sick'

(b)   *I mBetlehem arL   dhúirt na targaireachtaí goN
        In   COMP said the prophecies   COMP

       mbéarfaí   an Slánaitheoir
       would-be-born the Saviour

'It was in Bethlehem that the prophecies said the Saviour would be born.'

Instances of this second pattern are cited in (18)–(20).[4]

(18)   **Aird ní   thabharfadh sé ar na mná   , aN   raibh amhras**
        heed NEG would-give   he on the women COMP was   doubt

        tagtha   air   faoi seo   goN   mba iad   bun
        come(past part) on-him by-this-time COMP Cop them bottom

        agus barr gach donas ... .
        and top every evil

        'He would pay no attention to women, whom he had begun to suspect by this time were the root of every evil.'

(19)   **agus gan   ceol   de chineál ar bith ag na daoine aN**
        and without music of kind   any   at the people COMP

        rabhthas   ag maíomh gurL   díobh é
        be(past impersonal) at claiming COMP+Cop of-them him

        'when the people that it was being claimed he belonged to had no music at all'

(20)   **Buta beag fir   ... nár   léir goN   raibh**
        butt little of-a-man   COMP+NEG+Cop clear COMP was

        muineál ar bith idir   a cheann agus a ghuaillí
        neck   any   between his head and his shoulders

        *' ... a stocky little man that it wasn't clear that he had any neck between his head and his shoulders'

We must allow then for two patterns:

(21) $\bar{\bar{X}}_j [_{\bar{s}} aL \ldots [_{\bar{s}} aL \ldots [_{\bar{s}} aL \ldots -_j \ldots]]]$

(22) $np_j [_{\bar{s}} aN \ldots [_{\bar{s}} goN \ldots [_{\bar{s}} goN \ldots Pro_j \ldots]]]$

(22) diagrams relative clauses and questions with resumptive pronouns. (21) diagrams any construction involving the binding of a gap (including relatives and constituent questions without resumptive pronouns, clefts, comparatives and so on). We will also want to account for the much simpler cases where the relative clause consists of a single clause, where there is also

of course a connection between the form of the complementizer and the question of whether the relativization-site is marked by a gap or a resumptive pronoun. As has been amply illustrated by now, the complementizer **aN** turns up when the clause has a resumptive pronoun; **aL** turns up when the clause has a gap:

(23) $np_j [_{\bar{s}} \textbf{ aL } \ldots -_j \ldots]$

(24) $np_j [_{\bar{s}} \textbf{ aN } \ldots \text{Pro}_j \ldots]$

How are we to deal with these facts?

Suppose we assume that the distribution of the non-interrogative complementizers is determined by the principles in (25):

(25) (i) unless otherwise specified, COMP = **goN**
      (ii) in the configuration
           $\ldots \bar{\bar{X}}_j \ldots [_{\bar{s}} \text{COMP} \ldots [_{\bar{\bar{x}}} -_j] \ldots \bar{s}] \ldots$
           COMP = **aL**
      (iii) in the configuration
           $\ldots np_j [_{\bar{s}} \text{COMP} \ldots \underset{[+\text{Pro}]}{\text{NP}}{}_j \ldots \bar{s}] \ldots$
           COMP = **aN**

(In (25), as previously, $[_{\bar{\bar{x}}} -_j]$ is to be taken as an empty node of category $\bar{\bar{X}}$ indexed with the subscript $_j$.)

These principles are stated a little informally, and it is not quite clear where they fit in the pantheon of formal devices made available by a generative syntax, but they will, I think, account for all the data we have discussed so far.

Given the rule of Relative Deletion, the principles in (25) must be construed as filters that check post-transformational structures, since of course they depend crucially on being able to tell if a bound pronoun has been deleted or not. Given that assumption, condition (ii) will guarantee the patterns (21) and (23) ((23) being simply the case where the variable in (ii) between the binder $\bar{\bar{X}}$ and the Complementizer is null), while condition (iii) will guarantee the patterns in (22) and (24). Since (ii) is stated in terms of the supercategory $\bar{\bar{X}}$, it generalizes to cover the other binding constructions we have discussed, predicting the data in (9)–(15).

Notice too that the principles in (25) allow the right degree of correlation between the appearance of **aL** and the binding relationship – that is, (ii) does not say that **aL** occurs *only* under the conditions defined there. Recall that in Chapter Two we argued against identifying **aL** as a wh-pronoun by pointing out that it turned up in constructions which could not plausibly be analyzed as involving binding – in the constructions illustrated in (26), for example.[5]

(26a)   **Is   amhlaidh aL   d'fhill   siad 'na bhaile**
        Cop thus   COMP returned they home
        'Actually, they returned home'.

(b)   **Nuair aL   shíleas duine   goN   bhfuil sé féin   maith is**
      when COMP   thinks a-person COMP is   he reflex. good   Cop

      é rud   aL   bhíos sé dall   ar a   chuid lochtanna
      it a-thing COMP is   he blind on his share faults

      'When a person thinks that he is good, actually he is blind to his faults'.

(c)   **Níl fhios agam céacu   aL   tháinig sé nó aL**
      I don't know   which-of-them COMP came   he or COMP

      d'fhan   sé sa bhaile
      remained he at home

      'I don't know whether he came or stayed at home'.

If we take 'unless otherwise specified' in (25)(i) to include 'unless otherwise specified by subcategorization', we can account for the appearance of **aL** in these collocations by specifying in the lexical entries for **amhlaidh**, **rud** and **céacu** that they have a subcategorization feature $[\_[_{\overline{s}} \text{ aL } S]]$, just as we do in the case of certain conjunctions.

5.3. FURTHER PREDICTIONS

The three conditions in (25) then deal correctly with all the data so far discussed, but they also predict the correct distribution of complementizers in a variety of other cases as well.

Consider first the ways in which the complementizers distribute when the relative or questioned clause is a cleft. When questioning or relativizing into a cleft, pronoun-retention is normally obligatory, as in examples like (27a)–(27d).

(27a) **filí   ar   mar mhaithe le h-airgead aL   chum**
       poets COMP+Cop for-the sake-of money   COMP composed

       siad a   gcuid   dánta
       they their portion poems

       'poets that it was for the sake of money that they wrote their
       poems'

(b)   **Cén   fear ar   dó   aL   thug tú an t-airgead**
       which man COMP+Cop to-him COMP gave you the money
       'Which man was it you gave the money to?'

(c)   **amhráin arbh   é   Ó Cearnaigh féin   aL   chum**
       songs   COMP+Cop him Carney   reflex. COMP composed

       iad
       them

       'songs that it was Carney himself who composed them'

(d)   **an file arbh   é   aL   chum   na h-amhráin sin**
       the poet COMP+Cop him COMP composed those songs
       'the poet that it was him who composed those songs'

The conditions in (25) predict correctly the distribution of complementizers
in (27). To illustrate this, we should begin by saying something about the
rather complicated matter of the morphological interaction between the
copula and the various complementizers. The copula normally forms an
amalgam with the complementizers – both interrogative and declarative. The
items **ar** in (27a) and (27b) and **arbh** in (27c) and (27d) both represent
amalgams of the Indirect Relative complementizer **aN** with the copula – in
the past tense, this amalgam has the form **ar** before words with initial con-
sonants and **arbh** before words with initial vowels (for a discussion of these
matters, see, for instance, the Christian Brothers' Grammar, pp. 188–192).
For our purposes then, it seems reasonable merely to ask our syntactic rules
to predict the appearance of **aN** as the first complementizer in such examples,
and to leave it to some unspecified morphological device to produce the
actually occurring forms. All of the examples in (27) then, have **aN** as the
topmost (leftmost) complementizer and **aL** as the second. How the principles
of (25) guarantee this result is illustrated in figures (27a′)–(27d′). I ignore
the problem of the pronominal augment é in (27c) (*cf.* Ahlqvist 1978).

(27a′)

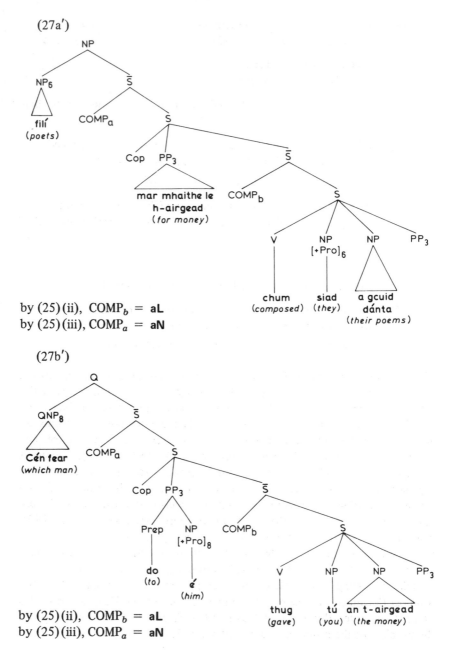

by (25)(ii), COMP$_b$ = **aL**
by (25)(iii), COMP$_a$ = **aN**

(27b′)

by (25)(ii), COMP$_b$ = **aL**
by (25)(iii), COMP$_a$ = **aN**

(27c′)

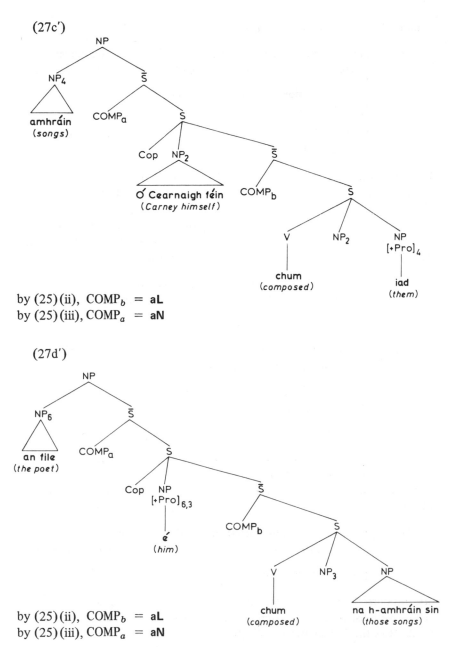

by (25)(ii), COMP$_b$ = **aL**
by (25)(iii), COMP$_a$ = **aN**

(27d′)

by (25)(ii), COMP$_b$ = **aL**
by (25)(iii), COMP$_a$ = **aN**

A more complex example[6] (28) is worked out in (28′).

(28)   beagán i dtaobh cogaí thar lear ar   as   na nuachtáin
         a-little about   wars abroad   COMP+Cop from the newspapers

         is   dóiche aL   baineadh é
         COMP+Cop probable COMP was-taken it

         'a little about foreign wars that it is probable that it was from the
         newspapers that it was taken'

ar is the form taken by the amalgam of the copula and the Indirect Relative
complementizer **aN** in both the present and past tenses (Christian Brothers'
Grammar, p. 188); **is** is the form taken by the amalgam of the copula with
the Direct Relative complementizer **aL** in the present tense. Therefore, the
complementizer sequence we want to predict in (28) is **aN** ... **aL** ... **aL**.
The simple sentence upon which (28) is based is (29):

(29)   is   dóiche   gurL   baineadh as   na nuachtáin é
         Cop probable COMP was-taken from the papers   it

         'It is probable that it was taken from the papers.'

Note the presence of the (past tense form of) the complementizer **goN** in the
complement of **dóiche**. The clefted version of (29) is (30):

(30)   is   as na nuachtáin is   dóiche aL   baineadh é
         Cop from the papers COMP+Cop probable COMP was-taken it

         'It is from the newspapers that it is probable it was taken'.

Finally, if (30) is embedded as a relative clause, with binding of the object
é in the lowest clause, the result is (28).

Consider next the case of relativizing or questioning into a Complex NP
island:

(31)   daoine arL   labhair achan duine aL   bhain leo   Gaeilge
         people COMP spoke   everyone   COMP took with-them Irish

         'people that every one connected with them spoke Irish'

arL of course is the past tense form of the Indirect Relative complementizer
aN, so we must predict the topmost complementizer to be **aN**, the second to
be **aL**. How this is guaranteed is illustrated in (31′).

(28')

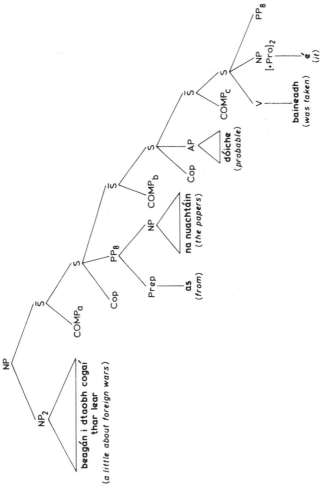

by (25)(iii), COMP$_a$ = aN
by (25)(ii), COMP$_b$ = aL
by (25)(ii), COMP$_c$ = aL

(31')

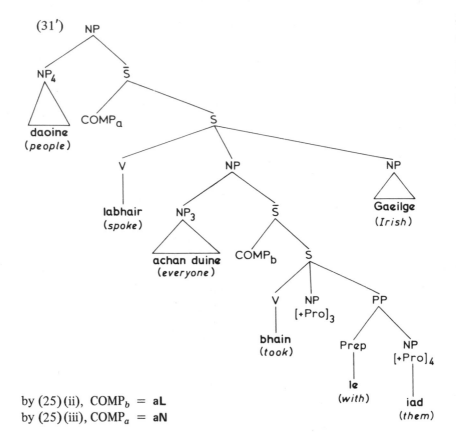

by (25)(ii), COMP$_b$ = **aL**
by (25)(iii), COMP$_a$ = **aN**

How the more complicated example (32) works is illustrated in (32').

(32)   **Cén   file   arL   dhúirt tú   gurL   léigh tú   achan dán**
        which poet COMP said   you COMP read you every poem

        aL   scríobh sé?
        COMP wrote   he

        'Which poet did you say you had read every poem he wrote?'

Examples involving relativizing or questioning in to an Embedded Question
island will work identically, as the reader may verify for him or herself
with reference to the examples (90)–(94) of Chapter 2.

Finally note that (ii) of (25) accounts for the fact that clefts and

(32')

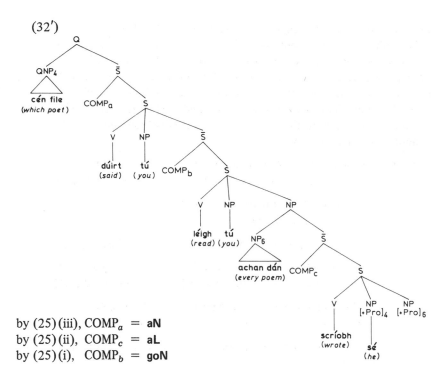

by (25)(iii), COMP$_a$ = **aN**

by (25)(ii), COMP$_c$ = **aL**

by (25)(i), COMP$_b$ = **goN**

comparative clauses are introduced by **aL** rather than any other of the complementizers. This has one particularly interesting consequence in the case of comparative clauses. Irish has just one word – **chomh** – corresponding to English *so ... that* and *as ... as*. Witness the examples in (33) and (34).

(33)   **Bhí sé chomh fuar sin   gurL   fhan   achan duine   sa bhaile**
       was it   cold demon. COMP stayed every person at-home

       'It was so cold that everybody stayed at home'.

(34)   **Bhí sé chomh fuar agus   aL   bhí sé anuraidh**
       was it   cold CONJ COMP was it last-year

       'It was as cold as it was last year'.

Now one of the essential differences between *so ... that* clauses and *as ... as* clauses is that the latter but not the former involve binding. *As ... as* clauses involve the binding of an anaphoric element corresponding to adjective or adverb phrases, as is indicated, for instance, by the

fact that the compared clause in (34) contains an AP-gap. Principle (ii) of
(25) predicts that we should find the complementizer **aL** in the clause that
involves binding (i.e. in the construction corresponding to English *as* . . . *as*);
principle (i) predicts that we should find **goN** in the case that does not
involve binding (i.e. in the construction corresponding to English *so* . . .
that). These predictions are borne out, as illustrated by (33) and (34).

Similar facts hold in the case of the word **oiread** (amount) which is used
in another comparative construction:

(35)   **Thug a athair a oiread airgid   dó   agus aL**
        gave   his father its amount money (gen) to-him CONJ COMP

        cheannódh leath Bhaile Átha Cliath
        would-buy half Dublin

        'His father gave him as much money as would buy half of Dublin'.

(36)   **Thug a athair a oiread airgid   dó   agus goN**
        gave   his father its amount money (gen) to-him CONJ COMP

        dtiocfadh leis leath Bhaile Átha Cliath a cheannach
        he could   half Dublin   to buy

        'His father gave him so much money that he could buy half of
        Dublin'.

Once again in that construction that involves binding ((35)) we find that the
clause is introduced by the complementizer **aL**, as predicted by condition
(ii) of (25), while in (36), the construction that does not involve binding,
we find the complementizer **goN**, which we would expect, given condition
(i) of (25).

The three conditions in (25) deal then with a fairly broad range of data
in a fairly straightforward way. These are also the areas in which intuitions
are clear and where there is no disagreement among speakers, that I have
observed at any rate, as to what the facts are. Things are not, of course, so
simple or so clear-cut. In the next section we consider some contexts in
which the simple rules in (25) break down, and in which there is considerable idiolectal variation concerning the crucial examples.

5.4. DISPUTED DATA

At the end of Chapter Three we discussed one respect in which relative
clauses differed syntactically from nominal constituent questions. This

difference consists in the fact that in nominal constituent questions but not in relative clauses, it is possible to front a prepositional phrase containing a bound pronoun to a position between an interrogative pronoun and the complementizer. So we have both (37) and (38):

(37)   **Cé aN   raibh tú ag caint leis?**
          Who COMP were you at talking with-him

          'Who were you talking to?'

(38)   **Cé leis aN raibh tú ag caint?**

          'Who were you talking to?'

Some speakers (but not all) allow this process over unbounded contexts, accepting (40) as well as (39):

(39)   **Cé arL   shíl   tú gurL labhair tú leis?**
          Who COMP thought you COMP spoke you with-him

          'Who did you think you spoke to?'

(40)   **Cé leis   arL   shíl   tú aL   labhair tú?**
          Who with-him COMP thought you COMP spoke you

          'Who did you think you were talking to?'

The curious thing about the distribution of complementizers in such example is that if one looks only at the examples in (38) and the first complementizer of examples like (40), then it seems that the distribution of complementizers is settled in the same way as in the (what I take to be) more basic examples (37) and (39) – as if the fronting rule applied after the matter of complementizer-distribution was settled and therefore could not affect the result. But then of course one finds the **aL** of (40) which indicates quite the opposite.

A second problem is the apparent existence for some speakers of another pattern of complementizer-distribution that turns up in the case of a relative or questioned clause with a retained pronoun. The type is illustrated in (41).

(41a)   **an fear aL   mheas tú aN   raibh ocras air**
        the man COMP thought you COMP was hunger on-him

        'the man that you thought was hungry'

(b)   **an fear aL   dúirt tú aL   mheas tú aN   raibh**
the man COMP said   you COMP thought you COMP was

ocras   air
hunger on-him

'the man that you said you thought was hungry'

That is, the pattern is essentially as diagrammed in (42):

(42) $np_j [_{\bar{s}} aL \ldots aL \ldots aN \ldots Pro_j \ldots]$

Examples of such constructions are usually given in grammars (see the Christian Brothers' Grammar, p. 343, Section 677b, for instance), but many speakers will not accept them. It also seems to be exceedingly rare in writing and speech. In two years of casual listening and careful reading, I have not managed to find any examples. What one hears and reads is the pattern in (43) already discussed and accounted for by (25):

(43a)   **an fear arL   mheas tú goN   raibh ocras   air**
the man COMP thought you COMP was   hunger on-him

(b)   **an fear arL   dhúirt tú gurL   mheas tú goN   raibh**
the man COMP said   you COMP thought you COMP was

ocras   air
hunger on-him

Another curious fact about (42) is that it is impossible if the bound pronoun is subject or object in its clause. Even those speakers who accept examples like (41) vehemently reject (43):

(43a)   ***an bhean aL   mheas tú aN   raibh sí   tinn**
the woman COMP thought you COMP was   she ill

'the woman that you thought was ill'

***an bhean aL   mheas tú aN   bpósfadh Feidhlimidh í**
the woman COMP thought you COMP would-marry   her

'the woman that you thought Feidhlimidh would marry'

The third difficult and disputed area involves the Prepositional Relative – the slightly marginal relative construction discussed in the final section of Chapter 2:

(44)   **an seomra inaN   bhfuil siad**
         the room   in+rel.ptc. are   they
         'the room in which they are'

Recall that when this strategy is used to reach into an embedded clause, there are two possibilities:

(45a)   **an seomra aL   mheasann sé inaN   bhfuil siad**
         the room   COMP thinks   he in+rel.ptc. are   they

(b)   **an seomra inaN   measann sé aN   bhfuil siad**
         the room   in+rel.ptc. thinks   he COMP are   they

         'the room in which he thinks they are'

None of these three problematical areas can be handled by the rules in (25), and I have nothing to offer by way of solutions but ad hocery. Given though the uncertainty and variability of the data, perhaps a piece of ad hocery is what is required. In any case, I am reasonably sure that whatever system is ultimately developed to handle such facts, the rules in (25), or something rather like them at any rate, will be at the heart of the system.

Before leaving the question though, one other, slightly more manageable problem should be mentioned. There are certain nouns which appear in relative clauses and questions which seem to involve a different kind of binding than we have so far provided for. I have in mind examples like (46).

(46a)   **an lá aL   bhí muid i nDoire**
         the day COMP were we   in Derry
         'the day we were in Derry'

(b)   **Cén   fáth   aN   dtáinig tú**
         which reason COMP came   you
         'Why did you come?'

(c)   **Cén   uair aL   tháinig siad 'na bhaile**
         which time COMP came   they home
         'When did they come home?'

I assume that such examples involve the binding of a null adverbial element, roughly as in (47):

(47)

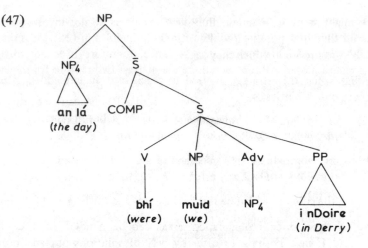

Temporal NP occur quite freely as adverbs in Irish, as illustrated in (48):

(48a) **Tháinig muid 'na bhaile an lá   ina dhiaidh sin**
       came   we   home   the day after that
       'We came home the following day.'

(b)   **D'imigh siad an oíche sin**
       left   they that night
       'They left that night.'

There is therefore independent need for a Phrase Structure rule Adv → NP
as required by the analysis suggested in (47) (constrained in the appropriate
ways perhaps by the kind of feature-filtering mechanisms proposed by
Bresnan and Grimshaw (1978)). As far as I can tell, there is no general way
to predict for this class of nouns which complementizer (**aN** or **aL**) will turn
up with which noun – it seems to be a matter of arbitrary subcategorization.
Fáth (reason) and **dóigh** (way) take **aN** for instance (*cf.* (46b)); **lá** (day), **oíche**
(night) and most temporal nouns can take either an **aL**-clause or an **aN**-clause;
uair (time), however, takes only **aL**-clauses (*cf.* (46c)). (For a discussion of
these matters, cf the Christian Brothers' Grammar pp. 336–337.) It seems
then that such nouns impose a subcategorizational restriction on the complementizer of any relative or questioned clause that modifies them. But of
course, principle (ii) of (25) demands the complementizer **aL** in all these
examples, because they all involve the binding of a gap.

One might want to maintain that such examples do not involve binding at all, and therefore pose no problem for the principles in (25). Adverbs are normally optional constituents of a sentence, therefore it is not obvious when a clause has an AP-gap. But there are at least two reasons for believing that these examples do involve binding. Firstly, in those cases where the clause contains a verb which does demand an AP, one can 'see' the gap. The verb to be, for example, has as one of its subcategorization frames [_ NP AP] . So in an example like (49), the gap is more obvious:

(49)   **an áit   aN   raibh muid** _
        the place COMP were we
        'the place we were'

Secondly, we find the **goN/aL** alternation which we have argued is a diagnostic for the binding-relationship in Irish. Consider (50).

(50a)   **Cén   fáth   arL   dhúirt tú   aL   tháinig sé**
        which reason COMP said   you COMP came   he

   (b) **Cén   fáth   arL   dhúirt tú   goN   dtáinig sé**
                                          COMP

Both of these examples are translated by the ambiguous English sentence (51):

(51)   Why did you say he came?

(50a) corresponds to the reading on which the interrogative adverbial is construed with the lower clause (i.e. when it is his reason for coming that is being questioned); (50b), on the other hand, corresponds to the reading of (51) on which the interrogative adverb is construed with the matrix clause (i.e. the reading on which it is your reason for saying something that is being questioned). This very strongly suggests that these examples do involve binding; that what accounts for the appearance of **aL** in (50a) is the fact that the binding between **Cén fáth** and the empty AP-node must reach into the lower clause and thus invoke principle (ii) of (25) which forces the appearance of **aL**. In (50b) the binding reaches only into the matrix clause and therefore principle (i) will guarantee the appearance of **goN**.

Given that these examples involve binding, what they seem to require is that we let the requirements of subcategorization over-ride those of (25). Notice that **fáth** requires an **aN**-clause (i.e. has the feature [_[ₛ aN S]])

and that this requirement is met even in the double-relative case (50a). This
seems to be generally the case. The noun **caoi** (way, manner) requires an
aN-clause, and we find examples like (52).[7]

> (52)   **ach cen   chaoi aN   gceapann tú aL   tá mise ag dul ag**
>   *but which way   COMP think   you COMP am I   going to*
>
>   **maireachtáil**
>   *make a living*
>
>   'but how do you think I am going to live?'

The principles in (25) then are to be thought of as default conditions, which
are called into play if no other device imposes its requirements on COMP.

NOTES

* For an interesting alternative account of some of these facts, see Hale 1978.

[1] (5a) from **An Druma Mór**, Seosamh Mac Grianna, p. 8; (6a) from **Mo Bhealach Féin**
by the same author, p. 95; (7a) from **Lig Sinn i gCathú** by Breandán Ó hEithir, p. 77;
(8a) from **An Druma Mór**, Seosamh Mac Grianna, p. 31.

[2] (11a) is from a Raidio Éireann news broadcast, April 11th, on the occasion of the
parting of the ways of the **punt Gaelach** and the pound sterling; (12a) is from **Is Glas
na Cnoic**, by Sean 'ac Fhionnlaoich, p. 200; (13a) is borrowed from O'Nolan (1934)
p. 141.

[3] For discussion of the construction that I have called here (perhaps misleadingly) the
Pseudo-Cleft, and of the function of the particle **ná** in such constructions see Malone
1977.

[4] (18) from **An Díthreabhach agus Scéalta Eile as Comhar** ed. Eoghan Ó hAnluain,
Mercier Press, (1977) p. 124; (19) from **Gura Slán le m'Óige**, by Fionn Mac Cumhail,
Oifig an tSoláthair, Dublin, (1967) p. 20; (20) from **Lig Sinn i gCathú** by Breandán
Ó hEithir, p. 10.

[5] (26b) is from **Mo Bhealach Féin**, Seosamh Mac Grianna, p. 41.

[6] From the Introduction (p. ix) to **Cín Lae Amhlaoibh**, ed. Tomás de Bhaldraithe.

[7] (52) is from **Lig Sinn i gCathú**, Breandán Ó hEithir, p. 34.

CHAPTER 6

DEEP STRUCTURE SYNTAX

6.1. INTRODUCTION

The discussion so far has been on a fairly informal level. In the second half of this study I want to do two things – to put the syntactic description on a level of precision approaching that required by Montague's general theory and, that done, to define a model-theoretic semantics on that syntactic base.

The formal fragment that I will present will exclude some of the material that has been discussed in the first half of the study. Exclusions are made on the basis of two kinds of considerations – for some of the data discussed in the first section (AP-Questions for instance) I have no semantic theory of sufficient breadth and precision to be worth presenting. Another set of phenomena is excluded simply for convenience – in that, although their inclusion would not raise any particularly nasty problems, it would give rise to clutter and distract attention from the issues upon which I wish to focus. There will, for instance, be no treatment of tense or of negation, nor of quantifier-scope. In this last case I believe that a treatment along the lines of Cooper 1975 can be added without any particular difficulty. These exclusions, as well as the limitations I will impose on the lexicon, will sometimes give rise to a certain artificiality in the examples discussed. I would ask the reader to remember that this is a consequence only of these decisions of convenience and not of any defect of the grammar to be presented here.

The fragment will include a detailed and thorough treatment of relative clauses, of nominal constituent questions and of Yes/No questions. These topics will be the focus of the discussion, but to be able to treat them we must, obviously, include a fairly substantial treatment of simple declarative sentences – both as constituents out of which relatives and questions can be constructed and as contexts in which they can be embedded. The fragment must then be large enough to include verbs which take sentence complements and question complements. Since Irish makes substantial use of prepositions to mark argument-positions, this will raise some interesting questions about the semantic analysis of prepositional phrases.

The model of grammar that I will work with here can be schematized as in the box diagram (1). Phrase Structure Rules and the lexicon in combination

173

(1)

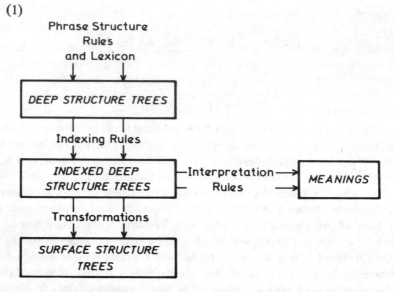

generate a set of Phrase Structure trees – to be called *deep structures*. A set of indexing rules convert these trees into *indexed deep structure trees*. This set of structures forms the input to both the transformational component and the rules of semantic interpretation. This model has much in common with the model of 'I-Grammar' developed in Cooper and Parsons (1976) – with the rather important difference that, in that model, transformations are denied access to the indexing. It is a crucial part of the analysis of relatives and questions and of the analysis of the complementizer system to be proposed here, that transformations be allowed to refer to the indices assigned by indexing rules.

One of the interesting facets of this model, and of much work within the framework of Montague Grammar in general is that it incorporates an attempt to interpret the syntax of natural language directly – rather than making use of an auxiliary language like 'semantic representation' or 'logical form' to mediate between syntax and semantic interpretation. Rather, semantic values are assigned directly to syntactic representations of phrases of natural language. The claim that this represents a 'direct' interpretation of natural language is interesting to the extent that the syntactic base on which the interpretation is defined has independent syntactic motivation. I hope to have demonstrated in the first half of this study that the base on which the semantics is to be defined here is well-motivated syntactically.

The theory of semantic interpretation incorporated in Montague Grammar draws on the logical tradition of truth-conditional semantics. Within that tradition, the purpose of a semantic interpretation is to provide a precise characterization of the notions 'true sentence under a given interpretation' and logical consequence. This is achieved by assigning meanings to well-formed expressions of every category and by giving a set of rules which specify recursively how the meanings of complex expressions are constructed from the meanings of their parts, where 'meanings' are taken to be functions – some simple, some complex – defined among possible worlds, individuals and the two truth values. For discussion and defence of this general approach to semantics, see Thomason (1974a), Partee (1975), Cooper (1977).

Semantic values may be assigned in one step to expressions of the language being interpreted (as in Montague (1974c) or Cresswell (1973)) or, alternatively, interpretation may be induced by the device of 'translating' expressions of natural language into expressions of a formal logic (some version of intensional logic) for which the task of semantic interpretation has already been accomplished. It should be stressed that the use of intensional logic in this way is merely an expository convenience. The rationale behind constraining the 'translation relation' (the relation that holds between the object language and the interpreted formal language) in the very strict way that Montague does, is to ensure that any system using such an intermediary stage will be provably equivalent to a system in which semantic values are assigned directly. (For an elucidating discussion of this issue, see Halvorsen and Ladusaw (to appear).) Thus, the use of intensional logic in this way is not equivalent to or parallel to the use of such levels of representation as 'logical form' – as it has been discussed in some recent work by Chomsky and others (Chomsky 1973, 1975, 1977, Sag 1976a, b, Williams 1977, May 1977). Logical form is a significant level of linguistic representation, derived, it seems, by transformational or transformation-like rules from surface structures, and whose syntactic properties may play a crucial role in determining the grammaticality of sentences.

In this study the translation method of assigning interpretations will be used. I will state a set of translation rules which map indexed deep structure trees onto expressions of intensional logic. I will use that version of intensional logic defined by Montague in PTQ, and I will assume a certain degree of familiarity with the syntax and interpretation of that language.

For this to be a genuine case of 'direct interpretation', it must be demonstrable that the fragment to be defined here is actually a valid instance of Montague's general theory as presented in "Universal Grammar". How this can be done for the kind of model assumed here has been demonstrated by

Cooper and Parsons (1976), so I will not go into the matter here. A demonstration for a fragment like the one defined here in all relevant respects is given in McCloskey (1977b).

The remainder of the book will be organized as follows: I begin in this chapter by presenting the PS-Rules and lexicon that generate deep structure trees. This is the syntactic base on which the semantic interpretation is to be defined. Then in Chapter 7 the translation rules are defined – first for simple sentences, then for complex NP, finally for questions.

The techniques for interpreting transformational grammars within Montague's framework that I will be using here were developed originally by Robin Cooper and Terence Parsons. For a more detailed explication of this system and certain alternatives, the reader should consult Cooper (1975) and Cooper and Parsons (1976).

6.2. PHRASE STRUCTURE RULES

I gather here the set of Phrase Structure rules that generate deep structure trees.

I will state the rules in terms of a simple $\bar{X}$-framework, borrowing notational conventions from Bresnan (1976a) and Davis and Hellan (MS). I use the $\bar{X}$ theory here because some of the proposals I have made depend crucially on the decomposition of the traditional syntactic categories into bundles of syntactic features, and I wish to show that these proposals can actually be realized within a theory of PS-syntax that incorporates such a decomposition. This programme of decomposition is, of course, one of the essential elements of the $\bar{X}$ framework.

The fundamental aim of the $\bar{X}$ theory is to provide a theoretical framework in which systematic regularities in internal structure, distribution and transformational behaviour across categories can be given formal expression. To this end, traditional category names are replaced by an ordered pair whose first element is its *type* (usually represented by the number of bars or primes in its representation – N, $\bar{N}$, $\bar{N}$ etc.) and whose second element is a feature matrix. This bifurcation allows for the statement of regularities along two dimensions – categories of the same type (e.g. NP, PP, AP, ($\bar{\bar{N}}$, $\bar{\bar{A}}$, $\bar{\bar{P}}$)) will be predicted (correctly, it seems) to behave similarly in some respects, and categories with the same feature-matrix (or which merely have certain feature-values in common) will also have certain things in common.

I will use a system in which the major syntactic categories occur in three types – X, $\bar{X}$, $\bar{\bar{X}}$ (types 0, 1, and 2 respectively). Those categories that do not participate in this stratification (Det and COMP, for instance) will, following Bresnan 1976a, be regarded as being of type Ø. The categories I use here will be built up out of the following elements:

Features: [± V] [± N] [± Q] [± clause] [± D] [± Pro] [± def]
            [± C] [± Poss]

Types: 0, 1, 2, Ø

One of the central concerns of those who have worked on this theory has been to specify general principles of how categories are constructed out of such elements and particularly to define general constraints on how PS-rules can in turn be constructed from such complex categories. This research has produced very little in the way of agreement about what these principles are, and since I will have nothing to add here to the various debates being waged on these matters,[1] it will be simpler for my purposes simply to stipulate that certain of the possible combinations of features and types shall be the syntactic categories of the fragment and then to regard these combinations as being (rather elaborate) category names.

A list of the categories to be used is given in (2). Beside each category is an informal description of its contents and a shorter and more familiar name for it. The PS-rules, indexing rules and translation rules are stated in terms of these more manageable abbreviations.

(2)   *Syntactic Categories*

1. $\left\langle 0, \begin{bmatrix} + \text{clause} \\ - Q \end{bmatrix} \right\rangle$ S   Declarative clauses

2. $\left\langle 1, \begin{bmatrix} + \text{clause} \\ - Q \end{bmatrix} \right\rangle$ $\bar{S}$ Embedded Declaratives

3. $\left\langle 1, \begin{bmatrix} + \text{clause} \\ + Q \end{bmatrix} \right\rangle$ Q   Interrogative Clauses

4. $\left\langle 0, \begin{bmatrix} + V \\ - N \end{bmatrix} \right\rangle$ V   Verbs

5. $\left\langle 2, \begin{bmatrix} - V \\ + N \\ - Q \\ - \text{Pro} \end{bmatrix} \right\rangle$ $\begin{matrix} \text{NP} \\ [-\text{Pro}] \end{matrix}$ Non-pronominal Noun Phrases

6. $\left\langle 2, \begin{bmatrix} -V \\ +N \\ -Q \\ +Pro \end{bmatrix} \right\rangle$ NP [+Pro] Pronouns

7. $\left\langle 2, \begin{bmatrix} -V \\ +N \\ +Q \\ -Pro \end{bmatrix} \right\rangle$ QNP [−Pro] Non-Pronominal Interrogative Noun Phrases

8. $\left\langle 2, \begin{bmatrix} -V \\ +N \\ +Q \\ +Pro \end{bmatrix} \right\rangle$ QNP [+Pro] Interrogative Pronouns

9. $\left\langle 1, \begin{bmatrix} -V \\ +N \\ -Q \end{bmatrix} \right\rangle$ Nom Nominals

10. $\left\langle 0, \begin{bmatrix} -V \\ +N \\ -Q \end{bmatrix} \right\rangle$ N Nouns

11. $\left\langle \emptyset, \begin{bmatrix} +D \\ +Q \\ -def \end{bmatrix} \right\rangle$ QDet Interrogative Determiners

12. $\left\langle \emptyset, \begin{bmatrix} +D \\ -Q \\ +def \end{bmatrix} \right\rangle$ Det [+def] Definite Article

13. $\left\langle \emptyset, \begin{bmatrix} +D \\ -Q \\ -def \end{bmatrix} \right\rangle$ Det [−def] Indefinite Article

14. $\left\langle 2, \begin{bmatrix} -V \\ +N \\ -Q \\ +Pro \\ +Poss \end{bmatrix} \right\rangle$ NP $\begin{bmatrix} +Pro \\ +Poss \end{bmatrix}$ Possessive Pronouns

15. $\left\langle 2, \begin{bmatrix} -V \\ -N \end{bmatrix} \right\rangle$ PP Prepositional Phrases

16.	$\left\langle 0, \begin{bmatrix} -V \\ -N \end{bmatrix} \right\rangle$	Prep	Prepositions
17.	$\left\langle 0, \begin{bmatrix} +V \\ +N \end{bmatrix} \right\rangle$	Adj	Adjectives
18.	$\left\langle \emptyset, \begin{bmatrix} +C \\ -Q \end{bmatrix} \right\rangle$	COMP [−Q]	Declarative Complementizers
19.	$\left\langle \emptyset, \begin{bmatrix} +C \\ +Q \end{bmatrix} \right\rangle$	COMP [+Q]	Interrogative Complementizers

The use of the two features [V] and [N] to distinguish nominal, verbal, prepositional and adjectival categories is taken from Bresnan 1976a but originates ultimately with Chomsky. The feature [Q], as discussed previously, distinguishes interrogative from non-interrogative pronouns, interrogative from non-interrogative determiners, and interrogative from declarative clauses. $\bar{S}$ and Q in this system have the feature [+ clause] in common so that any transformation which applies to both categories (Extraposition is a likely candidate, if it is a rule of Irish) can be stated in terms of this feature.

The $\bar{X}$ framework makes available a great number of useful abbreviations over categories – this is precisely its function. We will make use of the following in the syntactic and semantic rules to be presented here:

(3)				
	1.	$\langle 2, \alpha \rangle$	$\bar{\bar{X}}$	NP, AP, PP (for α any feature matrix)
	2.	$\left\langle 2, \begin{bmatrix} -V \\ +N \\ -Q \end{bmatrix} \right\rangle$	NP	Non-Interrogative Noun Phrases (Pronominal and Non-Pronominal)
	3.	$\left\langle 2, \begin{bmatrix} -V \\ +N \\ +Q \end{bmatrix} \right\rangle$	QNP	Interrogative Noun Phrases (Pronominal and Non-Pronominal)
	4.	$\left\langle 2, \begin{bmatrix} -V \\ +N \end{bmatrix} \right\rangle$	np	Interrogative and Non-Interrogative Noun Phrases
	5.	$\left\langle 2, \begin{bmatrix} -V \\ +N \\ -Pro \end{bmatrix} \right\rangle$	np [−Pro]	Non-Pronominal Noun Phrases (Interrogative and Non-Interrogative)

			Interrogative and
6.	$\langle \emptyset\, [+\text{D}] \rangle$	det	Non-Interrogative Determiners
7.	$\left\langle \emptyset, \begin{bmatrix} +\text{D} \\ -\text{Q} \end{bmatrix} \right\rangle$	Det	Non-Interrogative Determiners
8.	$\langle \emptyset,\, [+\text{C}] \rangle$	COMP	Complementizers

We can take these to be abbreviations for disjunctions of categories. The supercategory np, for instance, is to be regarded as a name for that set that contains all well-formed expressions of the categories $\dfrac{\text{NP}}{[+\text{Pro}]}$' $\dfrac{\text{NP}}{[-\text{Pro}]}$' $\dfrac{\text{QNP}}{[+\text{Pro}]}$ and $\dfrac{\text{QNP}}{[-\text{Pro}]}$ and nothing else.

Using these categories and super-categories, we can define the following set of PS-rules:

(4a) $\quad$ S $\rightarrow$ V NP $\left(\left\{ \begin{matrix} \text{NP} \\ \overline{\text{S}} \\ \text{Q} \end{matrix} \right\} \right)$ (PP) (PP)

(b) $\quad \left\langle 1, \begin{bmatrix} +\text{ clause} \\ \alpha\text{Q} \end{bmatrix} \right\rangle \rightarrow \left\langle \emptyset, \begin{bmatrix} +\text{C} \\ \alpha\text{Q} \end{bmatrix} \right\rangle$ S

(c) $\quad$ Q $\rightarrow$ QNP $\overline{\text{S}}$

(d) $\quad \begin{bmatrix} \text{np} \\ -\text{Pro} \\ \alpha\text{Q} \end{bmatrix} \rightarrow \left\{ \begin{matrix} \begin{matrix} \text{det} \\ [\alpha\text{Q}] \end{matrix} & \text{Nom} \\ \begin{matrix} \text{np} \\ [\alpha\text{Q}] \end{matrix} & \overline{\text{S}} \end{matrix} \right\}$

(e) $\quad$ Nom $\rightarrow \left\{ \begin{matrix} \text{Nom} & \text{Adj} \\ \text{N} \end{matrix} \right\}$

(f) $\quad$ PP $\rightarrow$ Prep NP

(g) $\quad$ Det $\rightarrow \begin{bmatrix} \text{NP} \\ +\text{Pro} \\ +\text{Poss} \end{bmatrix}$

We can interpret the PS-rules in the following way.

First we define a set of structural operations $F_1, F_2, \ldots F_n$ each of which is of the form $F_n \langle \text{Cat}_1, \text{Cat}_2 \ldots \text{Cat}_n, \text{Cat}_{n+1} \rangle$. Every F_n is an operation of n

places on phrase structure trees which when given as input trees rooted by Cat_1, Cat_2 ... Cat_n yields as output a tree in which the sub-trees Cat_1, Cat_2 ... Cat_n are sister-adjoined in the left-to-right order $1, 2, \ldots n$ under the category label Cat_{n+1}. We define a PS-rule by specifying a structural operation F_n and a sequence of $n + 1$ categories. So for instance, the rule which generates (5) is (6):

(5)

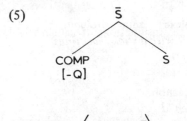

(6) $F_2 \left\langle \begin{matrix} COMP, S, \bar{S} \\ [-Q] \end{matrix} \right\rangle$

This way of formalizing PS-grammars builds trees from the bottom up but is clearly equivalent to more traditional formulations. The theoretical interest of looking at PS-grammars in this light is that it allows them to be interpreted as disambiguated languages in the technical sense defined in UG (Montague 1974a). This in turn allows a demonstration that the system of PS-grammar, indexing system and translation rules is a valid instance of Montague's general theory of semantic interpretation. This demonstration is due to Robin Cooper and Terence Parsons (1976).

Most of these rules, I believe, should be familiar from previous discussion. Perhaps (4a) requires some comment. It will provide the following expansions:

[$_S$ V NP]

Imíonn an sagart
leaves   the priest
'The priest leaves'.

[$_S$ V NP PP]

Imíonn an sagart i ndiaidh an Aifrinn
                    after   the Mass

[$_S$ V NP PP PP]

Imíonn an sagart i ndiaidh an Aifrinn ar a   rothar
                                on his bicycle

[$_S$ V NP NP]

Mharaigh an stócach a   athair
killed   the youth   his father
'The youth killed his father

[$_S$ V NP NP PP]

mharaigh an stócach a athair le   bata   droighin
                                with a stick blackthorn

[$_S$ V NP NP PP]

Thug siad úll   don   leanbh
gave they an apple to the child

[$_S$ V NP NP PP PP]

Thug siad úll don leanbh i   nDoire
                            in Derry

[$_S$ V NP $\bar{S}$]

Creideann sí   nachN bhfuil aon Dia ann
believes   she that there is no God

[$_S$ V NP Q]

D'fhógraigh siad cé aL fuair deontaisí na bliana seo
announced   they who got this year's grants

Some of these rules require that there be scrambling rules that rearrange the order of some constituents depending on their heaviness.[2] For example, any member of the disjunction NP, $\bar{S}$, Q of rule (4a) which is sufficiently heavy normally appears in clause-final position:[3]

[$_S$ V NP NP PP]

Thug siad don   leanbh an capall aL cheannaigh siad
gave they to the child   the horse that they bought

i n-Annagaire
in Annagry

[s V NP S̄ PP]

Dúirt an t-Aire   Oideachais   liom
said   the Minister of Education with me

goN mbeadh obair le fáil
that work would be available

'The Minister for Education told me that there would be work.'

[s V NP S̄ PP PP]

Dúirt an t-Aire Oideachais liom i   mBaile Átha Cliath
                                        in Dublin

goN mbeadh obair le fáil

'The Minister of Education told me in Dublin that there would
be work.'

[s V NP Q PP]

D'fhiafraigh mé den   Aire   cá h-uair aL
asked   I   of the Minister when there

bheadh obair le fáil
would be work available

[s V NP Q PP PP]

D'fhiafraigh mé den Aire sa Dáil
I asked the Minister   in Parliament

cá h-uair aL bheadh obair le fáil
when work would be available

'I asked the Minister (in Parliament) when work would be
available.'

I will not attempt to formulate the relevant principles here.

6.3. THE LEXICON

The lexicon to be presented here will have a fairly orthodox look, although
the fact that we are dealing with a VSO language will force us to modify in a
number of respects the classical theory of subcategorization, as presented in
Chomsky (1965).

We will take each lexical entry to be a pair (D, C) where D is a phonological representation of the item in question (here treated simply as its standard orthographic representation) and C is a set of syntactic features. There are two kinds of syntactic features – category features and subcategorization features. Category features are constructed from the set of syntactic category names given in (2) by placing either a+ or a— in front of a category name. Every lexical item is positively specified for at least one category feature, and by convention negatively specified for all others. This positively-specified feature determines what syntactic category the item belongs to and determines what node the item must be dominated by in a PS tree. Subcategorization features – as is traditional – are taken to specify those syntactic contexts into which a lexical item can be inserted – thereby defining 'subcategories' such as the subcategory of intransitive verbs, the subcategory of question-embedding verbs and so on. The subcategory of transitive verbs, for instance, is that sub-set of lexical items which has as its members all those verbs which are marked [+ _ NP NP]. This feature in turn says that any verb so marked must be inserted under V in a tree of the form:

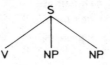

That is, the verb must take both a subject and a direct object. The only items liable to subcategorization in the present fragment are verbs.

Subcategorization in a VSO language like Irish poses certain problems for the theory of verb-subcategorization as presented in Chomsky 1965. Chomsky maintains there that all and only the immediate constituents of VP are relevant for the subcategorization of verbs. Subject NP, auxiliaries and certain classes of adverbial are all claimed to be irrelevant and are analyzed as being external to VP. In a VSO language, there is apparently no way to make this structural distinction between those constituents which are liable to be sub-categorized by a verb and those which are not. One of the awkwardnesses that this leads to is that every verb must be supplied with a subcategorization-feature corresponding to every optional adverbial constituent which can appear in a sentence with it. One reasonably economic way in which to do this is to subcategorize every verb explicitly only for those categories that participate in subcategorization and then to state a lexical redundancy rule which associates with every subcategorization frame another frame which

includes the optional adverbials. In the present fragment we will, for simplicity's sake deal only with adverbials that take the form of a prepositional
phrase:

(7)   If α is a lexical item which has the features [+ V, +_A B ... N],
        then α also has a feature [+_A B ... N PP].

So, for instance, the class of intransitive verbs is defined by the subcategorization feature [+ _ NP]. This will require such verbs to occur in clauses like
(8):

(8)   **Imíonn an garda**   'The policeman leaves'
        leaves   the policeman

The convention (7) will also give them the feature [+ _ NP PP] which will
allow them to occur in clauses like (9):

(9)   **Imíonn na fir óga   ar a gcuid rothar**
        leave   the men young on their bicycles
        'The young men leave on their bicycles'.

Notice that there is a recursion implicit in the convention (7). That is, given
the feature [+ _ A B ... N PP], the rule can 're-apply' to add a third feature
[+ _ A B ... N PP PP] allowing the verb to occur in frames like (10):

(10)   **Imíonn na fir óga ar a gcuid rothar   i dtreo Mín na Leice**
        the young men leave on their bicycles towards Meenaleck

And so on indefinitely.

   Another departure from the assumptions of Chomsky (1965) is required
by the fact that the domain of subcategorization for verbs must be S. This
allows – or rather requires – that we subcategorize verbs for subject position.
We need this possibility to define the subcategory of verbs which take sentential subjects. One such verb is **tarla** ('happen'):

(11)   **Tharla   goN   raibh mé ar an Chlochán Liath an lá sin**
        happened COMP was I   in Dunloe   that day
        'It happened that I was in Dunloe that day'.

One of the subcategorization frames associated with **tarla** will be [+ _ $\bar{S}$].
   We are now in a position to define the following lexicon:

(12a)

$[+ \text{N}]$: fear ('man'), bean ('woman'), garda ('police-man'), bangharda ('policewoman'), rothar ('bicycle'), pingin ('penny'), scian ('knife'), litir ('letter')

(b) $\left[+ \begin{matrix} \text{NP} \\ [-\text{Pro}] \end{matrix} \right]$: Ciarán, Seán, Nollaig, Máire, Deirdre, Aingeal

(c) $\left[+ \begin{matrix} \text{NP} \\ [+\text{Pro}] \end{matrix} \right]$: sé ('he, it'), sí ('she, it'), é ('him, it'), í ('her, it')

(d) $\left[+ \begin{matrix} \text{QNP} \\ [+\text{Pro}] \end{matrix} \right]$: cé ('who'), caidé ('what')

(e) $\left[+ \begin{matrix} \text{Det} \\ \begin{bmatrix} -\text{Q} \\ +\text{def} \end{bmatrix} \end{matrix} \right]$: an ('the')

(f) $\left[+ \begin{matrix} \text{Det} \\ \begin{bmatrix} -\text{Q} \\ -\text{def} \end{bmatrix} \end{matrix} \right]$: Ø ('a')

(g) $\left[+ \begin{matrix} \text{Det} \\ \begin{bmatrix} +\text{Q} \\ -\text{def} \end{bmatrix} \end{matrix} \right]$: cén ('which')

(h) $[+ \text{Prep}]$: ar ('on'), le ('with'), de ('of'), ó ('from'), do ('*Dative* to'), i ('in')

(i) $\left[+ \begin{matrix} \text{COMP} \\ [-\text{Q}] \end{matrix} \right]$: aL, aN, goN

(j) $\left[+ \begin{matrix} \text{COMP} \\ [+\text{Q}] \end{matrix} \right]$: anN

(k) $\left[+ \begin{matrix} \text{NP} \\ \begin{bmatrix} +\text{Pro} \\ +\text{Poss} \end{bmatrix} \end{matrix} \right]$: a ('her'), aL ('his')

(l) $[+ \text{Adj}]$: mór ('great'), clúiteach ('famous'), cróga ('courageous'), álainn ('beautiful'), fada ('long')

(m) $[+ \text{V}, + \_\_ \text{NP}]$: éirigh ('rise'), rith ('run'), imigh ('leave'), tig ('come') goid ('steal'), póg ('kiss'), pós ('marry'),

(n)   [+ V, + _ NP NP] : maraigh ('kill'), scríobh ('write'), gortaigh
                            ('hurt'), tí ('see')

(o)   [+ V, + _ NP $\bar{S}$]   : creid ('believe'), síl ('think')

(p)   [+ V, + _ NP Q]   : fógraigh ('announce')

(q)   [+ V, + _ NP [PP[Prep le] NP]]   : cuidigh ('help')

(r)   [+ V, + _ NP [PP[Prep ar] NP]]   : feall ('betray')

(s)   [+ V, + _ NP NP [PP[Prep ar] NP]]   : iarr ('ask')

(t)   [+ V, + _ NP NP [PP[Prep do] NP]]   : tabhair ('give')

(u)   [+ V, + _ NP $\bar{S}$ [PP[Prep le] NP]]   : deir ('say')

(v)   [+ V, + _ NP $\bar{S}$ [PP[Prep do] NP]]   : inis ('tell')

(w)   [+ V, + _ NP Q [PP[Prep de] NP]]   : fiafraigh ('ask')

(x)   [+ V, + _ NP Q [PP[Prep do] NP]]   : inis ('tell')

A few comments on some of these categories:

12b: I treat proper names as lexical members of the category NP. This ensures – correctly – that they will never be modified by determiners or adjectives. It does not ensure that they will not be modified by relative clauses, since we have opted for the NP $\bar{S}$ structure for relatives.

12m–x define the various subcategories of verbs. (12m) and (12n) represent intransitive and transitive verbs respectively. (12o) and (12p) represent the classes of sentence-embedding and question-embedding verbs respectively. (12q)–(12x) represent various different subcategories that all have one thing in common – they mark one of their argument positions with a preposition. The verb cuidigh (12q) uses the preposition le ('with') to mark the NP that is, semantically, its direct object:

(13)   **Chuidigh siad le   Ciarán**   'They helped Ciaran'.
        helped   they with

The verb feall ('betray, let down, fail') marks its semantic direct object with the preposition ar:

(14)   **Ná   feall   orm!**   'Don't let me down!'
        NEG IMP betray on me

(12s) and (12t) represent classes of three-place verbs with NP objects that mark the indirect object position with a particular preposition:

(15)   **D'iarr sé cipín   orm**   'He asked me for a match'
         asked he a match on me

(16)   **Thug sé cipín   dom**   'He gave me a match'
         gave he a match to me

(12u) and (12v) represent the class of verbs which take sentential objects and indirect objects and mark the indirect object position with a particular preposition:

(17)   **Deireann an t-Aire   liom   goN   bhfuil an   cogadh thart**
         says   the Minister with me COMP is   the war   over

         'The Minister tells me that the war is over'.

(12w) and (12x) embed questions:

(18)   **D'fhiafraigh an t-Aire   díom anN raibh an   cogadh thart**
         asked   the Minister of me INT was   the war   over

         'The Minister asked me if the war was over'.

6.4. GENERATING DEEP STRUCTURE TREES

In the kind of bottom-to-top grammar we are constructing here, we can construe lexical insertion in the following way:

(19)   If α is a lexical item with the feature $[+ X]$,
        then X is a Phrase Structure Tree.
           |
          α

From this we can go on to define the set of trees generated by the PS-rules. The set of Phrase Structure Trees is the union of the following sets:

(20)   (i)   the set of lexical items
        (ii)   the set of trees derived from lexical items by (19)
       (iii)   the set of trees derived by applying the rules in (4)

The set of trees defined by (20) is not the set of Deep Structure Trees. This set is much too large because it takes no account yet of subcategorizational restrictions. The set of Deep Structure Trees, those structures upon which the indexing rules operate, will be a subset of the set of Phrase Structure Trees which meet a certain condition. Intuitively, that restriction will say that every lexical item in the tree must occur in a syntactic frame which is provided for by one of the subcategorization features in that item's lexical entry.

Our subcategorization features are not strictly local in the sense of Chomsky (1965) because they are required to look down into categories like PP which are sisters to a verb and require not just that the verb be followed by a PP, but rather by a PP that is headed by a particular preposition. Our interpretation of subcategorization features must then be a little more elaborate than that in Chomsky (1965), and also more elaborate than that of Cooper (1975), which is a reconstruction of the *Aspects* system in a framework much like the one articulated here.

We interpret subcategorization features in the following way: Take a subcategorization feature to be an ordered sequence of structural conditions in the sense of Peters and Ritchie (1973). On this account, a feature like (20) is an abbreviation for the sequence of structural conditions in (21):

(20) $[+ \_ \text{NP} \, [_{PP}[_{Prep} \, \text{le}] \, \text{NP}]]$

(21) $\_ \text{NP}^1_1; \text{PP}^2_{1-2} \, \& \, \text{Prep}^2_1 \, \& \, \text{le}^2_1 \, \& \, \text{NP}^2_2$

That is, following the dash there is a sequence of two structural conditions – the first a trivially simple one that is satisfied by any tree that is a NP, the second being a two-term structural condition which will be satisfied by a tree of the form in (22):

(22)

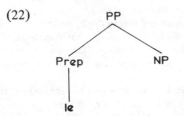

Intuitively what our well-formedness condition will require is that when a lexical item is inserted into a tree, its sisters must be sub-trees which are satisfied by the structural conditions in the subcategorization frame. So for instance the subcategorization feature (20)/(21) requires that its verb be inserted into a tree followed first by a sub-tree that is a NP and then by a sub-tree of the form (22). This condition is stated formally in (23).[4]

(23)   A Phrase Structure Tree ϕ is well-formed iff every lexical item α
         in ϕ which has the features $[+ X, [+ \_ A B \ldots N]]$ appears in a
         tree of the following form:

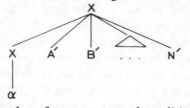

where for any structural condition C, C′ is a tree which admits of
a factorization of which the structural condition C is true.

The set of Deep Structure Trees can now be defined as the smallest set that
contains all members of the set of Phrase-Structure Trees which meet the
well-formedness condition (23).

NOTES

[1] It is perhaps worth pointing out however that the system presupposes (following
Hornstein 1977) that S, $\bar{S}$ and Q are not verbal categories. It is difficult to see how the
idea that a sentence is a verbal category whose head is VP is compatible with VSO syntax
– or indeed how the putative internal structural parallelism between S and NP, which is
the principle motivation for the analysis of S as a verbal category, can be maintained in a
VSO language. Our analysis of NP with relative clause modifiers (i.e. in terms of a rule
NP → NP $\bar{S}$) also assumes (contra Jackendoff 1977) that expansions of the form $X^n \rightarrow$
$\ldots X^n \ldots$ (where X^n is the head of the larger constituent) are valid.

[2] This is a little misleading as no $\bar{S}$- or Q-constituent will ever be 'light' enough not to be
extraposed. It may be wrong to assume that the same principles that determine that
'heavy' NP's appear in clause-final position also account for the fact that embedded
clauses normally appear in clause-final position, but nothing very crucial turns on that
here.

[3] For a discussion of the normal patterns of word-order in Ulster Irish, see Sommerfelt
1965.

[4] Actually our decision to base-generate the focus-constituent of a cleft, together with
our decision to use subcategorization to handle governed prepositions, forces on us a
more elaborate non-local treatment of subcategorization, since governed prepositions can
appear in the focus of a cleft, as in (i):

(i)   **Is   liom   aL   d'éirigh go maith**
           Cop with-me COMP rose   well

           'It's me that did well'.

We can allow for these cases by modifying (23) as follows:

(23')   '... where for any structural condition C, C' is a tree which admits of a
           factorization of which the structural condition C is true, or is an empty
           node co-indexed with a tree which admits of a factorization of which the
           structural condition C is true'.

CHAPTER 7

SEMANTIC INTERPRETATION

7.1. INTRODUCTION

In Chapter 6 the task of defining the syntax was accomplished. Here we turn to the task of providing a semantic interpretation for that syntactic base.

Within the terms of Montague's general theory, an interpretation of a language L consists of the following:

1.   an interpretation for each lexical item of L

2.   an interpretation rule corresponding to each syntactic rule of L

Together (1) and (2) define recursively:

3.   an interpretation for each of the well-formed expressions of L

When interpretation is induced by translation into intensional logic, as it will be here, (1) consists of a function mapping lexical items of L onto meaningful expressions (basic or derived) of intensional logic. (2) consists of a set of operations – one associated with each syntactic rule of L – which associate with each complex expression of L a *translation* – an expression of intensional logic which is itself a function of the translations of its constituent parts and of the syntactic rule of L which puts those parts together.

To ensure that such a system is equivalent to one in which semantic values are assigned directly to expressions of L, Montague placed certain restrictions on the 'translation relation' – the relation holding between the logic and the natural language. These restrictions are designed to ensure that the disambiguated version of natural language and the formal logic (construed as algebras) are homomorphic (in a technical sense defined in UG). In particular:

1. There must be just one category of the logic corresponding to each syntactic category of the language being interpreted. So it can never be the case, for instance, that some instances of $\bar{S}$ will have one semantic value and in other cases a different value. There need not, however, be a one-to-one correspondence between syntactic categories and semantic types. It can perfectly well be the case that two independent syntactic categories will

192

map on to the same semantic type. In the present fragment, for instance, both S and $\bar{S}$ will denote truth values – i.e. they will both be of type t.

2. The translation rules are subject to the following requirement of compositionality: the translation of any given complex expression of natural language must contain as sub-parts the translation expressions of all its immediate constituents. More formally: in any given pair of syntactic rule and translation rule, there must be just one syntactic operation in intensional logic that corresponds to the syntactic operation of natural language. This is not a very strong version of the thesis of compositionality, because a very simple operation in the syntax may correspond to a very complex operation in the semantics (or vice versa). The effect of this is that the translation expression of an expression of natural language may contain much more than the translation of its immediate constituents. What this relative freedom amounts to is a recognition of the role of what is traditionally known as 'grammatical meaning' – elements of meaning that are contributed not by the meanings of the constituent parts of some phrase but rather by the syntactic configuration in which those constituent parts find themselves.

There have been various attempts within the framework of Montague Grammar to develop stricter versions of the requirement of compositionality. Much of Thomason's work, for instance, is informed by a desire to limit the available semantic operations to functional application and intensional functional application (Thomason 1976, MS). Barbara Partee (to appear) has also proposed limits on the set of semantic operations available to translation rules. The rules presented here will not meet these stricter requirements but will make crucial use at several points of the relative freedom granted by Montague's original formulation.

To define an interpretation for this fragment then, we define:

1.   a function f that maps the syntactic categories of Irish onto the categories of intensional logic.

2.   a function g that maps lexical items of Irish onto expressions of intensional logic.

3.   a set of translation rules, one for each phrase structure configuration generated by the PS-rules and indexing procedure.

7.2. TYPE ASSIGNMENT

The function f has as its domain the set of category names of Irish (as in (2) of Chapter 6) and as its range the set of types of intensional logic. Following

Cooper (1975), we do not define the function for lexical categories, but rather for subcategories as defined by bundles of subcategorization features. It is crucial semantically to be able to distinguish the various different subcategories of the category 'verb' since the functional requirements of, for instance, intransitive verbs, transitive verbs and question-embedding verbs are quite different. Defining the function f in terms of subcategories allows us to make the crucial distinctions and to maintain the essence of Montague's requirement that there be a unique denotation type for each syntactic category, while still maintaining the syntactic and morphological unity of the category 'verb'. For the non-lexical categories, the function is defined in the normal way.

(2a) $f(S)$ $= t$

(b) $f(\bar{S})$ $= t$

(c) $f(Q)$ $= \langle\langle s, t\rangle, t\rangle$

(d) $f(np)$ $= \langle\langle e, t\rangle, t\rangle$

(e) $f(Nom)$ $= f(N) = \langle e, t\rangle$

(f) $f(Adj)$ $= \langle\langle s, f(Nom)\rangle, f(Nom)\rangle$

(g) $f(det)$ $= \langle f(Nom), f(np)\rangle$

(h) $f(PP)$ $= \langle\langle s, \langle e, t\rangle\rangle, \langle e, t\rangle\rangle$

(i) $f(Prep)$ $= \langle\langle s, f(np)\rangle, f(PP)\rangle$

(j) $f(COMP) = \langle\langle s, f(S)\rangle, f(\bar{S})\rangle$
      $[-Q]$

(k) $f(COMP) = \langle\langle s, f(S)\rangle, f(Q)\rangle$
      $[+Q]$

The values of f for the categories (all verbal) that involve subcategorization are given in (2l)–(2s). These are presented in the same order as in the lexicon of (12) in Chapter 6:

(l) $f([+V, + \_ NP])$ $= \langle e, t\rangle$ (intransitives)

(m) $f([+V, + \_ NP\ NP]) = \langle\langle s, f(np)\rangle, \langle e, t\rangle\rangle$ (transitives)

(n) $f([+V, + \_ NP\ \bar{S}])$ $= \langle\langle s, f(\bar{S})\rangle, \langle e, t\rangle\rangle$

(o) $f([+V, + \_ NP\ Q])$ $= \langle\langle s, f(Q)\rangle, \langle e, t\rangle\rangle$

(p) $f([+ V, + \_ NP\ PP])$ $= \langle e, t \rangle$

(q) $f([+ V, + \_ NP\ NP\ PP]) = \langle\langle s, f(\text{np})\rangle, \langle e, t \rangle\rangle$

(r) $f([+ V, + \_ NP\ \bar{S}\ PP])$ $= \langle\langle s, f(\bar{S})\rangle, \langle e, t \rangle\rangle$

(s) $f([+ V, + \_ NP\ Q\ PP])$ $= \langle\langle s, f(Q)\rangle, \langle e, t \rangle\rangle$

The notation here, and the type assignment, is taken, for the most part, from PTQ but we have eliminated (following Thomason MS) the systematic appeal to intensional types found in that paper. A word on the notation first: e is the type of individuals, t is the type of truth values (0 and 1). For any type α, $\langle s, \alpha \rangle$ is the type of functions from possible worlds to things of type α. For any types α and β, $\langle \alpha, \beta \rangle$ is the type of functions from things of type α to things of type β. So for instance $\langle s, t \rangle$ is the type of functions from possible worlds to truth values – i.e. the type of propositions. $\langle\langle s, t \rangle, t \rangle$ is the type of functions from propositions to truth values – i.e. the type of sets of propositions.

A few words on the actual assignments are probably in order here, although the usefulness of particular decisions is probably best seen in the treatment of actual examples. Clauses, both embedded and unembedded, are taken to have truth values as their extension (and hence propositions as their intensions), as is traditional. Noun phrases (both interrogative and non-interrogative) are taken to denote sets of sets of individuals. (For a discussion of some of the advantages to be gained in this way, see Cooper (1977a).) Prepositional Phrases are treated essentially as adverbs–adverbs that have the equivalent of VP-scope in that they never include the subject of their sentence within their scope. The semantic properties of PP's will be discussed in some detail shortly. Questions are not, of course, treated in PTQ. They are taken here (following Karttunen (1977a)) to denote sets of propositions. This matter too will be discussed in some detail shortly. The types assigned to other categories can for the most part be determined from the phrase structure configurations in which they are found. Determiners, both interrogative and non-interrogative, for instance, always appear in the configuration (3):

(3)

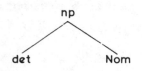

Determiners must then be of such a type as to take a Nom-extension as argument and yield a np-extension as value. That is, they must denote functions from things of type $f(\text{Nom})$ to things of type $f(\text{np})$. The appropriate type assignments for Prepositions, complementizers and adjectives can be determined in the same way.

Categories (i–o) represent those verbal subcategories that do not govern prepositions; categories (p–s) represent those that do. The type assigned to a verb can be regarded as a sort of semantic subcategorization of that verb. Every verb requires certain kinds of arguments – the subcategorization of a verb represents the syntactic side of this coin, while the denotation type represents the semantic side. There is a certain redundancy in giving both for a verb, in that once certain decisions are made (for example, once it is decided what types are to be assigned to the various argument categories), then the type of any verb is in large part predictable from its subcategorization feature. Irish has no syntactic VP but in the course of building up the translations of sentences, we build up a 'semantic VP' to which is applied the translation of the subject NP. This means that the translation of a verb along with its subcategorizational requirements must be of the semantic type of VP's – i.e. sets of individuals. The verb itself then must denote a function from things of the intensional type of its complement (in this fragment NP, $\bar{\text{S}}$ and Q) to things of type $\langle e, t \rangle$. The denotation types assigned to all the verbs in (i–o) of (2) are all determined in this way. A verb like **creid** ('believe') for instance has the subcategorization feature [_ NP $\bar{\text{S}}$] – it requires a subject and an embedded clause. Therefore **creid** must correspond in the logic to a constant which denotes a function from $\bar{\text{S}}$-intensions (propositions) to sets of individuals. **Creid** then associates a proposition with a set of individuals – namely those that believe that proposition.

Verbs subcategorized to take a particular preposition behave a little differently. PP's are taken to be VP-scope adverbs. Therefore they represent functions which take the 'semantic VP' as an argument rather than being themselves an argument of the verb. How this idea is compatible with the semantics of preposition-governing verbs will be discussed shortly. For now what it means is that the fact that a verb is subcategorized for a particular preposition will not be reflected in its denotation type – notice that the subcategories in (p–s) all have the same types as their counterparts which do not govern prepositions (in (i–o)).

7.3. TRANSLATING THE LEXICON

Having defined the assignment of denotation types to syntactic categories, we go on to define the function g which maps lexical items of Irish onto expressions of intensional logic.

First though, I should say something about the notation we will use. I will assume here the syntax and interpretation of that version of intensional logic defined in Montague's PTQ. But since the type assignment we have defined in the preceding section is different in a number of respects from that defined in PTQ, it will be convenient to distinguish a different class of variables. So:

> P, Q, R will be the first, second, and third variables of type $\langle e, t \rangle$ respectively. That is, they are variables over sets of individuals.
>
> x, y, z will be the first, third and fifth variables of type $\langle e \rangle$ respectively. That is, they are variables over individuals.
>
> x_n will be the $2n$-th variable of type $\langle e \rangle$.
>
> $\mathscr{P}$ will be the first variable of type $\langle s, \langle\langle e, t \rangle, t \rangle\rangle$. That is, it is a variable over np-intensions (Properties of sets).
>
> $\mathscr{P}_n$ will be the $2n$-th variable of type $\langle s, f(\text{np})\rangle$
>
> p, q will be the first and second variables of type $\langle s, t \rangle$ respectively. That is, they are variables over propositions.

Formally, g is a fixed biunique function such that:

(i) the domain of g is the set of lexical items of our fragment except the members of the category $\underset{[+\text{Pro}]}{\text{NP}}$. And,

(ii) whenever α is a lexical item of category A, and α is in the domain of g, then $g(\alpha) \in \text{ME}_{f(A)}$, where for any type β, ME_β is the set of meaningful expressions of intensional logic of type β.

Pronouns are excluded from the domain of g because we need a special convention to interpret them. Many lexical items will be translated by constants of intensional logic of the appropriate type. For these I will adopt the convention that the name of the constant shall be their standard English translation. So $g(\textbf{fear})$ is 'man' for instance, were 'man' is a constant of intensional logic of type $\langle e, t \rangle$, $g(\textbf{fiafraigh})$ is 'ask' where 'ask' is a constant of type $\langle\langle s, f(Q)\rangle, \langle e, t\rangle\rangle$ and so on. All of the lexical items in the fragment will be treated in this way except the following:

(4) $g(\textbf{Ciarán})\ =\ \lambda PP(c)$

         $g(\textbf{Deirdre})\ =\ \lambda PP(d)$

         $g(\textbf{Nollaig})\ =\ \lambda PP(n)$,   etc.

That is, proper names translate to expressions denoting sets of sets of individuals. 'P' and 'Q' represent distinguished variables of type $\langle e, t\rangle$. That is, they are variables over sets of individuals. 'c', 'd', and 'n' etc. are constants of type $\langle e\rangle$ which pick out the individuals **Ciarán**, **Deirdre**, and **Nollaig** respectively. Expressions of the form $\lambda v[\phi]$ (where v is a variable of any type and ϕ is any well-formed expression of the logic) denote functions from things of type v to things of type ϕ. Where ϕ is of type t, the expression $\lambda v[\phi]$ will denote the characteristic function of a set of things of the type of v. So $\lambda PP(c)$ denotes the characteristic function of a set of sets – all those sets of which **Ciarán** is a member.

(5) $g(\textbf{aL}) = g(\textbf{aN}) = g(\textbf{goN}) = \lambda p(\check{\ }p)$

This translation reflects a decision to treat non-interrogative complementizers as semantically empty. Its effect is to pass through the translation of any S-constituent to which it is applied unchanged.

(6) $g(\textbf{cé})\quad =\ \lambda P\, \exists x[\text{person}(x) \wedge R(x) \wedge P(x)]$

         $g(\textbf{caidé}) =\ \lambda P\, \exists x[\neg\text{person}(x) \wedge R(x) \wedge P(x)]$

         $g(\textbf{anN})\ =\ \lambda q\lambda p[\check{\ }p \wedge ((p{=}q) \vee (p{=}\hat{\ }\neg\check{\ }q))]$

These represent the translations of 'who', 'what' and the interrogative complementizer respectively. They will be discussed in the section on questions.

(7) $g(\textbf{an})\ =\ \lambda P\lambda Q\, \exists x[\forall y[(P(y) \wedge R(y)) \leftrightarrow x{=}y] \wedge Q(x)]$

         $g(\emptyset)\ =\ \lambda P\lambda Q\, \exists x[P(x) \wedge R(x) \wedge Q(x)]$

These translations represent the standard interpretations of the definite and indefinite articles respectively, except that they both contain an occurrence of a free set-variable R. The function served by this variable will be discussed when we discuss the semantics of relative clauses.

7.4. TRANSLATION RULES

We will define the rules for translation on the set of trees generated by the PS-rules in combination with the indexing procedures – that is, on the set of indexed deep structure trees.

We will use the following notation in stating the rules:

(8)

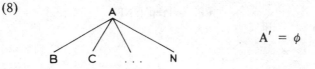

$$A' = \phi$$

The schema (8) is to be interpreted as follows: any tree rooted by the node A which has as its immediate constituents trees rooted by the nodes B, C, ... N respectively in that order, has the translation ϕ, (where by the requirement of compositionality ϕ will contain B', C', N' etc.). In general X' will denote the translation of a tree rooted by the node X.

We begin by defining some general translation conventions. First one for preterminal nodes which dominate lexical items:

(9) $\begin{matrix} X \\ | \\ a \end{matrix}$ $X' = g(a)$ if a is in the domain of g.

We need two conventions for the interpretation of pronouns – one for unindexed pronouns (those used deictically) and one for indexed pronouns (those bound to a controller by one of the indexing rules discussed in Chapter 6.)

(10) $\begin{matrix} NP \\ [+Pro]_n \end{matrix}$ translates to $\lambda PP(x_n)$

(11) $\begin{matrix} NP \\ [+Pro] \\ | \\ a \end{matrix}$ translates to $\lambda PP(x_n)$ where n is any natural number

(10) and (11)[1] ensure that pronouns denote sets of sets of individuals – all the sets to which the individual picked out by the indexed variable belongs.

The translation rules corresponding to the PS-rules in (4) of Chapter 5 are given under (12). The letter identifying each set of rules is keyed to that of the corresponding PS-rule in (4), Chapter 6.

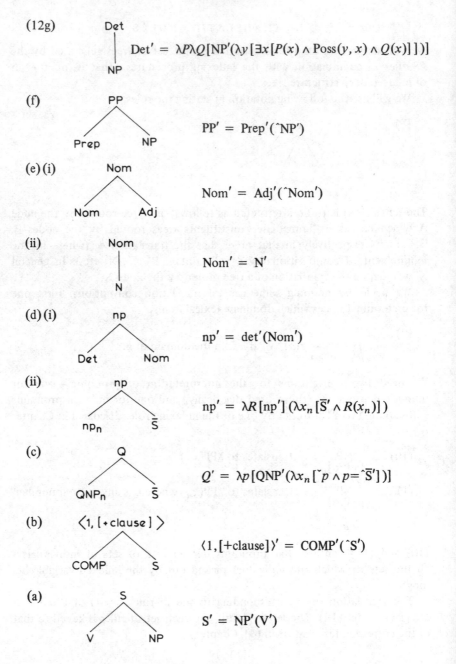

(12g) Det

$$\text{Det}' = \lambda P \lambda Q [\text{NP}'(\lambda y\,[\exists x\,[P(x) \wedge \text{Poss}(y,x) \wedge Q(x)]\,])]$$

NP

(f) PP

$$\text{PP}' = \text{Prep}'(\char94 \text{NP}')$$

Prep   NP

(e)(i) Nom

$$\text{Nom}' = \text{Adj}'(\char94 \text{Nom}')$$

Nom   Adj

(ii) Nom

$$\text{Nom}' = \text{N}'$$

N

(d)(i) np

$$\text{np}' = \text{det}'(\text{Nom}')$$

Det   Nom

(ii) np

$$\text{np}' = \lambda R\,[\text{np}']\,(\lambda x_n\,[\bar{\text{S}}' \wedge R(x_n)]\,)$$

np_n $\bar{\text{S}}$

(c) Q

$$Q' = \lambda p [\text{QNP}'(\lambda x_n\,[\check{\ }p \wedge p = \char94 \bar{\text{S}}'])]$$

QNP_n $\bar{\text{S}}$

(b) ⟨1, [+clause]⟩

$$\langle 1, [+\text{clause}]\rangle' = \text{COMP}'(\char94 \text{S}')$$

COMP   S

(a) S

$$\text{S}' = \text{NP}'(\text{V}')$$

V   NP

(12a) (ii)

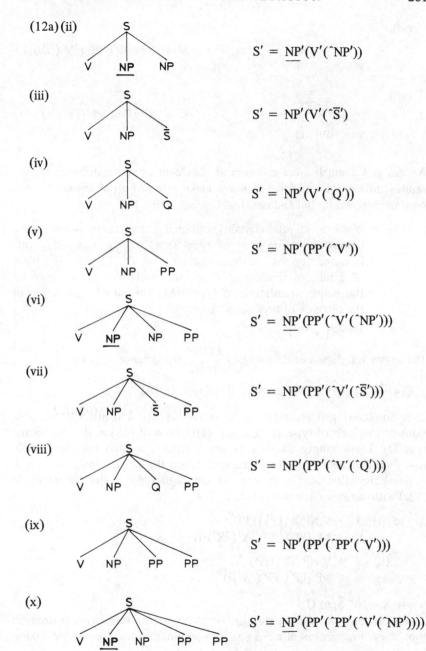

$$S' = \underline{NP}'(V'(^\wedge NP'))$$

(iii)

$$S' = NP'(V'(^\wedge\bar{S}')$$

(iv)

$$S' = NP'(V'(^\wedge Q'))$$

(v)

$$S' = NP'(PP'(^\wedge V'))$$

(vi)

$$S' = \underline{NP}'(PP'(^\wedge V'(^\wedge NP')))$$

(vii)

$$S' = NP'(PP'(^\wedge V'(^\wedge\bar{S}')))$$

(viii)

$$S' = NP'(PP'(^\wedge V'(^\wedge Q')))$$

(ix)

$$S' = NP'(PP'(^\wedge PP'(^\wedge V')))$$

(x)

$$S' = \underline{NP}'(PP'(^\wedge PP'(^\wedge V'(^\wedge NP'))))$$

(xi)

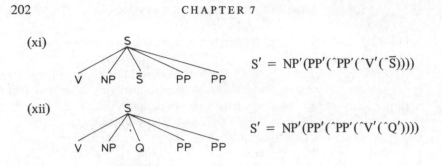

$$S' = NP'(PP'(\hat{}PP'(\hat{}V'(\hat{}\bar{\bar{S}}))))$$

(xii)

$$S' = NP'(PP'(\hat{}PP'(\hat{}V'(\hat{}Q'))))$$

We can give a much more economical statement of the translation for the various different expansions of S by making use of an abbreviatory convention proposed by Bill Ladusaw (*cf.* Ladusaw (1978):

(13)   When a PS-rule contains optional constituents whose trans-
       lations are expressions of type $\langle\langle s, \alpha\rangle, \alpha\rangle$, the translation rule
       is stated for the maximal expansion of the PS-rule. The place
       of a missing constituent δ in the translation rule is taken by
       the empty translation of type $f(\delta)$. The empty translation of
       the category of type $\langle\langle s, \alpha\rangle, \alpha\rangle$ is:

$$\lambda v^{\langle s, \alpha\rangle}[\check{}v^{\langle s, \alpha\rangle}]$$

The empty translation of the category $\dfrac{\text{COMP}}{[-Q]}$, for instance, is (14):

(14) $\lambda p[\check{}p]$ (*p* is a variable of type $\langle s, t\rangle$)

since non-interrogative complementizers have as their semantic values expres-
sions of the logic of type $\langle\langle s, t\rangle, t\rangle$ (*cf.* (2j)). So α of (13) in this case is the
type $\langle t\rangle$. These 'empty translations' are essentially identity functions which
pass their arguments through unchanged. Given this convention and using X
as an abbreviation over categories, we can replace the twelve statements in
(12a) with the two statements in (15):

(15)(i) S → V NP X (PP) (PP)
         S' = NP'(PP'(\hat{}PP'(\hat{}V'(\hat{}X'))))

(ii) S → V NP (PP) (PP)
      S' = NP'(PP'(\hat{}\overline{PP'}(\hat{}V')))

where X = NP, $\bar{\bar{S}}$, or Q

Translation rules can be thought of as processing trees from bottom to
top: they first assign meanings to pre-terminal nodes dominating lexical

items, then move up the tree to the root S, assigning meanings to each constituent as they go.

The rest of this section will be devoted to illustrating certain properties
of the interpretations assigned by these rules and to justifying them in certain
respects. Many of the rules presented here are designed simply to duplicate
certain characteristics of the PTQ fragment. The only essential difference
is that since we must do without a VP-node, translations of sentences must be
assembled directly from the translations of the verb, its arguments and any
optional adverbials that the sentence may contain. Some simple illustrations
of the operation of these rules are given in (16). From these we move on to
consider the innovations of the fragment – possessive pronouns, the problem
of interpreting PP's built around a governed preposition, complex NP containing relative clauses and finally Yes/No and Constituent Questions. I
assume throughout the abbreviatory conventions and Meaning Postulates of
PTQ.

(16a)

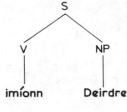

'Deirdre leaves'
$[_{NP}$ **Deirdre**$]' = \lambda PP(d)$
$[_V$ **imíonn**$]' = $ leave

$$S' = NP'(V')$$

$[_S$ **imíonn Deirdre**$]' = \lambda PP(d)$ (leave)
$\equiv$ leave(d)

(16b)   'Deirdre marries Ciarán'

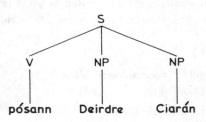

$[_{\text{NP}} \textbf{Deirdre}]' = \lambda PP(d)$
$[_{\text{NP}} \textbf{Ciarán}]' = \lambda PP(c)$
$[_{\text{V}} \textbf{pósann}]' = \text{marry}$
$S' = NP'(V'(\char"5E NP'))$
$[_S \textbf{pósann Deirdre Ciarán}]' = \lambda PP(d)(\text{marry}(\char"5E \lambda PP(c)))$
$\phantom{[_S \textbf{pósann Deirdre Ciarán}]'} \equiv \text{marry}(\char"5E \lambda PP(c))(d)$
$\phantom{[_S \textbf{pósann Deirdre Ciarán}]'} \equiv \text{marry}(d, \char"5E \lambda PP(c))$
$\phantom{[_S \textbf{pósann Deirdre Ciarán}]'} \equiv \text{marry}_*(d, c)$

(16c)   'Ciarán leaves with Deirdre'

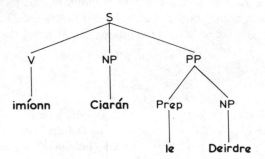

$[_{\text{NP}} \textbf{Deirdre}]' = \lambda PP(d)$
$[_{\text{PP}} \textbf{le Deirdre}]' = \text{with}(\char"5E \lambda PP(d))$
$[_{\text{NP}} \textbf{Ciarán}] = \lambda PP(c)$
$S' = NP'(PP'(\char"5E V'))$
$[_S \textbf{imíonn Ciarán le Deirdre}] = \lambda PP(c)(\text{with}(\char"5E \lambda PP(d))(\char"5E \text{leave}))$
$\phantom{[_S \textbf{imíonn Ciarán le Deirdre}]} \equiv \text{with}(\char"5E \lambda PP(d))(\char"5E \text{leave})(c)$
$\phantom{[_S \textbf{imíonn Ciarán le Deirdre}]} \equiv \text{with}_*(d)(\char"5E \text{leave}(c))$

As mentioned before, complementizers are treated as being semantically null by being assigned the empty translation of type $f(\text{COMP})$. How this will work is illustrated in (17).

(17)   **creideann Ciarán goN   ngortaíonn sé Máire**
         believes   Ciaran COMP hurts   he Mary
         'Ciarán believes that he hurts Mary'.

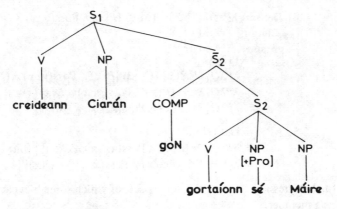

$$NP'_{[+Pro]} = \lambda PP(x_6)$$

$$S'_2 = \lambda PP(x_6)(hurt(\hat{}\lambda PP(m)))$$
$$\equiv hurt_*(x_6, m)$$

$$\bar{S}_2 = COMP'(\hat{}S')$$

$$COMP' = \lambda p[\check{}p]$$

$$\bar{S}_2 = \lambda p[\check{}p](\hat{}hurt_*(x_6, m))$$
$$\equiv hurt_*(x_6, m)$$

$$S' = NP'(V'(\hat{}\bar{S}'))$$

$$S'_1 = \lambda PP(c)(believe(\hat{}hurt_*(x_6, m)))$$
$$\equiv believe(\hat{}hurt_*(x_6, m))(c)$$
$$\equiv believe(c, \hat{}hurt_*(x_6, m))$$

In the final expression of (17), the free variable x_6 will pick out the same individual as the constant c in some contexts of use, a different individual in others. This accounts for the ambiguity (or vagueness) of (17).

The rule for treating possessive modifiers (12g) is an innovation. Its effect is illustrated in (18).[2]

(18)

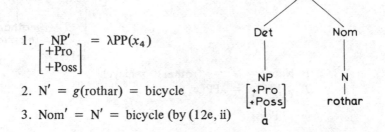

1. $\begin{bmatrix} NP' \\ +Pro \\ +Poss \end{bmatrix} = \lambda PP(x_4)$

2. $N' = g(rothar) = bicycle$

3. $Nom' = N' = bicycle$ (by (12e, ii)

4. $\text{Det}' = \lambda P\lambda Q[\begin{bmatrix} \text{NP}' \\ +\text{Pro} \\ +\text{Poss} \end{bmatrix}(\lambda y\exists x[P(x)\wedge\text{Poss}(y,x)\wedge Q(x)])]$

   (12g)

   $\equiv \lambda P\lambda Q[\lambda RR(x_4)(\lambda y\exists x[P(x)\wedge\text{Poss}(y,x)\wedge Q(x)])]$

   $\equiv \lambda P\lambda Q[\lambda y\exists x[P(x)\wedge\text{Poss}(y,x)\wedge Q(x)](x_4)]$

   $\equiv \lambda P\lambda Q[\exists x[P(x)\wedge\text{Poss}(x_4,x)\wedge Q(x)]]$

5. $\text{NP}' = \text{Det}'(\text{Nom}')$ (12d, i)

   $\equiv \lambda P\lambda Q[\exists x[P(x)\wedge\text{Poss}(x_4,x)\wedge Q(x)]]\,(\text{bicycle})$

   $\equiv \lambda Q[\exists x[\text{bicycle}(x)\wedge\text{Poss}(x_4,x)\wedge Q(x)]]$

This final expression denotes the set of sets of which some bicycle belonging to x_4 is a member.

Two more complex examples are worked out in (19a) and (19b). In this last case we can derive only the narrow scope reading for the existential associated with the possessive. The de re reading with respect to 'his knife' would be derived by assigning the NP **a scian** wide scope.

(19a)   'Deirdre leaves on her bicycle'.

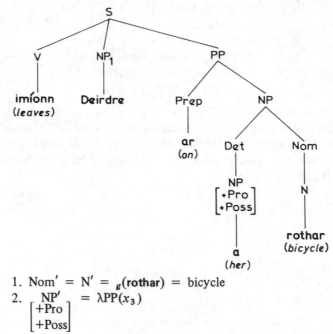

1. $\text{Nom}' = \text{N}' = {}_g(\textbf{rothar}) = \text{bicycle}$
2. $\begin{bmatrix} \text{NP}' \\ +\text{Pro} \\ +\text{Poss} \end{bmatrix} = \lambda P P(x_3)$

3. Det′ $= \lambda P\lambda Q[\lambda RR(x_3)(\lambda y[\exists x[P(x) \wedge \mathrm{Poss}(y,x) \wedge Q(x)]])]$
   $\equiv \lambda P\lambda Q[\exists x[P(x) \wedge \mathrm{Poss}(x_3,x) \wedge Q(x)]]$ (12g)

4. np′ $=$ det′(Nom′)
   $= \lambda P\lambda Q[\exists x[P(x) \wedge \mathrm{Poss}(x_3,x) \wedge Q(x)]]$(bicycle)
   $\equiv \lambda Q[\exists x[\mathrm{bicycle}(x) \wedge \mathrm{Poss}(x_3,x) \wedge Q(x)]]$

5. PP′ $=$ Prep′(ˆNP′)
   $= \mathrm{on}(\hat{\ }\lambda Q[\exists x[\mathrm{bicycle}(x) \wedge \mathrm{Poss}(x_3,x) \wedge Q(x)]])$

6. NP′$_1$ $= \lambda \mathrm{PP}(d)$

7. S′ $=$ NP′(PP′(ˆV′))
   $= \lambda \mathrm{PP}(d)(\mathrm{on}(\hat{\ }\lambda Q[\exists x[\mathrm{bicycle}(x) \wedge \mathrm{Poss}(x_3,x)$
   $\wedge Q(x)]])(\hat{\ }\mathrm{leave}))$
   $\equiv \mathrm{on}(\hat{\ }\lambda Q[\exists x[\mathrm{bicycle}(x) \wedge \mathrm{Poss}(x_3,x) \wedge Q(x)]])$
   $(\hat{\ }\mathrm{leave}(d))$
   $\equiv \exists x[\mathrm{bicycle}(x) \wedge \mathrm{Poss}(x_3,x) \wedge \mathrm{on}_*(x)(\hat{\ }\mathrm{leave}(d))]$

(19b) 'Ciarán thinks that he kills Seán with his knife'.

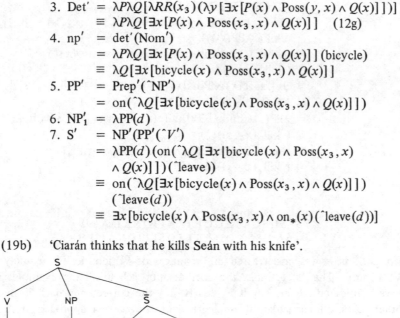

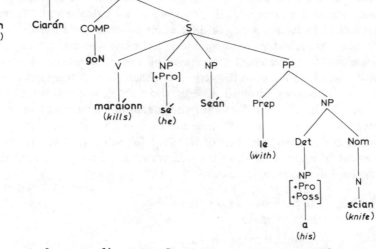

1. [$_{NP}$ a scian]′ $= \lambda Q\exists x[\mathrm{knife}(x) \wedge \mathrm{Poss}(x_4,x) \wedge Q(x)]$
2. [$_{PP}$ le a scian]′ $= \mathrm{with}(\hat{\ }\lambda Q\exists x[\mathrm{knife}(x) \wedge \mathrm{Poss}(x_4,x) \wedge Q(x)]$
3. [$_{NP}$ sé]′ $= \lambda \mathrm{PP}(x_4)$
4. [$_{NP}$ Seán] $= \lambda \mathrm{PP}(s)$

5. $S' = NP'(PP'(\hat{\ }V'(\hat{\ }NP')))$
   $= \lambda PP(x_4)(\text{with}(\hat{\ }\lambda Q \exists x[\text{knife}(x) \wedge \text{Poss}(x_4,x) \wedge Q(x)])$
   $(\hat{\ }\text{kill}(\hat{\ }\lambda PP(s))))$
   $\equiv \text{with}(\hat{\ }\lambda Q \exists x[\text{knife}(x) \wedge \text{Poss}(x_4,x) \wedge Q(x)])$
   $(\hat{\ }\text{kill}_*(x_4,s))$
   $\equiv \exists x[\text{knife}(x) \wedge \text{Poss}(x_4,x) \wedge \text{with}_*(x)(\hat{\ }\text{kill}_*(x_4,s))]$

6. $S' = NP'(V'(\hat{\ }\overline{S}'))$
   $= \lambda PP(c)(\text{think}(\hat{\ }\exists x[\text{knife}(x) \wedge \text{Poss}(x_4,x) \wedge \text{with}_*(x)$
   $(\hat{\ }\text{kill}_*(x_4,s))]))$
   $\equiv \text{think}(\hat{\ }\exists x[\text{knife}(x) \wedge \text{Poss}(x_4,x) \wedge \text{with}_*(x)$
   $(\hat{\ }\text{kill}_*(x_4,s))])(c)$

7.5. SUBCATEGORIZATIONAL AND ADVERBIAL USES OF PREPOSITIONAL PHRASES

Up until now we have treated all instances of PP identically – namely as VP-adverbs. This is, I think, the correct approach in all the examples we have considered so far, but it is clearly not the correct approach in many other cases. In particular, it is clearly not the correct approach in those cases where the preposition is governed by a particular verb. There are a number of important semantic differences between the adverbial uses of a PP and the subcategorizational use. Intuitively, the preposition, when it is part of the subcategorization frame of a verb, serves only to mark one of the argument places of the verb rather than contributing to the construction of a complex adverbial. One of the ways in which this distinction is reflected is in the fact that when the preposition is not part of the verb's subcategorization, it has a discrete meaning which contributes to the meaning of the complex adverbial of which it forms a part. There is a common element of meaning in all of the following uses of the preposition **ar**, however hard it may be to tie down:

(20a) **Tá Seán ina sheasamh ar Chiarán**
       is   standing   on
       'John is standing on Ciaran'.

(b)   **Tá an long ar an fharraige**
       is the ship on the sea
       'The ship is on the sea'.

(c) **D'imigh siad ar an bhus**
left   they on the bus
'They left on the bus'.

However this element of meaning does not appear in those instances where the preposition is governed by a particular verb. The verb **iarr** ('ask (for something)') for example, marks its direct object with the same preposition. **Feall** marks its (semantic) direct object and **theip** marks its (semantic) subject:

(21a) **D'iarr mé maithiúnas ar Dhia**
asked I   forgiveness on God
'I asked God for forgiveness'.

(b) **D'fheall sibh   orm**
betrayed you(pl) on me
'You betrayed me'.

(c) **Theip orm   bean   Ghaelach a phósadh**
failed on me a woman Irish   to marry
'I failed to marry an Irish woman'.

I think that it is clear that it is important to distinguish these two cases (*cf.* Bresnan (1978) for a discussion of some similar cases in English). The interesting question is where the distinction should be made. It seems clear that it should not be made in the syntax – there are, as far as I am aware, no syntactic correlates in Irish to the distinction being made here. The internal structure of the two kinds of PP is identical, the constraints on their position in the sentence are identical,[3] and PP-selecting rules or constructions like Clefting treat both kinds identically (*cf.* the discussion of Clefts in Chapter 4). The problem then is to treat both kinds of PP identically in the syntax but to distinguish them somehow in the semantics. As we have set things up so far, both the syntactic rules and the translation rules are blind to the distinction between the two uses. I propose that we let things stand as they are in this respect and to make the necessary distinctions by means of a Meaning Postulate. Actually we will need two schemata of postulates – one for three-place verbs like **deir** ('say'), **tabhair** ('give'), **iarr** ('ask') and one for two-place verbs like **cuidigh** ('help'), **feall** ('betray').

They will work in the following way: the postulates will be associated with any verb that is subcategorized for a particular preposition. What they will say – to speak very informally – is that there is something peculiar about

the semantics of PP's when they happen to co-occur with a verb subcategorized for their preposition – namely that the preposition makes no
semantic contribution to the sentence at all, that the PP does not 'really'
contribute an adverbial to the semantics of the sentence, and that the prepositional object is 'really' an argument of the verb. It says all this by stipulating that in all admissible models a sentence containing one of these verbs
and a PP of the appropriate form is logically equivalent to another sentence
which contains no preposition and no complex adverbial and in which the
translation of the verb is replaced by a new constant – a predicate of the
appropriate number of places, one of whose argument positions is occupied
by the prepositional object.

The postulate schema for 3-place verbs is stated in (22); that for 2-place
verbs in (23).

(22a)   If δ is the translation of a lexical item with the features [+ V,
        $+ \_ NP X [_{PP} \alpha NP]]$ where X is any category and α is a pre-
        position with translation α', then:

$$\exists T \, \forall \mathscr{P} \, \forall v^{\langle s, f(X)\rangle} \forall x \, \Box[\alpha'(\mathscr{P})(\hat{\ }\delta(v^{\langle s, f(X)\rangle}))(x)$$

$$\leftrightarrow \mathscr{P}\{\lambda y[[\check{\ }T](x, y, v^{\langle s, f(X)\rangle})]\}]$$

where: T is a variable of type $\langle s, \langle\langle s, f(X)\rangle, \langle e, \langle e, t \rangle\rangle\rangle\rangle$
       $\mathscr{P}$ is a variable of type $\langle s, f(NP)\rangle$
       x and y are variables of type $\langle e\rangle$

(b)   For all δ as defined in (a), δ' is an expression of type $\langle\langle s, f(X)\rangle,$
       $\langle e, \langle e, t\rangle\rangle\rangle$ which is defined in terms of δ as follows:

$$\delta' = \lambda v^{\langle s, f(X)\rangle} \lambda y[\alpha'(\hat{\ }\lambda PP(y))(\hat{\ }\delta(v^{\langle s, f(X)\rangle})))]$$

The joint effect of (a) and (b) is to make (c) a logical truth:

(c) $\Box[\alpha'(\mathscr{P})(\hat{\ }\delta(v^{\langle s, f(X)\rangle}))(x) \leftrightarrow \mathscr{P}\{\lambda y[\delta'(x, y, v^{\langle s, f(X)\rangle})]\}]$

(23a)   If β is the translation of a lexical item with the features [+ V,
        $+ \_ NP [_{PP} \alpha NP]]$, where α is a preposition with translation
        α', then:

$$\exists S \, \forall \mathscr{P} \, \forall x \, \Box[\alpha'(\mathscr{P})(\hat{\ }\beta)(x) \leftrightarrow [\check{\ }S](x, \mathscr{P})]$$

where S is a variable of type $\langle s, \langle\langle s, f(NP)\rangle, \langle e, t \rangle\rangle\rangle$
      $\mathscr{P}$ is a variable of type $\langle s, f(NP)\rangle$
      x is a variable of type $\langle e\rangle$

(b)   For all β as defined in (23a), β' is an expression of type $\langle\langle s, f(NP)\rangle,$ $\langle e, t\rangle\rangle$ which is defined in terms of β as follows:

$$\beta' = \lambda\mathscr{P}[\alpha'(\mathscr{P})(\hat{}\beta)]$$

The joint effect of (a) and (b) is to make (c) a logical truth:

(c) $\Box[\alpha'(\mathscr{P})(\hat{}\beta)(x) \leftrightarrow \beta'(x,\mathscr{P})]$

The syntax of intensional logic is so set up that we cannot collapse these two statements into one. The necessity of making two statements however turns out to be useful because the semantics of the NP governed by the preposition turns out to be quite different in the two cases. The indirect object position of a three-place verb seems always to be extensional. This is reflected in Meaning Postulate (24ab) in the fact that both the first and second argument positions of the 3-place predicate δ' are filled by individual variables. In this way it is ensured that any quantifiers that occur in the prepositional object position of a verb like **tabhair** ('give') or **deir** ('say') will always have wider scope than the verb itself, thus ensuring extensionality.

The two-place verbs behave quite differently in this respect. The verb **tráchtaim** ('I discuss'), for instance, governs the preposition **ar**:

(24)   **Thrácht muid ar leabharthaí Uí Bhriain**
         discussed we   on books   O'Brien's
         'We discussed O'Brien's books'.

But it is clear from examples like (25) that we must let the second argument position be intensional:

(25)   **Tráchtann siad ar lúchorpán**
         discuss   they on a leprechaun
         'They talk about a leprechaun'.

We allow for the intensional reading of such examples by filling the object position of β' in (23c) with the higher type variable $\mathscr{P}$ – a variable over NP-intensions. This will mean that the entire NP (including its quantifiers) can be inside the scope of β', thus allowing for de dicto readings.

Examples requiring these meaning postulates in their interpretation are worked out in (26a) and (26b).

(26a)   **Tabharann Seán a   scian do Mháire**
         gives   his knife to Mary
         'John gives his knife to Mary'.

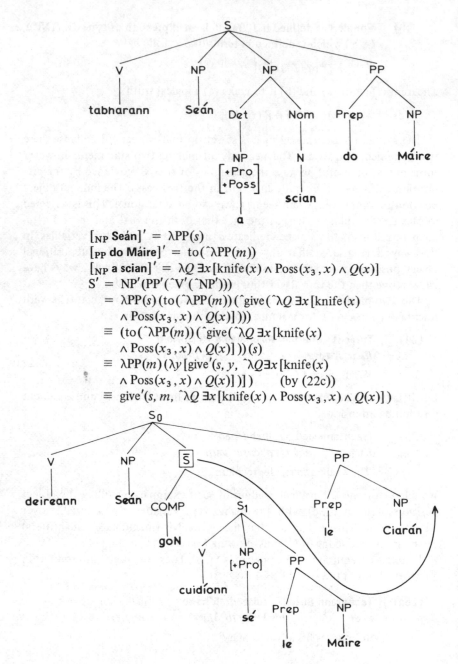

$[_{NP} \text{ Seán}]' = \lambda PP(s)$

$[_{PP} \text{ do Máire}]' = to(^{\frown}\lambda PP(m))$

$[_{NP} \text{ a scian}]' = \lambda Q\, \exists x\,[\text{knife}(x) \wedge \text{Poss}(x_3, x) \wedge Q(x)]$

$S' = NP'(PP'(^{\frown}V'(^{\frown}NP')))$

$\quad = \lambda PP(s)\,(to(^{\frown}\lambda PP(m))\,(^{\frown}\text{give}\,(^{\frown}\lambda Q\, \exists x\,[\text{knife}(x)$
$\qquad \wedge \text{Poss}(x_3, x) \wedge Q(x)]\,)))$

$\quad \equiv (to(^{\frown}\lambda PP(m))\,(^{\frown}\text{give}\,(^{\frown}\lambda Q\, \exists x\,[\text{knife}(x)$
$\qquad \wedge \text{Poss}(x_3, x) \wedge Q(x)]\,))\,(s)$

$\quad \equiv \lambda PP(m)\,(\lambda y\,[\text{give}'(s, y,\ ^{\frown}\lambda Q\exists x\,[\text{knife}(x)$
$\qquad \wedge \text{Poss}(x_3, x) \wedge Q(x)]\,)]\,)\qquad \text{(by (22c))}$

$\quad \equiv \text{give}'(s, m,\ ^{\frown}\lambda Q\, \exists x\,[\text{knife}(x) \wedge \text{Poss}(x_3, x) \wedge Q(x)]\,)$

(26b) **Deireann Seán le Ciarán go   gcuidíonn sé le Máire**
     says   *with*   *COMP helps*   *he with*

'Sean tells Ciarán that he helps Mary'.

$$S' = NP'(PP'(\hat{\ }V'))$$
$$S'_1 = \lambda PP(x_6)(\text{with}(\hat{\ }\lambda PP(m))(\hat{\ }\text{help}))$$
$$\equiv \text{with}(\hat{\ }\lambda PP(m))(\hat{\ }\text{help}))(x_6)$$
$$\equiv \text{help}'(x_6, \hat{\ }\lambda PP(m)) \qquad [\text{by } (23c)]$$
$$\bar{S}' = S'_1$$
$$S' = NP'(PP'(\hat{\ }V'(\hat{\ }\bar{S}')))$$
$$S'_0 = \lambda PP(s)(\text{with}(\hat{\ }\lambda PP(c))(\hat{\ }\text{say}(\hat{\ }\bar{S}')))$$
$$\equiv \text{with}(\hat{\ }\lambda PP(c))(\hat{\ }\text{say}(\hat{\ }\bar{S}'))(s)$$
$$\equiv \lambda PP(c)(\lambda y[\text{say}'(s, y, \hat{\ }\bar{S}')]) \qquad [\text{by } (22c)]$$
$$\equiv \text{say}'(s, c, \hat{\ }\bar{S}')$$
$$\equiv \text{say}'(s, c, \hat{\ }\text{help}'(x_6, \hat{\ }\lambda PP(m)))$$

For those 2-place verbs subcategorized for a preposition, whose second argument position is extensional (**cuidigh** ('help') and **feall** ('betray') in the present fragment, for instance) we can adapt the Meaning Postulate of PTQ that guarantees the extensionality of certain transitive verbs:

(27a)   If β is the translation of **cuidigh** or **feall** then:

$$\exists S \forall x \forall \mathscr{P} \Box [\beta'(x, \mathscr{P}) \leftrightarrow \mathscr{P}\{\lambda y[[\hat{\ }S](x, y)]\}]$$

where S is a variable of type $\langle s, \langle e, \langle e, t\rangle\rangle\rangle$ and other variables are as before.

(b)   For all β as defined in (a), β'_* is an expression of type $\langle e, \langle e, t\rangle\rangle$ which is defined in terms of β' as follows:

$$\beta'_* = \lambda x \lambda y \, \beta'(y, \hat{\ }\lambda PP(x))$$

Once again, the joint effect of (a) and (b) is to make (c) a logical truth:

(c) $\Box[\beta'(x, y, \mathscr{P}) \leftrightarrow \mathscr{P}\{\lambda y[\beta'_*(x, y)]\}]$

The β' of (27) is the constant defined in the original postulate (23). The new constants associated at double remove with **cuidigh** and **feall** are help$'_*$ and betray$'_*$ and are of type $\langle e, \langle e, t\rangle\rangle$. That is, they denote sets of ordered pairs – the sets of ordered pairs that stand in the helping and the betraying relation respectively to one another. Postulate (27) allows a further reduction of the translation expression of (26b). By (27c) the final expression of (26b) is equivalent to (28):

(28) $\text{say}'(s, c \ \text{help}'_*(x_6, m))$

Similarly, for those 3-place verbs whose direct object position is extensional (e.g. **tabhair** ('give') or **iarr** ('ask (for)')), we can define a meaning postulate that guarantees their extensionality in this respect:

(29a)   If δ is the translation of **tabhair** or **iarr** then:

$$\exists D \forall \mathscr{P} \ \forall x \forall y \Box [\delta'(x, y, \mathscr{P}) \leftrightarrow \mathscr{P}\{\lambda z \, [[\check{~} D] \, (x, y, z)]\}]$$

where $\mathscr{P}$ is a variable of type $\langle s, f(\text{NP}) \rangle$
x, y are variables of type $\langle e \rangle$
D is a variable of type $\langle s, \langle e, \langle e, \langle e, t \rangle \rangle \rangle \rangle$

(b)   For all δ as defined in (29a) δ'_* is a constant of type $\langle e, \langle e, \langle e, t \rangle \rangle \rangle$ which is defined in terms of δ' as follows:

$$\delta'_* = \lambda x \lambda y \lambda z \ \delta'(x, y, \check{~}\lambda P P(z))$$

So (c) is a logical truth:

(c) $\Box [\delta'(x, y, \mathscr{P}) \leftrightarrow \mathscr{P}\{\lambda z \, [\delta'_*(x, y, z)]\}]$

This postulate in combination with the schema (22) reduces 3-place verbs like **tabhair** ('give') or **iarr** ('ask') to 3-place relations among individuals denoted by 'give$'_*$' and 'ask$'_*$' respectively. The final formula in (26a), for instance, can be further reduced to (30) by means of (29c):

(30) $\exists x \, [\text{knife}(x) \wedge \text{Poss}(x_3 x) \wedge \text{give}'_*(s, m, x)]$

The interest of this general approach to the problem of preposition government lies in the fact that by making use of the rich semantic apparatus made available by Montague Grammar, we can treat the syntactic facts in a maximally simple – maximally autonomous, if you like – way.

7.6. NOUN PHRASES

I argued earlier for the adoption of the NP $\bar{\text{S}}$ analysis of relatives for Irish. Evidence for this conclusion came from the syntax of relative clauses themselves and also from the fact that the NP $\bar{\text{S}}$ analysis allows us to capture the syntactic relation between relatives and nominal constituent questions.

The NP $\bar{\text{S}}$ structure for relatives is not, however, compatible with the standard semantic analysis of relative clauses within the framework of Montague Grammar (and logical semantics in general). The problem is this. For a complex NP like (31):

(31)   **achan fear aL phósann ＿ maighdean mara**
       every man   marries   a mermaid

'every man who marries a mermaid'

we want to end up with a translation expression like (32):

(32) $\lambda Q \forall x [(\text{man}(x) \wedge \text{marry}(x, \text{a-mermaid}')) \rightarrow Q(x)]$

This expression denotes the set of sets of which all those individuals that are men and who marry a mermaid are members. The problem that the NP $\bar{S}$ structure poses is that on the standard account, the NP **achan fear** has the translation (33):

(33) $\lambda Q \forall x [\text{man}(x) \rightarrow Q(x)]$

There is no way to combine this expression with the translation of a relative clause because there is no variable in (33) for which the set formed by the operation of lambda-abstraction from the translation of the relative clause can be substituted.

The solution to this problem proposed by Emmon Bach and Robin Cooper (Cooper 1975, Bach and Cooper 1978) is to include in the translation of all the determiners and quantifiers an occurrence of a free variable R (a variable over sets of individuals in our system) so that the translations of the definite article, the indefinite article and the quantifier **achan** (if it were included in the fragment) would be as in (34):

(34a) $g(\text{an})$ $= \lambda P \lambda Q \exists x [\forall y [(P(y) \wedge R(y)) \rightarrow x=y] \wedge Q(x)]$

  (b) $g(\emptyset)$ $= \lambda P \lambda Q \exists x [P(x) \wedge R(x) \wedge Q(x)]$

  (c) $g(\text{achan}) = \lambda P \lambda Q \forall x [(P(x) \wedge R(x)) \rightarrow Q(x)]$

The translation rule for combining the translation of the head NP with the translation of the clause binds the R-variable with a lambda-operator, and applies the resultant function to the set of individuals formed from the relative clause by lambda-abstraction. This set then substitutes in for the R-variable, yielding an expression like (32).

The translation rule must do a little more than this though. We must allow for iterative stacking of relative clauses. In the syntactic scheme proposed here the recursion is through NP:

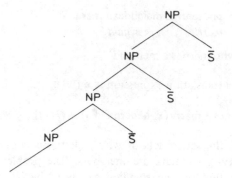

Once the translation of the lowest $\bar{\text{S}}$ goes in for the R-variable of the lowest NP, how will the translations of the higher clauses be introduced? There is no more room for another complex property in (32) than there is in (33).

To take care of this we have the translation rule bring in with the translation of the relative clause another occurrence of R which will hold a place for any other relative clauses that might be waiting up the tree. The final form of the rule is then as in (35):

(35)

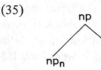 $np' = \lambda R[np'] \, (\lambda x_n \, [\bar{\text{S}}' \wedge R(x_n)])$

This rule deals with both interrogative and non-interrogative noun phrases which have relative clauses. In this secion though we will be concerned only with its non-interrogative aspect.

Recall that the NP-head is indexed to a pronoun under $\bar{\text{S}}$. The rule reads off this index to know what variable in the translation of the relative clause to form the lambda abstract over. This ensures in turn that the variable corresponding to the bound pronoun in the relative clause will be bound by the quantifier of the head NP. This pronoun is also of course the one that is deleted by Relative Deletion. Example (36) illustrates how the rule is supposed to work.

garda   aL phósann _ Deirdre
a policeman   marries

'a policeman that marries Deirdre'

(36)

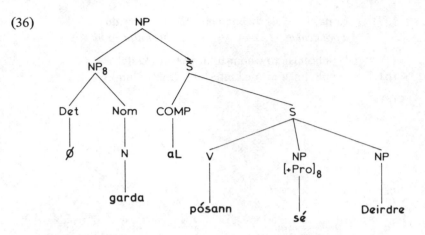

1. $\bar{S}' = S' = \text{marry}_*(x_8, d)$

2. $[_{NP_8}\emptyset\ \text{garda}]' = \lambda P\lambda Q\exists x\,[P(x) \wedge R(x) \wedge Q(x)]\ (\textit{policeman})$

        $\equiv \lambda Q\exists x\,[\text{policeman}(x) \wedge R(x) \wedge Q(x)]$

3. $NP' = \lambda R\,[\lambda Q\exists x\,[\text{policeman}(x) \wedge R(x) \wedge Q(x)]\,]$

        $(\lambda x_8\,[\text{marry}_*(x_8, d) \wedge R(x_8)]\,)$

        $\equiv \lambda Q\exists x\,[\text{policeman}(x) \wedge \text{marry}_*(x, d) \wedge R(x) \wedge Q(x)]$

Pronoun-retaining relative clauses are treated in exactly the same way. Both interpretations of an ambiguous example involving pronoun-retention are worked out in (37a) and (37b). The ambiguity of course turns on which of the two pronouns is interpreted as the bound pronoun. A complex example involving relativation into an embedded clause is treated in (38) and finally an example involving stacking is given in (39). The end result in this case is an expression of intensional logic which denotes the set of sets of which the unique individual that is a man, that is seen by Sean that writes a letter and that has some unspecified property R is a member.

One result of setting things up in this way is that every NP that has a determiner or a quantifier will have a free variable R in its translation expression. This will mean that they will be interpreted demonstratively – their meanings will depend in part on the context in which they are used. In Montague (1974a) a context of use is defined as consisting in part of an assignment of values to free variables. Thus the variable R will be assigned

(37)   **garda   aN dtabharann Seán a   scian dó**
        a policeman   gives   his knife to him

(a)   'a policeman to whom John gives his knife'
(b)   'a policeman whose knife John gives to him'

(a)

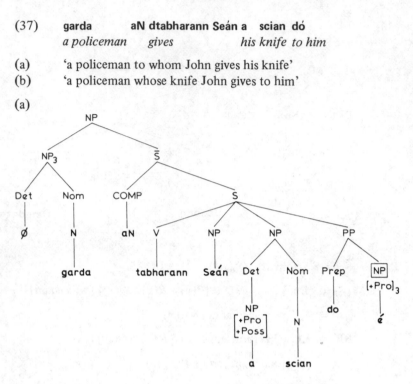

$$\overline{S}' \; = S' \; = \; \exists x \,[\mathrm{knife}(x) \wedge \mathrm{Poss}(x_6,x) \wedge \mathrm{give}'_*(s,x_3,x)]$$

$$\mathrm{NP}'_3 \; = \; \lambda Q \exists x\,[\mathrm{policeman}(x) \wedge R(x) \wedge Q(x)]$$

$$\mathrm{NP}' \; = \; \lambda R\,[\mathrm{NP}'_3]\,(\lambda x_3\,[\overline{S}' \wedge R(x_3)])$$

$$\equiv \; \lambda Q \exists x\,[\mathrm{policeman}(x) \wedge \exists y\,[\mathrm{knife}(y) \wedge \mathrm{Poss}(x_6,y)$$

$$\wedge \, \mathrm{give}'_*(s,x,y)] \wedge Q(x)]$$

(37b)

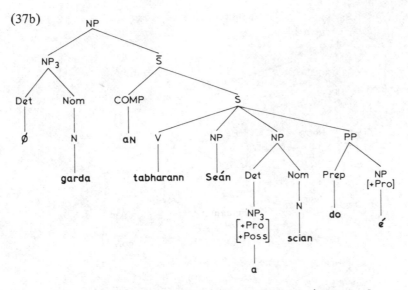

$$\bar{S}' = S' = \exists x\,[\text{knife}(x) \land \text{Poss}(x_3,x) \land \text{give}'_*(s,x_6,x)]$$
$$NP'_3 = \lambda Q\exists y\,[\text{policeman}(y) \land R(y) \land Q(y)]$$
$$NP' = \lambda R\,[NP'_3]\,(\lambda x_3\,[\bar{S}' \land R(x_3)])$$
$$\equiv \lambda Q\exists y\,[\text{policeman}(y) \land \exists x\,[\text{knife}(x) \land \text{Poss}(y,x)$$
$$\land \text{give}'_*(s,x_6,x)] \land Q(y)]$$

(38) **Imíonn an fear aN   gcreideann Ciarán goN   gcuidíonn Máire**
leaves   the man COMP believes   COMP helps

leis
with him

'The man leaves whom Ciarán believes that Mary helps'

$$\bar{S}'_2 = S'_2 = \text{help}'_*(m,x_7)$$
$$\bar{S}'_1 = S'_1 = \text{believe}\,(c,\,\hat{}\,\text{help}'_*(m,x_7))$$
$$NP'_7 = \lambda Q\exists x\,[\forall y\,[(\text{man}(y) \land R(y)) \leftrightarrow x{=}y] \land Q(x)]$$
$$NP' = \lambda R\,[NP'_7]\,(\lambda x_7\,[\bar{S}'_1 \land R(x_7)])$$
$$\lambda Q\exists x\,[\forall y\,[(\text{man}(y) \land \text{believe}\,(c,\,\hat{}\,\text{help}'_*(m,y))$$
$$\land R(y)) \leftrightarrow x{=}y] \land Q(x)]$$
$$S'_0 = NP'(V')$$
$$= \exists x\,[\forall y\,[(\text{man}(y) \land \text{believe}\,(c,\,\hat{}\,\text{help}'_*(m,y))$$
$$\land R(y)) \leftrightarrow x{=}y] \land \text{leave}(x)]$$

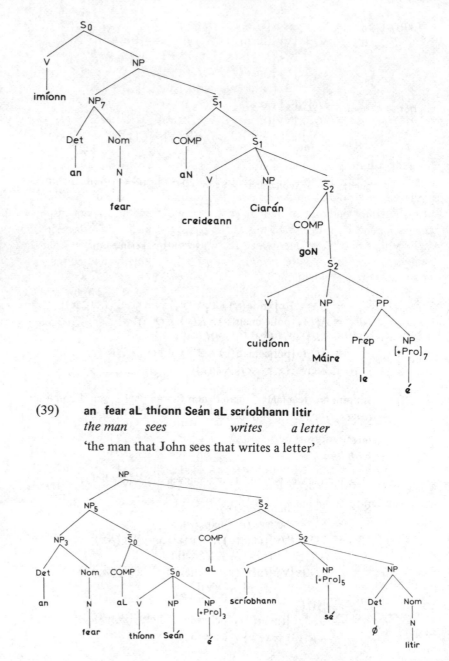

(39)   an fear aL thíonn Seán aL scríobhann litir
       the man   sees   writes   a letter
       'the man that John sees that writes a letter'

$$\bar{S}_0' = S_0' = \text{see}_*(s, x_3)$$
$$NP_3' = \lambda Q \exists x [\forall y [(\text{man}(y) \wedge R(y)) \leftrightarrow x=y] \wedge Q(x)]$$
$$NP_5' = \lambda R [NP_3'] (\lambda x_3 [\text{see}_*(s, x_3) \wedge R(x_3)])$$
$$\equiv \lambda Q \exists x [\forall y [(\text{man}(y) \wedge \text{see}_*(s, y) \wedge R(y)) \leftrightarrow x=y] \wedge Q(x)]$$
$$\bar{S}_2' = S_2' = \exists x [\text{letter}(x) \wedge \text{write}_*(x_5, x)]$$
$$NP' = \lambda R [NP_5'] (\lambda x_5 [\bar{S}_2' \wedge R(x_5)])$$
$$\equiv \lambda Q \exists x [\forall y [(\text{man}(y) \wedge \text{see}_*(s, y) \wedge \exists z [\text{letter}(z)$$
$$\wedge \text{write}_*(y, z)] \wedge R(z)) \leftrightarrow x=y] \wedge Q(x)]$$

different values in different contexts of use. In this way we can take it as specifying pragmatic limitations on the set that the quantifiers that occur in the Det-position of an NP can range over. It is an old observation that quantifiers and determiners require such pragmatic limitation. For instance, when someone says 'Everyone was at the party last night' there is clearly an implicit limit on the set over which the universal quantifier ranges. What the sentence means is that all the members of some contextually-defined set – the set of Linguistics students at UT, the set of common friends of the people talking, whatever – were at the party. Under our proposals, the sentence will have the translation in (40). This will

(40) $\forall x [(\text{person}(x) \wedge R(x)) \rightarrow H(\text{at-the-party}'(x)]$

count as true in some context of use just in case an appropriate value is assigned to R – the set of Linguistics students at UT, for instance.

Notice that NP containing relative clauses stand in need of this contextual restriction just as much as those that do not. In an example like the following – 'Everyone who drank champagne last night got hopelessly drunk' – the set over which the universal quantifier ranges must also be limited (imagine, for instance, the sentence being uttered on New Year's Day). Since on the analysis proposed here NP with relative clauses will also contain an occurrence of R (introduced by the relative clause interpretation rule) this pragmatic limitation is accounted for in exactly the same way as in the case of NP without relative clauses.

What this analysis amounts to is a formalization of the idea that the range of quantifiers in NP can be limited either explicitly by means of a relative clause or implicitly by means of a pragmatically given property which restricts membership in the set over which the quantifier is to range.[4] In this sense it can be thought of as a formalization of Vendler's (1967) proposal that every occurrence of the definite article be understood as containing an implicit relative clause.

(41)   **iarrann Seán úll**   **ar an fhear mhór chlúiteach aL phósann**
         asks   *an apple on the man great famous*   *marries*

         Máire _
         Mary

         'Seán asks the great famous man whom Mary marries for an apple'.

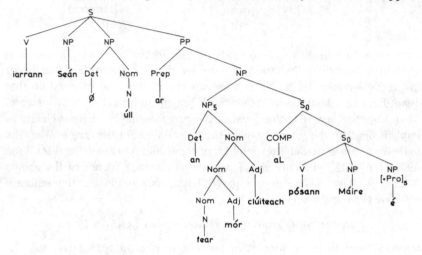

1. $\bar{S}'_0 = S'_0 = \text{marry}_*(m, x_5)$
2. $[_{\text{Nom}} \textbf{fear mór}]' = \text{great}(\hat{\ }\text{man})$
3. $[_{\text{Nom}} \textbf{fear mór clúiteach}]' = \text{famous}(\hat{\ }\text{great}(\hat{\ }\text{man}))$
4. $NP'_5 = \text{Det}'(\text{Nom}')$
        $= \lambda Q \exists x [\forall y [(\text{famous}(\hat{\ }\text{great}(\hat{\ }\text{man}))(y) \wedge R(y)) \leftrightarrow x=y]$
        $\wedge Q(x)]$
5. $NP' = \lambda R [NP'_5] (\lambda x_5 [\bar{S}'_0 \wedge R(x_5)])$
        $\equiv \lambda Q \exists x [\forall y [(\text{famous}(\hat{\ }\text{great}(\hat{\ }\text{man}))(y) \wedge \text{marry}_*(m, y)$
        $\wedge R(y)) \leftrightarrow x=y] \wedge Q(x)]$
6. $PP' = \text{on}(\hat{\ }NP')$
7. $S' = NP'(PP'(\hat{\ }V'(\hat{\ }NP')))$
8. $[_{NP} \emptyset \textbf{úll}] = \lambda Q \exists x [\text{apple}(x) \wedge R(x) \wedge Q(x)]$
9. $S' = \lambda PP(s)(PP'(\hat{\ }\text{ask}(\hat{\ }\lambda Q \exists x [\text{apple}(x) \wedge R(x) \wedge Q(x)])))$
        $\equiv PP'(\hat{\ }\text{ask}(\hat{\ }\lambda Q \exists x [\text{apple}(x) \wedge R(x) \wedge Q(x)]))(s)$
        $\equiv \hat{\ }\lambda Q \exists x [\forall y [(\text{famous}(\hat{\ }\text{great}(\hat{\ }\text{man}))(y) \wedge \text{marry}_*(m, y)$
        $\wedge R(y)) \leftrightarrow x=y] \wedge Q(x)] \{\lambda y [\text{ask}'(s, y, (\hat{\ }\lambda Q \exists x [\text{apple}(x)$
        $\wedge R(x) \wedge Q(x)]))]\}$ [by (22c)]

$$\equiv \exists x [\forall y [(\text{famous}(\hat{\ }\text{great}(\hat{\ }\text{man}))(y) \wedge \text{marry}_*(m, y)$$
$$\wedge R(y)) \leftrightarrow x{=}y] \wedge \text{ask}'(s, x, (\hat{\ }\lambda Q \exists x [\text{apple}(x) \wedge R(x)$$
$$\wedge Q(x)]))]$$
$$\equiv \exists x [\forall y [(\text{famous}(\hat{\ }\text{great}(\hat{\ }\text{man}))(y) \wedge \text{marry}_*(m, y)$$
$$\wedge R(y)) \leftrightarrow x{=}y] \wedge \exists z [\text{apple}(z) \wedge R(z) \wedge \text{ask}'_*(s, x, z)]]$$
$$[\text{by (29c)}]$$

I find this analysis intuitively appealing but there is much that is questionable about it semantically. In particular it requires a rather elaborate theory of the interpretation of free variables. Note that there can be many occurrences of the R-variable in a single sentence – every NP with a determiner will have one. Different values must be assigned to R then not just with respect to a context of use but also with respect to a particular occurrence in a formula of intensional logic – the third occurrence must receive (at least potentially) a different value than will the second and so on. The interpretation of indexicals may require such elaborate apparatus – Taylor (to appear) presents such a theory for the interpretation of demonstratives in English, though within a slightly different semantic framework than that assumed here.

Let me end this section with one final example to illustrate the flexibility of this system. In (42) we have an example in which the relative clause itself is a Cleft sentence:

(42)   **an fear arb é a rothar aL   ghoideann Seán _**
       the man COMP his bicycle COMP steals

       'the man whose bicycle it is that John steals'.

The item **arb** in COMP position in (42) is the regular morphological result of combining the copula with the complementizer **aN**. The pronoun following this element is the extra pronoun that regularly appears in copular sentences with definite NP's (*cf.* Chapter 3, Section 8, pp.90–91). If we can be allowed to suppress these details then example (42) derives from an indexed deep structure (43) (overleaf):

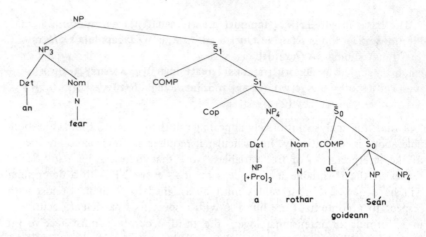

The indexing rule for Clefts ((27) of Chapter 4) binds the empty NP_4 of the lowest clause to the focus NP **a rothar**. The indexing rule for relatives and questions ((7) of Chapter 4) looks inside this NP and binds the possessive pronoun to the head of the relative clause ($[_{NP}$ **an fear**]). The semantics will work as in (44). We have not included a treatment of Clefts in the formal definition of the fragment but our proposed treatment is sketched in fair detail in Chapter 4.

(44) $NP_4' = {}^{\vee}\mathscr{P}_4$ [by (29) of Chapter 4]

$S_0' = \bar{S}_0' = \text{steal}(s, {}^{\wedge\vee}\mathscr{P}_4) \equiv \text{steal}(s, \mathscr{P}_4)$

$S_1' = \bar{S}_1' = \lambda\mathscr{P}_4[\bar{S}_0']\ ({}^{\wedge}[\textbf{a rothar}]')$ [by (31) of Chap. 4]

$\equiv \lambda\mathscr{P}_4[\text{steal}(s, \mathscr{P}_4)]\ ({}^{\wedge}\lambda Q\exists x[\text{bicycle}(x) \wedge \text{Poss}(x_3, x)$
$\wedge Q(x)])$

$\equiv \text{steal}(s, {}^{\wedge}\lambda Q\exists x[\text{bicycle}(x) \wedge \text{Poss}(x_3, x) \wedge Q(x)])$

$\equiv \exists x[\text{bicycle}(x) \wedge \text{Poss}(x_3, x) \wedge \text{steal}_*(s, x)]$

$NP_3' = \lambda Q\exists x[\forall y[(\text{man}(y) \wedge R(y)) \leftrightarrow x=y] \wedge Q(x)]$

$NP' = \lambda R[NP_3']\ (\lambda x_3[\bar{S}_1' \wedge R(x_3)])$

$\equiv \lambda Q\exists x[\forall y[(\text{man}(y) \wedge \exists z[\text{bicycle}(z) \wedge \text{Poss}(y, z)$
$\wedge \text{steal}_*(s, z) \wedge R(y)]) \leftrightarrow x=y] \wedge Q(x)]$

7.7. QUESTIONS

The account of the semantics of questions to be given here is based on recent work of Lauri Karttunen and Stanley Peters (Karttunen 1977a, 1977b, Karttunen and Peters 1976, Peters 19''7).

The basic insight in this approach to the semantics of questions is that questions of all kinds (Yes/No Questions, Alternative Questions, Constituent Questions) should be regarded as having the same denotation-type – they can be regarded as denoting sets of true propositions. More specifically, a question denotes the set of true propositions that jointly constitute a true and complete answer to that question.

This system has several important advantages over previous attempts to explicate the semantics of questions. One of the facts we stressed in the course of defending the existence of a syntactic category Q was that questions of all types share the same distribution. Having one syntactic category and therefore one semantic type embrace questions of all kinds lets us state this distribution in a maximally simple way. Having that semantic type be that of sets of true propositions provides an intuitively satisfying account of their semantics. Consider Alternative Questions first. It is natural to think of Alternative Questions as providing a list of propositions and enquiring about the membership of that set which contains only the true propositions of that list. So when a speaker asks (45) he can be thought of as asking for the membership of the

(45)   Is there someone in the next room or is the TV still on?

the set of true propositions in the list {'There is someone in the next room', 'The TV is still on'}. Here the alternatives presented to the listener are completely distinct propositions, although there is an assumption that only one of the presented alternatives is true. Yes/No questions can then be regarded as being the special case of an Alternative Question in which the relevant set from which the true propositions are to be selected contains a proposition and its negation. So when someone asks 'Is it raining?' he is asking for the membership of the unit set which contains whichever member of the set {'It is raining', 'It is not raining'} is true.

Constituent questions also fall into this schema. They too supply a list of propositions from which the set of true propositions is to be selected. Unlike Alternative Questions though, they define this set of propositions, not by means of a listing but in an open-ended way by quantification. So if I ask:

(46)   Which quartets did Beethoven write in 1826?

what I am asking for is the membership of the set of true propositions of the form 'Beethoven wrote x in 1826' where x ranges over string quartets.

This account generalizes in a very natural way to deal with the semantics of embedded questions. Consider (47) for instance:

(47)

$$
\text{John}
\begin{Bmatrix}
\text{didn't know} \\
\text{wondered}
\end{Bmatrix}
\begin{Bmatrix}
\text{whether or not it was raining} \\
\text{if there was someone in the next} \\
\text{room or if the TV was still on} \\
\text{which quartets Beethoven wrote} \\
\text{in 1826}
\end{Bmatrix}
$$

These sentences are true just in case John was ignorant of or curious about the membership of the set of propositions denoted by the embedded question.

Requiring that questions denote sets of *true* propositions accounts for some otherwise mysterious characteristics of some question-embedding verbs, such as *tell*. *Tell* is not normally factive. (48) neither entails nor presupposes that its complement is true:

(48)   John told me that Beethoven wrote the Grosse Fuge in 1826

(49) however, does entail that John told me the truth.[5]

(49)   John told me which quartets Beethoven wrote in 1826.

This fact falls out naturally from an account in which questions denote sets of *true* propositions. This requirement also provides a natural account of the meaning of question-embedding verbs like *depend*. On the analysis proposed here, a sentence like (50):

(50)   What theory you believe in depends on what department you were trained in

says that the membership of the set of true propositions of the form 'you believe in x' where x ranges over theories is a function of the membership of the set of true propositions of the form 'you were trained in y' where y ranges over departments. This is a satisfying account of the meaning of the verb *depend* which is missed by other proposals that have been made with respect to the semantics of questions.

For a more detailed defence of this general approach and for a discussion of alternative proposals see Karttunen (1977a).

One point that should be made before we turn to the formal details is that the semantics that we will define here is really a semantics for embedded questions. Karttunen's account is traditional in that it assumes that embedded questions are basic semantically and that the semantic properties of matrix questions are derivable in one way or another from the semantics of embedded questions.

There are various ways in which we could set this up. We could follow Karttunen (1977a) in proposing the existence of a special interrogative performative operator '?' which turns questions into declarative clauses of a certain kind – clauses that mean 'I ask you to tell me Q'.

Alternatively one could follow the line of Cresswell (1973)[6] and hold that such distinctions are not to be made in the formal theory of semantics but rather in a theory of language use. So just as we must give an account of how it is that the uttering of an expression of type $\langle t \rangle$ (a declarative clause) can count as an assertion of a proposition, so we must give an account as well of how it is that the uttering of an expression of type $\langle\langle s, t \rangle, t \rangle$ (an interrogative clause) can count as the asking of a question.

I am inclined to this second approach, but this is not a question I will go into here. It should be remembered though that the semantics I will be defining here is properly speaking a semantics for embedded questions and will have to be supplemented in one way or another to provide an account of matrix questions.

Technically the analysis will work as follows. Questions will be assigned translation expressions of the form $\lambda p(\phi)$ where ϕ is an expression of type $\langle t \rangle$. p is the proposition variable – that is, a variable of type $\langle s, t \rangle$. The whole expression will then denote a function from propositions to truth-values – that is to say a set of propositions.

Consider how this will work in the case of Yes/No Questions to begin with We want a question like (51) to denote the unit set containing either the proposition that Ciarán beats Deirdre or that he doesn't, whichever is true at a particular world and time. On our analysis, (51a) has the structure (51b).

(51a)   **AnN mbuaileann Ciarán Deirdre?**
        Int   beats

'Does Ciaran beat Deirdre?'

(b)

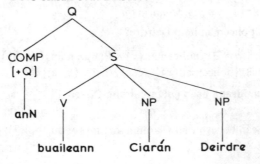

We assign to the interrogative complementizer the translation in (52).

(52) $\lambda q \lambda p [\check{\ } p \wedge [(p{=}q) \vee (p{=}\hat{\ }\neg\check{\ }q)]]$

We already have a rule that builds clause meanings out of the meanings of complementizers and S's. This is the simple rule of intensional functional application repeated in (53):

(53)

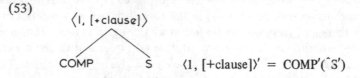

$\langle 1, [+\text{clause}]\rangle' = \text{COMP}'(\hat{\ }\text{S}')$

In the cases we have seen so far (that is, cases where the complementizer is non-interrogative – **aL**, **aN**, or **goN**) the effect of this operation is semantically trivial. Non-interrogative complementizers have what is in essence an identity function as their meaning. In the case of the interrogative complementizer though, the semantic effect is not trivial. In the case of (51) we get (54):

(54) $Q' = \text{COMP}'(\hat{\ }\text{S}')$
        $[{+}Q]$
        $= \lambda q \lambda p [\check{\ } p \wedge [(p{=}q) \vee (p{=}\hat{\ }\neg\check{\ }q)]] (\hat{\ }\text{beat}_*(c, d))$
        $\equiv \lambda p [\check{\ } p \wedge [(p{=}\hat{\ }\text{beat}_*(c, d)) \vee (p{=}\hat{\ }\neg\check{\ }\hat{\ }\text{beat}_*(c, d))]]$
        $\equiv \lambda p [\check{\ } p \wedge [(p{=}\hat{\ }\text{beat}_*(c, d)) \vee (p{=}\hat{\ }\neg\text{beat}_*(c, d))]]$

This expression denotes at a given world and time the unit set of propositions which contains either the proposition 'Ciarán beats Deirdre' or the proposition 'Ciarán does not beat Deirdre' whichever happens to be true at that world and time.

Some examples of the meaning assigned by this system are given in (55).

(55a)   **AnN gcuidíonn garda   le Deirdre**
        Int   helps   a policeman with

        'Does a policeman help Deirdre?'

        $\lambda p [\check{\ } p \wedge [(p{=}\hat{\ }\exists x [\text{policeman}(x) \wedge R(x) \wedge \text{help}_*(x, d)])$
        $\vee (p{=}\hat{\ }\neg\exists x [\text{policeman}(x) \wedge R(x) \wedge \text{help}_*(x, d)])]]$

(b)   **AnN gcreideann Seán goN n-iarrann Ciarán úll   air**
        Int   believes   asks   an apple on him

        'Does Seán believe that Ciarán asks him for an apple?'

$$\lambda p[\check{\ }p \wedge [(p=\hat{\ }\text{believe}(s, \hat{\ }\exists x[\text{apple}(x) \wedge R(x) \wedge \text{ask}'_*(c, x_5, x)]))$$
$$\vee (p=\hat{\ }\neg\text{believe}(s, \hat{\ }\exists x[\text{apple}(x) \wedge R(x) \wedge \text{ask}'_*(c, x_5, x)]))]]$$

One of the consequences of the analysis proposed here is that corresponding positive and negative Yes/No Questions will be assigned identical meanings. To see this, consider the negative question corresponding to (51):

(56)   **NachN   mbuaileann Ciarán Deirdre**
         NEG Int beats

         'Doesn't Ciarán beat Deirdre?'

I have not given a treatment of negation here but let's assume for a moment that we have one. The schematic structure for (56) will be (57a) (assuming for the moment an analysis of the negative forms of complementizers in which NEG begins under S and is hopped into COMP to derive **nachN** and **nárL** (the non-Past and Past forms respectively)).

(57a)

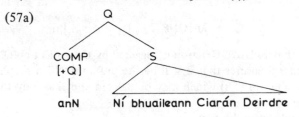

This structure will be interpreted as (b).

(b) $S' = [\neg\text{beat}_*(c, d)]$
       $Q' = \text{COMP}'(\hat{\ }[\neg\text{beat}_*(c, d)])$
       $[+Q]$
       $= \lambda p[\check{\ }p \wedge [(p=\hat{\ }\neg\text{beat}_*(c, d)) \vee (p=\hat{\ }\neg\check{\ }\hat{\ }\neg\text{beat}_*(c, d))]]$
       $\equiv \lambda p[\check{\ }p \wedge [(p=\hat{\ }\neg\text{beat}_*(c, d)) \vee (p=\hat{\ }\neg\neg\text{beat}_*(c, d))]]$
       $\equiv \lambda p[\check{\ }p \wedge [(p=\hat{\ }\neg\text{beat}_*(c, d)) \vee (p=\hat{\ }\text{beat}_*(c, d))]]$

This expression is of course equivalent to (54).

This is an appropriate result it seems. The Irish questions in (51) and (56) differ in meaning in much the same way as do the corresponding English questions. The difference is not one that has to do with the truth-conditional aspects of meaning. Both negative and positive questions ask for the same information – whether he beats her or not. At the level of truth-conditional meaning then, both should have the same value. The difference of course is that the utterer of the negative question expects the answer 'Yes' while

the positive question is neutral in this respect. That is, the two questions
are used appropriately only given different assumptions on the part of the
speaker – the differences are differences at the level of implicated meaning
rather than at the level of denotative meaning.

The rule for interpreting nominal constituent questions is similar in many
respects to that for relative clauses – as we might expect given the deep-
seated syntactic parallels that hold between the two constructions. What
happens here essentially is that the interrogative noun phrase is quantified
in to the translation of the questioned clause over a variable distinguished
by the indexing rule for relatives and questions. The resulting expression also
has its type raise to the level $\langle\langle s, t \rangle, t\rangle$ by the introduction of appropriate
syncategorematic material. The rule is restated in (58):

(58)

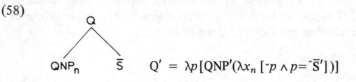

$$Q' = \lambda p\,[\mathrm{QNP}'(\lambda x_n\,[\,\check{}p \wedge p = \hat{}\,\bar{S}'])]$$

Once again the fact that Relative Deletion is triggered by the indices on QNP
and the pronoun under $\bar{S}$ ensures that it will be the pronoun which supplies
the distinguished variable for (58) which may be deleted and that only that
pronoun may be deleted.

Consider some simple examples first.

(59)   **Cé aL phósann __ Deirdre**
          who   marries
          'Who marries Deirdre?'

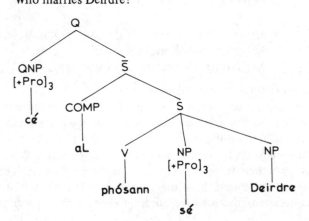

We assign to the interrogative pronouns **cé** ('who') and **caidé** ('what') the same translation as to indefinitely quantified NP:

(60) $g(\mathbf{c\acute{e}})$ $= \lambda P \exists x [\text{person}(x) \wedge R(x) \wedge P(x)]$ [7]

     $g(\mathbf{caid\acute{e}}) = \lambda P \exists x [\neg \text{person}(x) \wedge R(x) \wedge P(x)]$

The translation of the question will be built up as follows. By rules that should by now be familiar,

$$\bar{S}' = S' = \text{marry}_*(x_3, d)$$

By rule (58) then, the whole question will be interpreted as in (61):

(61) $Q' = \lambda p [\lambda P \exists x [\text{person}(x) \wedge R(x) \wedge P(x)]$
     $(\lambda x_3 [\check{\,} p \wedge p = \hat{\,} \text{marry}_*(x_3, d)])]$

     $\equiv \lambda p [\exists x [\text{person}(x) \wedge R(x) \wedge \check{\,} p \wedge p = \hat{\,} \text{marry}_*(x, d)]]$

This expression denotes the set of true propositions of the form 'x marries Deirdre' where x is a person and is a member of a contextually appropriate set.

A more complex example is worked out in (62). The final expression in (62) denotes the set of propositions that are true and are of the form 'John thinks that he$_5$ asks Noel for x' where x ranges over contextually relevant non-persons.

A different kind of complex example is worked out in (63). In this case we have a relative clause adjoined to the interrogative pronoun. Recall that the interpretation rule for relative clauses is stated in terms of np – that is, the same rule applies in both interrogative and non-interrogative noun phrases:

np

np$_n$ $\bar{S}$ $\text{np}' = \lambda R [\text{np}'] (\lambda x_n [\bar{S}' \wedge R(x_n)])$

Stage 3 of the interpretation (63) involves the interrogative aspect of this rule. The final translation expression for (63) denotes the set of propositions that are true and that are of the form 'He$_4$ marries x' where x ranges over the set of contextually relevant people that Ciaran kisses.

Finally we present an example, (64), in which the question is embedded under a question-embedding verb. The final translation for this example says that the policeman asks Mary for the membership of the set of true propositions of the form 'she$_3$ thinks that Sean steals x' where again x ranges over contextually relevant things.

(62)   **Caidé aL shíleann Seán aL iarrann sé ar Nollaig?**
what   thinks   asks   he on

'What does John think he asks Noel for?'

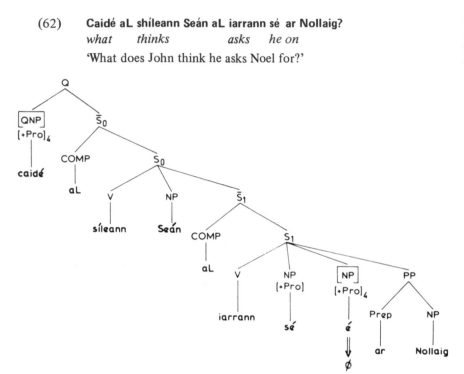

1. $\overline{S}'_1 = S'_1 = \text{NP}'(\text{PP}'(\hat{\ }\text{V}'(\hat{\ }\text{NP}')))$
            $= \text{on}(\hat{\ }\lambda\text{PP}(n))(\hat{\ }\text{ask}(\hat{\ }\lambda\text{PP}(x_4)))(x_5)$
            $\equiv \text{ask}'(x_5, n, \hat{\ }\lambda\text{PP}(x_4))$ [by (22c)]
            $\equiv \text{ask}'_*(x_5, n, x_4)$ [by (29c)]

2. $\overline{S}'_0 = S'_0 = \text{NP}'(\text{V}'(\hat{\ }\overline{S}'))$

            $= \lambda\text{PP}(s)(\text{think}(\hat{\ }\text{ask}'_*(x_5, n, x_4)))$
            $\equiv \text{think}(s, \hat{\ }\text{ask}'_*(x_5, n, x_4))$

3. $\text{Q}' = \lambda p[\text{QNP}'_4(\lambda x_4[\check{\ }p \wedge p = \hat{\ }\overline{S}'_0])]$
      $\text{QNP}'_4 = \lambda P \exists x[\neg\text{person}(x) \wedge R(x) \wedge P(x)]$
      $\text{Q}' = \lambda p[\lambda P \exists x[\neg\text{person}(x) \wedge R(x) \wedge P(x)]$
      $(\lambda x_4[\check{\ }p \wedge p = \hat{\ }\overline{S}'_0])]$
      $\equiv \lambda p[\exists x[\neg\text{person}(x) \wedge R(x) \wedge \lambda x_4[\check{\ }p \wedge p = \hat{\ }\overline{S}'_0](x)]]$
      $\equiv \lambda p[\exists x[\neg\text{person}(x) \wedge R(x) \wedge \check{\ }p \wedge p = \hat{\ }\text{think}$
      $(s, \hat{\ }\text{ask}'_*(x_5, n, x))]]$

(63)   **Cé aL phógann Ciarán aL phósann sé?**

       who   kisses   marries   he

       'Whom that Ciaran kisses does he marry?'

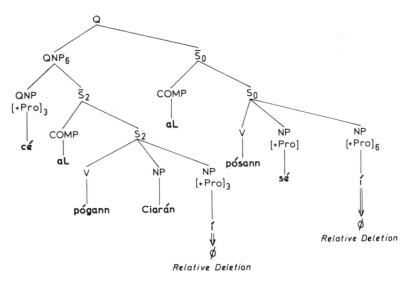

1. $\overline{S}'_2 = S'_2 = \text{kiss}_*(c, x_3)$
2. $\text{QNP}'_3 = \lambda P \exists x [\text{person}(x) \wedge R(x) \wedge P(x)]$
3. $\text{QNP}'_6 = \lambda R [\text{QNP}'_3] (\lambda x_3 [\overline{S}'_2 \wedge R(x_3)])$
     $\equiv \lambda P \exists x [\text{person}(x) \wedge \text{kiss}_*(c, x) \wedge R(x) \wedge P(x)]$
4. $\overline{S}'_0 = S'_0 = \text{marry}_*(x_4, x_6)$
5. $Q' = \lambda p [\text{QNP}'_6 (\lambda x_6 [{}^\vee p \wedge p = {}^\wedge \overline{S}'_0])]$
     $\equiv \lambda p [\exists x [\text{person}(x) \wedge \text{kiss}_*(c, x) \wedge R(x)$
     $\wedge {}^\vee p \wedge p = {}^\wedge \text{marry}_*(x_4, x)]]$

(64) **Fiafraíonn an garda   de Mháire caidé aL shíleann sí aL**
      asks   the policeman of   what   thinks   she

   ghoideann Seán
   steals

   'The policeman asks Mary what she thinks John steals.'

1. $\bar{S}'_0 = S'_0 = \text{steal}_*(s, x_7)$
2. $\bar{S}'_2 = S'_2 = \text{think}(x_3, \hat{\ }\text{steal}_*(s, x_7))$
3. $\text{QNP}'_7 = \lambda P \exists x [\neg \text{person}(x) \wedge R(x) \wedge P(x)]$
4. $Q' = \lambda p [\text{QNP}'_7(\lambda x_7 [\check{\ }p \wedge p = \hat{\ }\bar{S}'_2])]$
    $\lambda p [\exists x [\neg \text{person}(x) \wedge R(x) \wedge \check{\ }p \wedge p = \hat{\ }\text{think}(x_3, \hat{\ }\text{steal}_*(s, x))]]$
5. $S' = \text{NP}'(\text{PP}'(\check{\ }V'(\hat{\ }Q')))$
    $= [_{\text{NP}} \text{an garda}]'([_{\text{PP}} \text{de Máire}]'(\hat{\ }\text{ask}(\hat{\ }Q')))$
6. $[_{\text{NP}} \text{an garda}]' = \lambda Q \exists x [\forall y [(\text{policeman}(y) \wedge R(y)) \leftrightarrow x = y] \wedge Q(x)]$
7. $S' = \exists x [\forall y [(\text{policeman}(y) \wedge R(y)) \leftrightarrow x = y]$
    $\wedge \text{of}(\hat{\ }\lambda \text{PP}(m))(\hat{\ }\text{ask}(\hat{\ }Q))(x)]$
    $\equiv \exists x [\forall y [(\text{policeman}(y) \wedge R(y)) \leftrightarrow x = y] \wedge \text{ask}'(x, m, \hat{\ }Q')]$
    $[\text{by (22c)}]$
    $= \exists x [\forall y [(\text{policeman}(y) \wedge R(y)) \leftrightarrow x = y] \wedge \text{ask}'(x, m, \hat{\ }\lambda p$
    $[\exists z [\neg \text{person}(z) \wedge R(z) \wedge \check{\ }p \wedge p = \hat{\ }\text{think}(x_3, \hat{\ }\text{steal}_*(s, z))]])]$

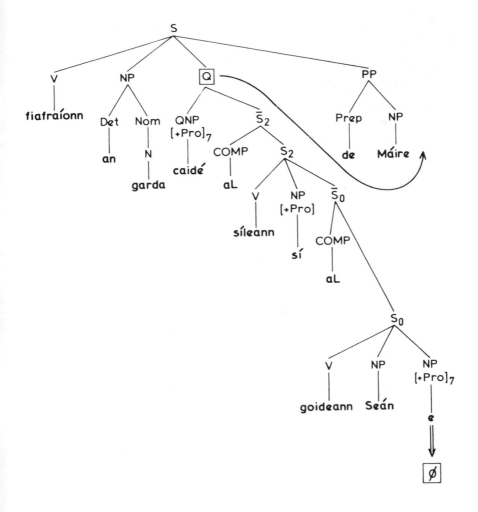

We come now to consider Constituent Questions with more complicated interrogative NP.

Consider first the situation where the interrogative phrase consists of an interrogative determiner and a nominal. (65) is such an example. The indexed deep structure tree from which it derives is given in (66).

(65)   **Cén   garda   aL   phósann Máire** —
        which policeman COMP marries

        'Which policeman does Mary marry?'

(66)

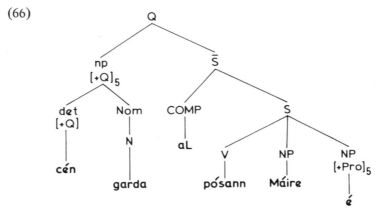

We have not yet assigned a meaning to the interrogative determiner. This is the only choice still to be made in interpreting these structures: we already have a rule for computing np-meanings from the meanings of determiners and nominals (12d(i)) and a rule for combining the meanings of interrogative noun phrases with the meanings of $\overline{S}$'s to derive question-meanings (12c)= (58). These decisions are made for us by the analyses we have already motivated for other structures.

The appropriate translation for **cén** is presented in (67):

(67) $\lambda P \lambda Q \exists x [P(x) \wedge R(x) \wedge Q(x)]$

(67) is the same meaning as is ascribed to the indefinite determiner. It is of course an old observation that there is a systematic relation between interrogative and indefinite determiners in many languages. The semantic relation suggested here (i.e. synonymy at least as far as the truth conditional aspects of their meanings[8] are concerned) goes some way towards explaining why there should be this morphological generalization.

Recall that the attempt to write the most general rule possible for determiners required us to give the interrogative determiner the features $\begin{bmatrix} +Q \\ -\text{def} \end{bmatrix}$. We can now make use of this apparently redundant feature to give a single translation rule for both the interrogative and indefinite determiners, as in (68):

(68) $g(\underset{[-\text{def}]}{\text{det}}) = \lambda P \lambda Q \exists x [P(x) \wedge R(x) \wedge Q(x)]$

How will all this aid us in interpreting an example like (66)? The rule for interpreting $[_{np}\,\text{det Nom}]$ structures is quite straightforward; it is simple functional application:

(69)

$$
\begin{array}{c}
\text{np} \\
\diagup\hspace{-0.2em}\diagdown \\
\text{det} \qquad \text{Nom}
\end{array}
\qquad \text{np}' = \text{det}'(\text{Nom}')
$$

So the interrogative noun phrase **cén garda** in (66) has the interpretation in (70):

(70) $[_{NP}\,\textbf{cén garda}]' = \lambda P \lambda Q \exists x [P(x) \wedge R(x) \wedge Q(x)]\,(policeman)$

$\equiv \lambda Q \exists x [\text{policeman}(x) \wedge R(x) \wedge Q(x)]$

The by-now familiar rules will interpret $\bar{\bar{S}}$ of (66) as in (71):

(71) $\bar{S}' = S' = \text{marry}_*(m, x_5)$

The rule for $[_Q\,\text{QNP}\,\bar{\bar{S}}]$ structures has been determined already by the simple cases. It is repeated for convenience as (72):

(72)

$$
\begin{array}{c}
\text{Q} \\
\diagup\hspace{-0.2em}\diagdown \\
\text{np}_n \qquad \bar{\bar{\text{S}}}
\end{array}
\qquad Q' = \lambda p\,[\text{np}'(\lambda x_n\,[\,\check{}\,p \wedge p = \hat{}\,\bar{S}'])]
$$

In the case of (66), this rule yields (73):

(73) $Q' = \lambda p\,[\lambda Q \exists x\,[\text{policeman}(x) \wedge R(x) \wedge Q(x)]$
$(\lambda x_5\,[\,\check{}\,p \wedge p = \hat{}\,\text{marry}_*(m, x_5)])]$

$\equiv \lambda p\,[\exists x\,[\text{policeman}(x) \wedge R(x) \wedge \check{}\,p \wedge p = \hat{}\,\text{marry}_*(m, x)]\,]$

This expression denotes at a given world and time the set of propositions that are of the form 'Mary marries x', where x ranges over policemen in some contextually relevant set (defined by the value assigned to R), and that are true at that world and time.

This decision as to how to treat the interrogative determiner is the last decision we need to make. We can increase the complexity of the illustrative examples to be discussed (as we will) but the rules already presented will deal with the more complex cases unaltered.

In (74) we present an example with several levels of embedding. The final translation expression in this case denotes the set of true propositions of the form 'Ciarán says that he$_5$ thinks that x helps he$_5$' where x is a man selected from some contextually relevant set (R). The possibility that x_5 may or may not be assigned the value Ciarán accounts for the fact that (74) has both coreferential and non-coreferential readings.

In (75) we are questioning into a question, so the Embedded Question Constraint forbids deletion of the bound pronoun sí$_3$. The bound pronoun é$_6$ is deleted by Relative Deletion under the control of QNP$_6$ – cé.

The last matter I will discuss in detail is example (76), which contains the most complex type of interrogative NP generable within the present fragment – namely one that contains an adjective and a relative clause.

(74)   **Cén   fear aL deireann Ciarán aL shíleann sé aL**
        which man   says   thinks

        chuidíonn __ leis
        helps   with him

        'Which man does Ciarán say he thinks helps him?'

$$\bar{S}_2' = S_2' = NP'(PP'(\hat{}V'))$$
$$= \lambda PP(x_4)(\text{with}(\hat{}\lambda PP(x_5))(\hat{}\text{help}))$$
$$\equiv (\text{with}(\hat{}\lambda PP(x_5))(\hat{}\text{help}))(x_4)$$
$$\equiv \text{help}'(x_4, \hat{}\lambda PP(x_5)) \qquad [\text{by (23c)}]$$
$$\equiv \text{help}'_*(x_4, x_5) \qquad [\text{by (27c)}]$$
$$\bar{S}_1' = S_1' = \text{think}(x_5, \hat{}\text{help}'_*(x_4, x_5))$$

$$\bar{S}_0' = S_0' = \text{say}(c, \hat{}\text{think}(x_5, \hat{}\text{help}'_*(x_4, x_5)))$$
$$Q' = \lambda p[\text{QNP}_4'(\lambda x_4[\check{}p \wedge p = \hat{}\bar{S}_0'])]$$
$$\text{QNP}_4' = \lambda P \exists x[\text{man}(x) \wedge R(x) \wedge P(x)]$$
$$Q' = \lambda p \exists x[\text{man}(x) \wedge R(x) \wedge \check{}p \wedge p = \hat{}\text{say}$$
$$(c, \hat{}\text{think}(x_5, \hat{}\text{help}'_*(x, x_5)))]$$

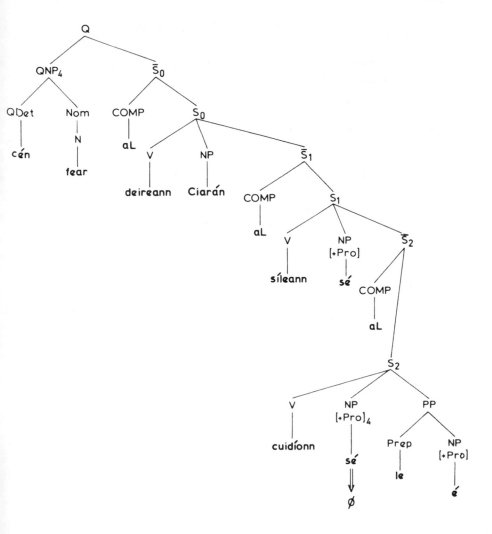

(75)   **Cén bhean aN n-insíonn Máire do Chiarán cé aL**
which woman COMP tells   to   who COMP

phógann sí _?
kisses   she

*'Which woman does Mary tell Ciarán who (she) kisses?'

1. $\bar{S}'_3 = S'_3 = \text{kiss}_*(x_3, x_6)$
2. $Q'_1 = \lambda p[\text{QNP}'_6(\lambda x_6[\check{} p \wedge p = \hat{} \bar{S}'_3])]$
3. $\text{QNP}'_6 = \lambda P \exists x[\text{person}(x) \wedge R(x) \wedge P(x)]$
4. $Q'_1 = \lambda p[\exists x[\text{person}(x) \wedge R(x) \wedge \check{} p \wedge p = \hat{}\text{kiss}_*(x_3, x)]]$
5. $\bar{S}'_2 = \text{NP}'(\text{PP}'(\hat{}\text{V}'(\hat{}\text{Q}')))$
       $= \lambda \text{PP}(m)(\text{to}(\hat{}\lambda \text{PP}(c))(\hat{}\text{tell}(Q'_1)))$
       $\equiv \text{to}(\hat{}\lambda \text{PP}(c))(\hat{}\text{tell}(\hat{}Q'_1))(m)$
6. $\equiv \text{tell}'(m, c, \hat{}Q'_1)$ [by (22c)]
7. $Q'_0 = \lambda p[\text{QNP}'_3(\lambda x_3[\check{} p \wedge p = \hat{} \bar{S}'_2])]$
8. $\text{QNP}'_3 = \lambda Q \exists x[\text{woman}(x) \wedge R(x) \wedge P(x)]$
9. $Q'_0 = \lambda p[\exists x[\text{woman}(x) \wedge R(x) \wedge \check{} p \wedge p = \hat{}\text{tell}'(m, c, \hat{}Q'_1)]]$
10. $= \lambda p[\exists y[\text{woman}(y) \wedge R(y) \wedge \check{} p \wedge p = \hat{}\text{tell}'(m, c, \hat{}\lambda q[\exists x[\text{person}(x) \wedge R(x) \wedge \check{} q \wedge q = \hat{}\text{kiss}_*(y, x)]])]]$

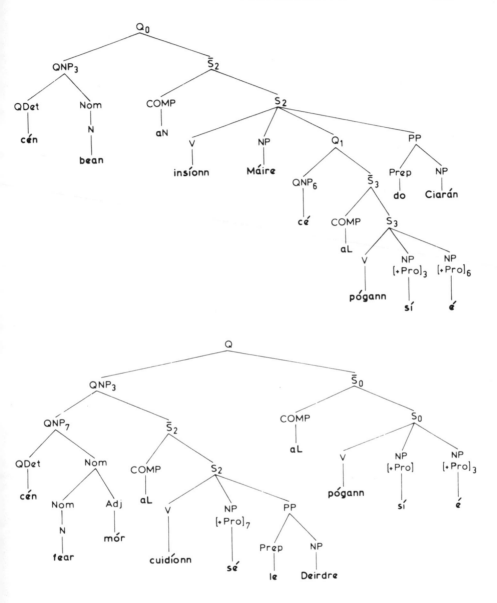

(76)   **Cén   fear mór aL chuidíonn le Deirdre aL phógann sí**
         which man big   helps   with   kisses   she
         'Which big man that helps Deirdre does she kiss?'

Consider first how the interpretation of the interrogative NP proceeds. As I have mentioned before, the interpretation of interrogative NP is accomplished in exactly the same way as that of non-interrogative NP:

(77)

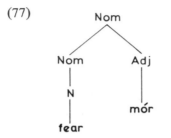

$$\text{Nom}' = \text{Adj}'(\hat{}\text{Nom}') = \text{big}(\hat{}\text{man})$$

QDet, as always, translates to:

$$\lambda P \lambda Q \exists x \, [P(x) \wedge R(x) \wedge Q(x)]$$

By rule (69), then, QNP_7 translates to:

(78) $\lambda Q \exists x \, [(\text{big}(\hat{}\text{man}))(x) \wedge R(x) \wedge Q(x)]$

The higher $\text{QNP} - \text{QNP}_3$ – is interpreted by the same rule which deals with any relative clause construction, namely (79):

(79)

np
— np$_n$ $\bar{\text{S}}$ $\text{np}' = \lambda R \, [\text{np}'] \, (\lambda x_n \, [\bar{\text{S}}' \wedge R(x_n)])$

In the case of (76):

(80) $\text{np}' = \text{QNP}_7' = \lambda Q \exists x \, [(\text{big}(\hat{}\text{man}))(x) \wedge R(x) \wedge Q(x)]$
         $\text{QNP}_3' = \lambda R \, [\text{QNP}_7'] \, (\lambda x_7 \, [\bar{\text{S}}_2' \wedge R(x_7)])$
         $\bar{\text{S}}_2' = \text{S}_2' = \text{help}_*'(x_7, d)$
         $\text{QNP}_3' = \lambda Q \exists x \, [(\text{big}(\hat{}\text{man}))(x) \wedge \text{help}_*'(x, d) \wedge R(x) \wedge Q(x)]$
         $Q' = \lambda p \, [\text{QNP}_3' (\lambda x_3 \, [\hat{}p \wedge p = \hat{}\bar{\text{S}}_0'])]$
         $\bar{\text{S}}_0' = \text{S}_0' = \text{kiss}_*(x_6, x_3)$
         $Q' = \lambda p \exists x \, [(\text{big}(\hat{}\text{man}))(x) \wedge \text{help}_*'(x, d) \wedge R(x) \wedge \check{}p$
         $\wedge p = \hat{}\text{kiss}_*(x_6, x)]$

This final expression denotes the set of true propositions of the form 'x kisses her$_7$' where x ranges over big relevant men who help Deirdre. As before x_7 may or may not pick out the same individual as 'Deirdre' depending on the context of use.

NOTES

[1] Notice that this convention will interpret both possessive and non-possessive pronouns, since $\begin{smallmatrix} \text{NP} \\ [+\text{Pro}] \end{smallmatrix}$ is unspecified for [Poss].

[2] This rule for interpreting possessives is quite general. In this fragment we have, for ease of explication, arbitrarily limited the class of NP that can occur under Det to possessive pronouns. But the rule (12g) will correctly interpret any NP in this position, as the reader may verify.

Actually the translations assigned to NP with possessive modifiers in this fragment are inaccurate in at least one respect. They are not definite enough. **A rothar** ('his bicycle') is given the interpretation in (i):

(i) $\lambda Q \exists x [\text{bicycle}(x) \wedge \text{Poss}(x_n, x) \wedge Q(x)]$

It would be closer to the truth to interpret them as in (ii):

(ii) $\lambda Q \exists x [\forall y [(\text{bicycle}(y) \wedge \text{Poss}(x_n, y)) \leftrightarrow x=y] \wedge Q(x)]$

(ii) is more appropriate because terms like **a rothar** or *his bicycle* pick out some *unique* bicycle owned by whatever individual the pronoun refers to. It would be a routine matter to fix the interpretation in the appropriate way by adjusting (12g) but since I introduce possessive pronouns into the fragment not for their intrinsic interest but only insofar as they play a role in relative and questioned clauses, I will persist in using the version of (12g) in the text since it makes for easier reading.

[3] The only difference is that subcategorized PP's normally precede non-subcategorized PP. But this is in any case required by the way in which the subcategorization features are set up – since they require that the first PP to follow the verb be the one which contains the governed preposition.

[4] It seems clear that quantifiers and the definite article require this kind of pragmatic limitation. It is perhaps less clear that the indefinite determiner requires it. It is not hard, however, to construct examples which indicate that it too must be restricted in the same way. Consider the following scenario: a man and woman are leaving home; she says to him 'Have you got a key?'. Clearly here the question being asked is not about any old key – but rather about a key that has the additional property of being a key to the house they are leaving.

[5] This observation is originally due to Baker 1968.

[6] There are, in fact, empirical issues that bear on this choice. Consider the ambiguity of a question like (i):

(i)   What did everyone read.

The fragment as set up so far yields only one reading for the Irish equivalent of these examples (incorrectly). There is no provision for assigning wider scope to *everyone* than to *what*, so we cannot derive the 'distributive' reading. Given the performative operator proposed by Karttunen, this reading can be derived by quantifying in *everyone* after the performative operator has been prefixed to the question. That is, the ambiguity will be treated as being exactly parallel to that found in (ii),

(ii)   I wondered what everyone read

in which *everyone* can be given wide scope by quantifying it into the matrix clause rather than into the embedded question. If we eschew the performative operator, we must formulate a new rule for quantifying into Q's. This turns out to be rather tricky. For a proposal along these lines and for an argument that Karttunen's analysis is wrong in this respect, see Belnap and Bennet (MS).

[7] Actually, the animateness part of the meaning of **cé** and the inanimateness part of the meaning of **caidé** are probably better treated as a matter of conventional implicature. This is also true for certain other things treated as a matter of truth-conditonal semantics here. The uniqueness part of the meaning of the definite article, for instance, should be treated as a matter of implicature I believe. There is no difficulty of principle here – I avoid presenting rules for conventional implicature only for the sake of clarity of exposition. For the necessary techniques see Karttunen and Peters (1975, 1976, to appear); Karttunen and Karttunen (1976, 1977), Karttunen (1977c).

[8] There is an important element of the meaning of this type of Constituent Question that is not dealt with here. Consider example (i).

(i)   **Cén scríbhneoir aL chuaigh _ thar lear?**
           Which writer went abroad?

One claim that a person who asks such a question is committed to, in Irish as in English, is that there is just one writer (in the contextually relevant set) who went abroad. Again, this is a matter of conventional implicature – a uniqueness implicature that arises from the interrogative determiner.

CHAPTER 8

THEORETICAL POSTSCRIPT

8.1. ON THE UNIVERSAL CHARACTERIZATION OF CONSTITUENT QUESTIONS

This study has had two major theoretical concerns. The first has been to demonstrate that unbounded deletion as well as unbounded leftward movement is a possible rule of Constituent Question Formation. The second has been to demonstrate the viability and attractiveness of a marriage between transformational syntax and Montague semantics. These two concerns are, of course, entirely independent and one could perfectly well be persuaded of the correctness of one thesis while remaining entirely unconvinced by the other. The two concerns do, however, meet in an interesting way when we come to consider the question of supplying a universal language-independent characterization of the class of constituent questions.

The thesis that Irish questions are derived by means of an unbounded deletion rule runs counter to a widely held view about the nature of constituent questions on a universal basis – namely that they are characterized by a universal rule of WH-Movement. Languages which obligatorily front interrogative phrases are assumed to have this rule, languages which do not are assumed to lack it. These are thought to be the only syntactic possibilities.

I hope to have demonstrated that this hypothesis is false by demonstrating that unbounded deletion is also a syntactic possibility. Must we then give up the attempt to give a universal definition of the class of constituent questions? I think not.

What we need is an essentially semantically-based definition. It seems that what is involved universally in the creation of a Constituent Question is the quantifying in of a phrasal category to an open sentence to create a new category of type $\langle\langle s, t \rangle, t \rangle$. The semantic operation of quantifying in has three possible syntactic analogues in a Montague Grammar with a transformational syntax. The phrasal category being quantified in can be the controller in an unbounded deletion rule; it can move unboundedly far to the left and bind the position from which it has been moved; or finally it can be left at the position it binds and be interpreted as having wide scope (as in the *de re* reading of 'John is looking for a mermaid'.). All of these syntactic possibilities (and only these?) turn up in various languages in the Constituent Question

245

construction: unbounded deletion in Irish, unbounded leftward movement in English and in situ interpretation in those languages – like Turkish or Japanese – in which interrogative phrases sit at the position they bind.

This characterization of Constituent Questions represents in a number of respects a more substantial hypothesis than the one that I have been arguing against implicitly throughout this paper – firstly in that it incorporates an hypothesis about the semantics of Constituent Questions on a universal basis; secondly in that it incorporates a prediction about the set of syntactic operations that will be characteristic of Constituent Questions on the basis of a more general hypothesis about a correlation between syntactic and semantic operations.

8.2. DEEP STRUCTURE VS. SURFACE STRUCTURE INTERPRETATION

The rules of semantic interpretation proposed in this study are defined on deep structures – more precisely, on indexed deep structure trees. There has been a good deal of debate in recent years on whether semantic interpretation should be defined at the level of deep structure, at the level of surface structure or whether both levels should contribute different elements of a semantic interpretation. It seems to me that this question diminishes rapidly in interest and importance as the differences between deep structure and surface structure diminish. It is perhaps worth pointing out though, that all of the main conclusions defended here are unaffected by the choice and that it would be easy to define the translation rules proposed here on 'surface structures' granted a couple of assumptions:

(1) that unbounded deletions leave 'traces' or 'structural residues' in the form of indexed nodes that dominate no terminal elements. So the rule of relative deletion would leave behind an indexed $\begin{smallmatrix} \text{NP} \\ [+ \text{Pro}] \end{smallmatrix}$ node. We would then need a general convention for translating such nodes:

$$
\begin{array}{l}
\text{NP} \\
[+ \text{Pro}]_n \qquad \text{NP}' = \lambda P P(x_n) \\
| \\
e
\end{array}
$$

Everything would then work as before.

(2) that 'surface structure' be defined in a more abstract way than is

traditional. Translation rules will operate on the output of unbounded extraction rules like Relative Deletion, but on structures that have not yet been subjected to the operation of rules like Extraposition from NP which break up constituents that need to be treated as such by the semantics. Interestingly, this is also the level at which island constraints need to be checked, given the analysis of clefts proposed in Chapter 4 and also the level at which the 'surface' filter (90) of Chapter 4 must apply.

Given the data that have been the subject matter of this study, I do not believe that there is anything that would decide between this alternative and the model that we have worked with in the body of the text.

BIBLIOGRAPHY

Ahlqvist, Anders (1978) 'On Preposed Adverbials', *Scottish Gaelic Studies* **XIII**, Part 1, 66–80.

Akmajian, A., Culicover, P. and Wasow, T., (eds.) (1977) *Formal Syntax*, Academic Press, New York.

Akmajian, A. and Kitagawa, C. (1976) 'Deep Structure Binding of Pronouns and Anaphoric Bleeding', *Language* **52**, 61–77.

Anderson, S. and Kiparsky, P., (eds.) (1973) *A Festschrift for Morris Halle*, Holt, Rinehart and Winston, New York.

Armstrong, J. (1975) 'A Note on Initial Mutation in Modern Irish', *Linguistic Inquiry* **6**, 317–323.

Bach, Emmon (1971) 'Questions', *Linguistic Inquiry* **2**, 153–166.

Bach, Emmon (1977) 'Comments on the Paper by Chomsky', in Akmajian, Culicover and Wasow 1977.

Bach, Emmon and Cooper, Robin (1978) 'The NP S Analysis of Relatives and Compositional Semantics', *Linguistics and Philosophy* **2**.

Bach, Emmon and Horn, George (1976) 'Remarks on Conditions on Transformations', *Linguistic Inquiry* **7**, 265–299.

Baker, C. L. (1968) *Indirect Questions in English*, unpublished doctoral dissertation, University of Illinois, Urbana, Ill.

Baker, C. L. (1970) 'Notes on the Description of English Questions The Role of an Abstract Question Morpheme', *Foundations of Language* **6**, 197–219.

Baltin, Mark (1978) *Toward a Theory of Movement Rules*, unpublished doctoral dissertation, MIT, Cambridge, Massachusetts.

Belnap, Nuel and Bennet, M. (1977) 'Questions in Montague Grammar', unpublished MS, University of Pittsburgh.

Böer, Stephen (1978) " 'Who' and 'Whether': Towards a Theory of Indirect Question Clauses", *Linguistics and Philosophy* **2**.

Brame, Michael (1967) 'A New Analysis of the Relative Clause: Evidence for an Interpretive Theory', unpublished MS.

Brame, Michael (1976) *Conjectures and Refutations in Syntax and Semantics*, North Holland, Amsterdam and London.

Brame, Michael (1977) 'Alternatives to the Tensed S and Specified Subject Conditions', *Linguistics and Philosophy* **1**, 3.

Brame, Michael (1978) *Base Generated Syntax*, Noit Amrofer, Seattle, Washington.

Brame, Michael (1979) 'Realistic Grammar', paper presented at the *Conference on Current Approaches to Syntax*, Milwaukee, Wisconsin, April 1979.

Breatnach, Liam (1979) 'Some Remarks on the Old Irish Relative', unpublished MS, Dublin Institute for Advanced Studies.

Bresnan, Joan (1972) *Theory of Complementation in English Syntax*, unpublished doctoral dissertation, MIT, Cambridge, Massachussetts.

Bresnan, Joan (1973a) 'Syntax of the Comparative Clause Construction in English', *Linguistic Inquiry* 4, 275–343.

Bresnan, Joan (1973b) 'Headless Relatives', mimeographed, University of Massachusetts, Amherst, Massachusetts.

Bresnan, Joan (1975) 'Comparative Deletion and Constraints on Transformations', *Linguistic Analysis* 1, 1.

Bresnan, Joan (1976a) 'On the Form and Functioning of Transformations', *Linguistic Inquiry* 7, 3–40.

Bresnan, Joan (1976b) 'Evidence for a Theory of Unbounded Transformations', *Linguistic Analysis* 2, 353–393.

Bresnan, Joan (1977a) 'Variables in the Theory of Transformations', in Akmajian, Culicover and Wasow 1977.

Bresnan, Joan (1978) 'A Realistic Transformational Grammar', in M. Halle, J. Bresnan and G. Miller, eds., *Linguistic Theory and Psychological Reality*, MIT Press, Cambridge, Massachusetts.

Bresnan, Joan and Grimshaw, Jane (1978) 'The Syntax of Free Relatives in English', *Linguistic Inquiry* 9, 331–391.

Carlson, G. (1977) 'Amount Relatives', *Language* 53, 520–542.

Chiba, S. (1972) "Another Case for 'Relative Clause Formation as a Copying Rule' ", *Studies in English Linguistics* 1, 1–12, Tokyo.

Chomsky, Noam (1965) *Aspects of the Theory of Syntax*, MIT Press, Cambridge, Massachusetts.

Chomsky, Noam (1970) 'Remarks on Nominalization', in R. Jacobs and P. Rosenbaum, eds., *Readings in English Transformational Grammar*, Ginn, Waltham, Massachusetts.

Chomsky, Noam (1973) 'Conditions on Transformations', in Anderson and Kiparsky, eds., 1973.

Chomsky, Noam (1975) *Reflections on Language*, Pantheon, New York.

Chomsky, Noam (1976) 'Conditions on Rules of Grammar', *Linguistic Analysis* 2, 303–351.

Chomsky, Noam (1977) 'On Wh-Movement', in Akmajian, Culicover and Wasow (eds.), 1977.

Chomsky, Noam (1978) 'On Binding', unpublished MS, MIT, Cambridge, Massachusetts.

Chomsky, Noam and Howard Lasnik (1977) 'Filters and Control', *Linguistic Inquiry* 8, 425–504.

Christian Brothers (1960) *Graiméar Gaeilge na mBráithre Críostaí*, M. H. Mac an Ghoill agus a Mhac, Tta, Dublin.

Cooper, Robin (1975) *Montague's Semantic Theory and Transformational Syntax*, unpublished doctoral dissertation, University of Massachusetts, Amherst, Massachusetts.

Cooper, Robin (1977a) 'Review of Formal Philosophy – Selected Papers of Richard Montague', R. H. Thomason, (ed.) Yale University Press, *Language* 53: 895–910.

Cooper, Robin (1977b) 'A Semantic Account of a Syntactic Constraint', paper presented at the Symposium on Montague Grammar, 52nd Annual Meeting of the Linguistic Society of America, Chicago, Ill., December 1977.

Cooper, Robin (1978) 'A fragment of English with Questions and Relative Clauses', unpublished MS, University of Wisconsin, Madison.

Cooper, Robin and Parsons, Terence (1976) 'Montague Grammar, Generative Semantics and Interpretive Semantics', in Partee 1976a.

Cresswell, M. J. (1973) *Logics and Languages*, London, Methuen.

Davis, Charles C. and Hellan, Lars (MS) 'The Syntax and Semantics of Comparative Constructions', unpublished MS, University of Massachusetts, Amherst, Massachusetts.

de Rijk, R. (1972) 'Relative Clauses in Basque: a Guided Tour', in *Chicago Which Hunt,
Papers from the Relative Clause Festival*, Chicago Linguistic Society, Chicago,
Illinois.

Dougherty, Ray (1969) 'An Interpretive Theory of Pronominal Reference', *Foundations
of Language* 5, 488–508.

du Plessis, Hans (1977) 'Wh-Movement in Afrikaans', *Linguistic Inquiry* 8, 723–726.

Emonds, Joseph (1976) *A Transformational Approach to English Syntax*, Academic
Press, New York.

Épée, Roger (1976) 'A Counterexample to the Q-Replacement and COMP-Substitution
Universals', *Linguistic Inquiry* 7, 677–686.

Fassi Fehri, A. (1978) 'Relatives Restrictives en Arabe: Déplacement de *wh* ou efface-
ment par dessus une variable', unpublished MS, Faculté de Lèttres, Rabat.

Fiengo, Robert (1977) 'On Trace Theory', *Linguistic Inquiry* 8, 35–61.

Frantz, Donald G. (1973) 'On Question Word Movement', *Linguistic Inquiry* 4, 4.

Grice, H. P. (1967) 'Logic and Conversation', in D. Davidson and G. Harman, eds., *The
Logic of Grammar*, Encino, California: Dickenson 1975.

Grimshaw, Jane (1975) 'Relativization by Deletion in Chaucerian Middle English', In
NELS V, Proceedings of the Fifth Annual Meeting of the North Eastern Linguistic
Society.

Grosu, Alexander (1974) 'On the Nature of the Left-Branch Condition', *Linguistic
Inquiry* 5, 308–319.

Hale, Kenneth (1978) 'Obviation in Modern Irish', unpublished MS, MIT. Cambridge,
Massachusetts.

Halvorsen, Per-Kristian (1978) *Syntax and Semantics of Cleft Constructions*, Texas
Linguistic Forum 11, Dept. of Linguistics, University of Texas at Austin.

Halvorsen, Per-Kristian and Ladusaw, William A. (to appear) 'Montague's 'Universal
Grammar': An Introduction for the Linguist', to appear in *Linguistics and Philosophy*.

Horn, George M. (1974) *The Noun Phrase Constraint*, unpublished doctoral dissertation,
University of Massachusetts, Amherst, Massachusetts.

Hornstein, Norbert (1977) 'S and X′ Convention', *Linguistic Analysis* 3, 137–176.

Jackendoff, Ray S. (1972) *Semantic Interpretation in Generative Grammar*, MIT Press,
Cambridge, Massachusetts.

Jackendoff, Ray S. (1973) 'The Base Rules for Prepositional Phrases', in Anderson and
Kiparsky 1973.

Jackendoff, Ray S. (1977) *X̄-Bar Syntax: A Study in Phrase Structure*, Linguistic Inquiry
Monograph 2, MIT Press, Cambridge, Massachussetts.

Jeanne, Laverne Masayesva (1978) *Aspects of Hopi Grammar*, unpublished doctoral
dissertation, MIT, Cambridge, Massachusetts.

Jespersen, Otto (1909–1949) *A Modern English Grammar on Historical Principles*,
London, Allen and Unwin.

Karttunen, Lauri (1977a) 'Syntax and Semantics of Questions', *Linguistics and Philosophy* 1, 3–44.

Karttunen, Lauri (1977b) 'Questions Revisited', paper presented at the Albany Conference on Montague Grammar, Albany, April 1977.

Karttunen, Lauri (1977c) 'Presupposition in Montague Grammar' paper presented to the

Symposium on Montague Grammar, 52nd Annual Meeting of the Linguistic Society of America, Chicago, Illinois, December 1977.

Karttunen, Frances and Karttunen, Lauri (1976) 'The Clitic -kin/-kaan in Finnish', in *Papers from the Transatlantic Finnish Conference*, Texas Linguistic Forum 5, Dept. of Linguistics, University of Texas at Austin.

Karttunen, Frances and Karttunen, Lauri (1977) *'Even* Questions', in Kegl, Nash and Zaenen (eds.), 1977.

Karttunen, Lauri and Peters, Stanley (1975) 'Conventional Implicature in Montague Grammar', in *BLS 1*, Proceedings of the First Annual Meeting of the Berkeley Linguistics Society, Berkeley, California.

Karttunen, Lauri and Peters, Stanley (1976) 'What Indirect Questions Conventionally Implicate', in *CLS 12*, Papers from the Twelfth Regional Meeting of the Chicago Linguistic Society, Chicago, Illinois.

Karttunen, Lauri and Peters, Stanley (to appear) 'Conventional Implicature', to appear in *Syntax and Semantics* vol. 10, Choon-Kyu Oh and Francis Dinneen (eds.)

Katz, J. and Postal, P. (1964) *An Integrated Theory of Linguistic Descriptions*, MIT Press, Cambridge, Massachusetts.

Keenan, Edward and B. Comrie (1977) 'Noun Phrase Accessibility and Universal Grammar', *Linguistic Inquiry* 8, 63–99.

Kegl, J., Nash, D. and Zaenen, A. (eds.) (1977) *NELS VII*, Proceedings of the Seventh Annual Meeting of the North Eastern Linguistic Society, MIT, Cambridge, Massachusetts.

Kuno, Susumu (1973) 'Constraints on Internal Clauses and Sentential Subjects', *Linguistic Inquiry* 4, 363–385.

Kuno, Susumu (1974) 'The Position of Relative Clauses and Conjunctions', *Linguistic Inquiry* 5, 117–136.

Ladusaw, William (1978) 'The Scope of Some Sentence Adverbs and Surface Structure', in *NELS VIII*, Proceedings of the Eighth Annual Meeting of the North Eastern Linguistic Society, University of Massachusetts, Amherst, Massachusetts.

Lasnik, Howard and Fiengo, Robert, (1976) 'Some issues in the Theory of Transformations', *Linguistic Inquiry* 7, 182–191.

Lightfoot, David (1976) 'Trace Theory and Twice-Moved NP', *Linguistic Inquiry* 7, 559–582.

McCloskey, James (1977a) 'Conditions on Transformations in Modern Irish', in Kegl, Nash and Zaenen (eds.) 1977.

McCloskey, James (1977b) 'A Fragment of a Grammar of Modern Irish', unpublished MS, Dept. of Linguistics, University of Texas at Austin.

McCloskey, James (1977c) 'An Acceptable Ambiguity in Modern Irish', *Linguistic Inquiry* 8, 604–609.

McCloskey, James (1978) 'The Internal Structure of NP in Modern Irish', unpublished MS, Dept. of Linguistics, University of Texas at Austin.

McCloskey, James (1979) 'Is There Raising in Modern Irish?', paper presented to the Sixth International Congress of Celtic Studies, University College Galway, July 1979.

McCloskey, James (to appear) 'A Note on Modern Irish Verbal Nouns and the VP-Complement Analysis', to appear in *Linguistic Analysis*.

Maling, Joan (1977) 'Old Icelandic Relative Clauses', in Kegl, Nash and Zaenen (eds.) 1977.

Maling, Joan (1978) 'An Asymmetry with Respect to Wh-Islands', *Linguistic Inquiry* 9, 75–89.

Malone, Joseph L. (1977) 'Irish ná, a Disambiguator of Perceptually Equivocal Surface Structures', unpublished MS, Barnard College, Columbia University.

May, Robert C. (1977) *The Grammar of Quantification*, unpublished doctoral dissertation, MIT, Cambridge, Massachusetts.

Montague, Richard (1974a) 'Universal Grammar', in Thomason (1974b).

Mongague, Richard (1974b) 'The Proper Treatment of Quantification in Ordinary English', in Thomason 1974b.

Montague, Richard (1974c) 'English as a Formal Language', in Thomason (1974b).

Montague, Richard (1974d) 'Pragmatics', in Thomason (1974b).

Montague, Richard (1974e) 'Pragmatics and Intensional Logic', in Thomason (1974b).

Morgan, J. (1972) 'Some Aspects of Relative Clauses in English and Albanian', in *Chicago Which Hunt, Papers from the Relative Clause Festival*, Chicago Linguistic Society, Chicago, Illinois.

Ó Cadhlaigh, Cormac (1940) *Gnás na Gaedhilge*, Govt. Publications Office, Dublin.

Ó Cadhlaigh, Cormac (19 –) *Ceart na Gaedhilge* (*A Treatise on Irish Syntax*), Mellifont Press, Dublin.

Ó Cuív, Brian (1944) *The Irish of West Muskerry, Co. Cork*, Dublin, The Institute for Advanced Studies.

O'Neill, John E. (1975) 'Irish Texts from South West Donegal', *Zeitschrift für Keltische Philologie* 34, 223–318.

O'Nolan, Gerald (1920) *Studies in Modern Irish*, The Educational Company of Ireland Ltd., Dublin.

O'Nolan, Gerald (1934) *The New Era Grammar of Modern Irish*, The Educational Company of Ireland Ltd., Dublin and Cork.

O'Rahilly, T. F. (1932) *Irish Dialects Past and Present*, Browne and Nolan, re-issued 1972 by the Dublin Institute for Advanced Studies.

Ó Searcaigh, Séamas (1939) *Coimhréir Ghaeilge an Tuaiscirt*, Govt. Publications Office, Dublin.

Partee, Barbara (1975) 'Montague Grammar and Transformational Grammar', *Linguistic Inquiry* 6, 203–300.

Partee, Barbara (1976a) *Montague Grammar*, Academic Press, New York (ed.).

Partee, Barbara (1976b) 'Some Transformational Extensions of Montague Grammar', in Partee (ed.) (1976a).

Partee, Barbara (1977) 'Comments on the Paper by Bresnan', in Akmajian, Culicover and Wasow (1977).

Partee, Barbara (to appear) 'Montague Grammar and the Well-Formedness Constraint', in the Proceedings of the Third Groningen Round Table (1976) (ed.) F. Heny and H. Schnelle.

Peters, Stanley (1977) 'The Semantics of Questions', paper presented to the Symposium on Montague Grammar, 52nd Annual Meeting of the Linguistic Society of America, Chicago, Illinois, December, 1977.

Peters, Stanley and R. W. Ritchie (1973) 'On the Generative Power of Transformational Grammars', *Information Sciences* 6, 49–83.

Postal, Paul M. (1970) 'On So-Called Pronouns in English', in R. A. Jacobs and P. S.

Rosenbaum (eds.) *Readings in English Transformational Grammar*, Ginn and Co., Waltham, Massachusetts.

Postal, Paul M. (1971) *Cross-Over Phenomena*, Holt, Rinehart and Winston, New York.

Postal, Paul M. (1976) 'On avoiding Reference to Subject', *Linguistic Inquiry* 7, 151–182.

Ross, John R. (1967) *Constraints on Variables in Syntax*, unpublished doctoral dissertation, MIT, Cambridge, Massachusetts.

Ross, John R. (1973) 'Nouniness', in Osamu Fujimura, (ed.) *Three Dimensions of Linguistic Theory*, TEC Co., Tokyo.

Sag, Ivan (1976a) 'A Logical Theory of Verb Phrase Deletion', in *CLS 12*, Papers from the Twelfth Regional Meeting of the Chicago Linguistic Society, Chicago, Illinois.

Sag, Ivan (1976b) *Deletion and Logical Form*, unpublished doctoral dissertation, MIT, Cambridge, Massachusetts.

Schachter, Paul (1973) 'Focus and Relativization', *Language* **49**.

Schmerling, Susan (1977) 'The Syntax of English Imperatives', unpublished MS, University of Texas at Austin.

Sommerfelt, Alf (1965) 'Sentence Patterns in the Dialect of Torr', *Lochlann: A Review of Celtic Studies*, Vol. 3, Universitetsforlaget, Oslo.

Sornhiran, Pasinee (1978) *Relative Clauses in Thai*, unpublished doctoral dissertation, University of Texas at Austin.

Stalnaker, Robert (1974) 'Pragmatic Presuppositions', in M. K. Munitz and P. K. Unger; eds., *Semantics and Philosophy*, New York University Press, New York, 197–214.

Stenson, Nancy (1976) 'Overlapping Systems in the Irish Comparative Construction', *Word* **28**, 78–95.

Taylor, Barry (MS) 'Truth Theory for Indexical Languages', unpublished MS, University of Melbourne.

Thomason, Richmond H. (1974a) 'Introduction' in Thomason (1974b).

Thomason, Richmond H. (1974b) *Formal Philosophy: Selected Writings of Richard Montague*, Yale University Press, New York and London.

Thomason, Richmond H. (1976) 'Some Extensions of Montague Grammar', in Partee (1976a).

Thomason, Richmond H. (MS) 'On the Semantic Interpretation of the Thomason 1972 Fragment', unpublished MS., University of Pittsburgh.

Van Riemsdijk, H. (1977) 'The Binding Nature of Prepositional Phrases', unpublished MS., University of Amsterdam.

Vendler, Zeno (1967) *Linguistics in Philosophy*, Cornell University Press, Ithaca, New York.

Vergnaud, J.-R. (1974) *French Relative Clauses*, unpublished doctoral dissertation, MIT, Cambridge, Massachusetts.

Wachowitz, Krystyna (1974) 'Multiple Questions', *Linguistica Silesiana* 1.

Wachowitz, Krystyna (1978) 'Q-Morpheme Hypothesis, Performative Analysis and an Alternative', in Henry Hiż, ed., *Questions*, Synthese Language Library, Reidel, Dordrecht and Boston.

Wasow, T. (1972) *Anaphoric Relations in English*, unpublished doctoral dissertation, MIT, Cambridge, Massachusetts.

Wheeler, Eric (1978) 'The *'Se 'Sann* Construction in Scottish Gaelic', in *NELS VIII*, Proceedings of the Eighth Annual Meeting of the North Eastern Linguistic Society.

Williams, Edwin (1977) 'Discourse and Logical Form', *Linguistic Inquiry* 8, 101–139.
Williams, Edwin (1978) 'Across the Board Rule Application', *Linguistic Inquiry* 9, 31–43.

INDEX

SYNTHESE LANGUAGE LIBRARY

Texts and Studies in Linguistics and Philosophy

Managing Editors:

JAAKKO HINTIKKA (Florida State University)
STANLEY PETERS (The University of Texas at Austin)

Editors:

EMMON BACH (University of Massachusetts at Amherst), JOAN BRESNAN
(Massachusetts Institute of Technology), JOHN LYONS (University of Sussex),
JULIUS M. E. MORAVCSIK (Stanford University), PATRICK SUPPES (Stanford
University), DANA SCOTT (Oxford University).

1. Henry Hiż (ed.), *Questions*. 1978.
2. William S. Cooper, *Foundations of Logico-Linguistics. A Unified Theory of Information, Language, and Logic*. 1978.
3. Avishai Margalit (ed.), *Meaning and Use*. 1979.
4. F. Guenthner and S. J. Schmidt (eds.), *Formal Semantics and Pragmatics for Natural Languages*. 1978.
5. Esa Saarinen (ed.), *Game-Theoretical Semantics*. 1978.
6. F. J. Pelletier (ed.), *Mass Terms: Some Philosophical Problems*. 1979.
7. David R. Dowty, *Word Meaning and Montague Grammar. The Semantics of Verbs and Times in Generative Semantics and in Montague's PTQ*. 1979.
8. Alice F. Freed, *The Semantics of English Aspectual Complementation*. 1979.
9. James McCloskey, *Transformational Syntax and Model Theoretic Semantics: A Case Study in Modern Irish*. 1979.
10. John R. Searle, Ferenc Kiefer, and Manfred Bierwisch (eds.), *Speech Act Theory and Pragmatics*. 1980. (Forthcoming.)

H 5